Communications in Computer and Information Science 2369

Rationale

The CCIS series is devoted to the publication of proceedings of computer science conferences. Its aim is to efficiently disseminate original research results in informatics in printed and electronic form. While the focus is on publication of peer-reviewed full papers presenting mature work, inclusion of reviewed short papers reporting on work in progress is welcome, too. Besides globally relevant meetings with internationally representative program committees guaranteeing a strict peer-reviewing and paper selection process, conferences run by societies or of high regional or national relevance are also considered for publication.

Topics

The topical scope of CCIS spans the entire spectrum of informatics ranging from foundational topics in the theory of computing to information and communications science and technology and a broad variety of interdisciplinary application fields.

Information for Volume Editors and Authors

Publication in CCIS is free of charge. No royalties are paid, however, we offer registered conference participants temporary free access to the online version of the conference proceedings on SpringerLink (http://link.springer.com) by means of an http referrer from the conference website and/or a number of complimentary printed copies, as specified in the official acceptance email of the event.

CCIS proceedings can be published in time for distribution at conferences or as post-proceedings, and delivered in the form of printed books and/or electronically as USBs and/or e-content licenses for accessing proceedings at SpringerLink. Furthermore, CCIS proceedings are included in the CCIS electronic book series hosted in the SpringerLink digital library at http://link.springer.com/bookseries/7899. Conferences publishing in CCIS are allowed to use Online Conference Service (OCS) for managing the whole proceedings lifecycle (from submission and reviewing to preparing for publication) free of charge.

Publication process

The language of publication is exclusively English. Authors publishing in CCIS have to sign the Springer CCIS copyright transfer form, however, they are free to use their material published in CCIS for substantially changed, more elaborate subsequent publications elsewhere. For the preparation of the camera-ready papers/files, authors have to strictly adhere to the Springer CCIS Authors' Instructions and are strongly encouraged to use the CCIS LaTeX style files or templates.

Abstracting/Indexing

CCIS is abstracted/indexed in DBLP, Google Scholar, EI-Compendex, Mathematical Reviews, SCImago, Scopus. CCIS volumes are also submitted for the inclusion in ISI Proceedings.

How to start

To start the evaluation of your proposal for inclusion in the CCIS series, please send an e-mail to ccis@springer.com

Vanessa Agredo-Delgado · Pablo H. Ruiz ·
Carlos Augusto Meneses Escobar
Editors

Collaboration in Knowledge Discovery and Decision Making

Third International Workshop, DECISIONING 2024
Pereira, Colombia, June 4–6, 2024
Proceedings

Springer

Editors
Vanessa Agredo-Delgado
Universidad del Cauca
Popayán, CAUCA, Colombia

Corporacion Universitaria Comfacauca
Unicomfacauca
Popayán, CAUCA, Colombia

Carlos Augusto Meneses Escobar
Universidad Tecnológica de Pereira
Pereira, RISARALDA, Colombia

Pablo H. Ruiz
Universidad del Cauca
Popayán, CAUCA, Colombia

ISSN 1865-0929 ISSN 1865-0937 (electronic)
Communications in Computer and Information Science
ISBN 978-3-031-91689-2 ISBN 978-3-031-91690-8 (eBook)
https://doi.org/10.1007/978-3-031-91690-8

This Springer imprint is published by the registered company Springer Nature Switzerland AG
The registered company address is: Gewerbestrasse 11, 6330 Cham, Switzerland

Preface

This book gathers the best papers presented at the event "Collaboration in Knowledge Discovery and Decision Making 2024" (DECISIONING 2024), held at the Universidad Tecnológica de Pereira, Colombia, from June 4–6, 2024. This event was a key meeting point for researchers, practitioners and academics interested in collaborative decision making and knowledge discovery, fostering interaction between academia and industry to address current challenges in this field.

Important decisions at all levels are based on a fundamental resource: knowledge. Improvement and innovation in organizations are based on the analysis of previous experiences and external events that constitute the knowledge base. Having knowledge bases with historical data and trends helps to predict behaviors and make decisions that generate competitive advantages.

In the knowledge society, organizations have managed to establish strategic alliances to share this resource and generate collaborative decisions that strengthen them. Collaborative decision making gathers knowledge from different groups, driving research and development in many productive sectors. In this context, sharing knowledge not only ensures its retention, but also catalyzes consensus building and allows better results to be achieved through decisions based on quality information.

Our perspective on collaborative decision making aims to improve the quality of the decision-making process and to ensure greater acceptance of the choices made. Shared decision making is a core activity in many disciplines, from organizational management to sustainable planning. We believe that knowledge sharing is essential to optimize this process and generate impact in the academic, business and social spheres.

DECISIONING 2024 was presented as the third edition of this international workshop, supported by six research teams from France, Argentina and Colombia. Its purpose was to explore recent advances in collaborative decision making and knowledge discovery, addressing topics including data analysis, artificial intelligence, decision models and industrial applications. The event facilitated the participation of experts from around the world, promoting debate and the exchange of ideas between academia and industry.

This volume brings together a selection of the best papers presented at DECISIONING 2024. A total of 54 papers were received, of which, after a rigorous peer review process, 18 were accepted for inclusion in this publication. The quality of these papers reflects the commitment of the scientific community to the advancement of knowledge in this field, offering innovative solutions and methodologies that enhance decision making in different sectors.

We are deeply grateful for the contribution of the authors, who shared their research and experiences; to the reviewers for their dedication in ensuring the quality of the content; to the organizing committee for their hard work in planning the event; and to the Universidad Tecnológica de Pereira for their invaluable support in the realization of DECISIONING 2024. We also extend our appreciation to Springer for allowing the publication of this book and contributing to the international dissemination of the event.

We hope that this publication will inspire new ideas, foster interdisciplinary collaborations and enrich knowledge in collaborative decision making and knowledge discovery. We are confident that DECISIONING 2024 will be a valuable reference for the scientific and professional community interested in these topics.

March 2025

Vanessa Agredo-Delgado
Pablo H. Ruiz
Carlos Augusto Meneses Escobar

Organization

General Chair

Julio César Chavarro	Universidad Tecnológica de Pereira, Colombia

Program Committee Chair

César Alberto Collazos	Universidad del Cauca, Colombia

Editorial Committee Chairs

Vanessa Agredo-Delgado	Universidad del Cauca and Corporación Universitaria Comfacauca Unicomfacauca, Colombia
Pablo H. Ruiz	Universidad del Cauca, Colombia
Cesar Augusto Jaramillo Acevedo	Universidad Tecnológica de Pereira, Colombia

Program Committee

Agredo Vanessa	Universidad del Cauca, Colombia
Arias Bibiana Patricia	Universidad Tecnológica de Pereira, Colombia
Bibbo Luis	Universidad Nacional de la Plata, Argentina
Besoain Pino Felipe	Universidad de Talca, Chile
Bolaños Manuel	Universidad de Nariño, Colombia
Carrillo Oscar	CPE Lyon, France
Chavarro Julio César	Universidad Tecnológica de Pereira, Colombia
Collazos Cesar	Universidad del Cauca, Colombia
Costaguta Rosanna	Universidad Nacional de Santiago del Estero, Argentina
Del Giorgio Horacio	Universidad Nacional de La Matanza, Argentina
Díaz Gloria	Instituto Tecnológico de Medellín, Colombia
Duque Néstor Darío	Universidad Nacional de Colombia, Colombia
Fernández Alejandro	Universidad Nacional de la Plata, Argentina
Franco Hugo	Universidad Central, Colombia
Gómez María Clara	Universidad de Medellín, Colombia

Contents

A Collaborative and Pattern-Based Training Approach to Knowledge Acquisition and Decision-Making During the Design of Software Architectures Courses: A Case Study

Wilson Libardo Pantoja Yepez[1](✉), Luis Mariano Bibbó[2], and Julio Ariel Hurtado Alegría[1]

[1] Universidad del Cauca, Popayán, Colombia
{Wpantoja,ahurtado}@unicauca.edu.co
[2] Universidad Nacional de la Plata, La Plata, Argentina
lmbibbo@lifia.info.unlp.edu.ar

Abstract. This article describes a collaborative learning experience on Software Architecture (SA) between Universidad del Cauca (UNICAUCA) in Colombia and Universidad Nacional de la Plata (UNPL) in Argentina. The goal was to apply and evaluate training patterns, identifying effective practices for replication in other contexts. During the planning phase, both universities compared learning objectives, curricula, and teaching strategies to find common ground for improving student training. Selected training patterns were implemented, and their impact on professors and students was measured. As an integrating activity, a global development experience was carried out in the final part of the course, merging the work teams of the two educational institutions in a development iteration. The evaluation of this experience focused on the competencies achieved through the training patterns, their perceived usefulness, and ease of use based on the Technology Acceptance Model (TAM). The training addressed industry needs for software architecture design skills despite challenges such as the abstract nature of architectures, prerequisite knowledge, difficulty in recreating realistic project environments, team collaboration challenges, and resource limitations. A catalog of training patterns was proposed to provide quality training. These patterns help simulate industry–like environments and structure architectural knowledge for incremental learning. The ability to make architectural decisions is developed over time and through multiple project experiences, emphasizing the need for practical, well-structured training programs.

Keywords: Knowledge in Software Architecture · Training · Collaborative Teaching · Training Patterns · Knowledge Acquisition · Decision Making

V. Agredo-Delgado et al. (Eds.): DECISIONING 2024, CCIS 2369, pp. 1–15, 2025.
https://doi.org/10.1007/978-3-031-91690-8_1

1 Introduction

Software architects are responsible for proposing the structure of software applications to satisfy the quality attributes and constraints of the system and make the applications easily adaptable to business changes. According to Sherman and Unkelos-Shpigel [1], the role of the architect is responsible for design and technical decisions in the software development process and has the function of solving a problem by defining the structures of a system that can be implemented using certain technologies. However, finding the right balance between software attributes such as security, performance, usability, availability, maintainability, and interoperability, among others, takes a lot of work. These attributes can conflict, so the software architect needs to know tactics, patterns, and principles to help them make the right design decisions. Therefore, architects must define systems by applying abstract knowledge, proven methods, and technologies to create a solution that balances quality expectations. Thus, architects' duties also include soft skills, such as leadership, communication, and training [2]. For example, a software architect must understand stakeholder expectations and communicate decisions to designers, programmers, testers, installers, and other users of the system's architectural specifications.

For example, undergraduate engineering programs, such as Computer Science and Engineering, Information Technology, Software Engineering, and Systems Engineering, include many courses in which skills are developed, and technical knowledge related to building software is imparted through the use of programming languages and development platforms [3]. However, students in these programs need more knowledge of Software Architecture (SA) and design issues despite their growing importance to the software industry [4]. Recent graduates especially need more skills in proper design decision-making, practices, and knowledge related to software design in the business context [4].

The existing literature on SA education and practice points to different reasons for this lack of skills related to software architecture and design. First, there is a considerable gap between the academic perception of software architecture and its practice in the industrial sector [5]. Sometimes, the problems that industries consider most critical and challenging are not given due importance for research or university training [5]. Second, there is a gap between the skills that the industry expects from graduates in Software Engineering and the skills taught in the curricula [6]. Third, many institutions need a clear vision of the topics in which software architects should be trained [4].

Although numerous virtual platforms provide training in technological development environments and programming languages, no courses help to form the systemic and strategic thinking of a software architect [4]. This situation has meant that most people interested in SA issues must embark on a long self-study path.

Decisions around SA go hand in hand with information and communication technology issues. A software architect must have a broad knowledge of technologies to decide which platforms, frameworks, and languages favor certain technical and business qualities and constraints. The problem lies in the speed at which these technologies evolve. Along with the rapid development of information and communication technology (ICT), the job skills required by ICT industries are also changing rapidly. It becomes difficult for all stakeholders to assess the gap between their skills and those needed in such an evolving context. Although universities conduct periodic assessments of the curriculum, the time gap between the assessments and their updates makes it quickly outdated, as it cannot cope with the accelerated and rapid changes occurring in the industry and the environment [7]. Moreover, the problem is not only to know the gap but also to work on concrete strategies to reduce it.

Through a review, we sought to investigate in depth the reasons for the complexity associated with teaching SA. As a result, we found several causes of the difficulty involved in the training in SA topics at the undergraduate level [8]. We classified these causes by categories defined through the reading of the summaries: (1) Software industry, (2) Curricular contents, (3) Professors, (4) Nature of the architectures, (5) Resources, and (6) Students. Some of these challenges have many causes: the abstract nature of the archfitectures, the bases required by the trainees, the difficulty in recreating projects and environments in training contexts with similar characteristics to those of the industry, the challenges of working in teams, the lack of resources and updated contents, among others [9].

This paper describes a shared teaching experience by executing a case study that allowed us to evaluate the impact of applying some training patterns articulated in a guide called SAGITA (Software Architecture: GuIdeline for TrAining) in two SA courses: the National University of La Plata, Argentina, and the University of Cauca. This case study was selected because it was a representative case, i.e., two undergraduate Software Architecture courses in which the professors involved were willing to test SAGITA and the training patterns, motivated to improve the courses and align them with industry needs. The case study design was conducted under the guidelines Runeson and Host [10] proposed.

2 Related Work

Giraldo et al. present and discuss the results obtained from a collaborative and distributed learning activity called CODILA (Collaborative and Distributed Learning Activity), which addresses the challenge of designing a software architecture for a communications infrastructure in a distributed manner [11].

Garousi et al. reviewed literature focusing on the challenges faced by software engineering graduates as they commence their professional journey, highlighting the mismatch between the skills acquired during their undergraduate studies and those demanded by the industry [12]. This examination enables educators and hiring managers to customize their educational and hiring strategies to equip the software engineering workforce better.

Niño and Anaya suggest a curriculum overhaul for the software engineering domain within systems engineering programs [13]. The primary outcome entails establishing a framework of professional competencies specific to software engineering, categorized into primary and secondary levels. Additionally, it delineates the foundational subjects crucial for fostering the competencies above.

Kiwelekar and Wankhede outline and categorize a series of learning objectives utilizing the Revised Bloom's Taxonomy (RBT) [14]. Their examination underscores the essential cognitive skills essential for architecture modeling. One of the critical advantages of categorizing learning objectives lies in the ability to align various educational processes, including instruction, learning, and assessment, more effectively, leveraging the framework proposed in this study.

Rupakheti and Chenoweth delineate a decade-long teaching experience within an undergraduate software architecture course integrated into a software engineering degree program [15]. They articulate their perspective on the practical objectives of instructing software architecture at this academic level. Emphasizing that the principal aim of the course is to equip students for advanced design scenarios encountered in the industry, they advocate for utilizing contemporary technologies and methodologies in student projects, along with rectifying architectural deficiencies in existing systems.

3 Training Patterns

This research presents a catalog of SA training patterns articulated in a guide called SAGITA (Software Architecture: Guideline for Training) that allows professors to design and execute courses at the undergraduate level. These patterns will enable the development of competencies in the creation, evaluation, and documentation of software architectures that align with the expectations of the software industry. The training patterns were extracted from the literature review, based on the experiences reported by professors proposing strategies to train their students with software architecture s.

The detailed description of SAGITA and the seven training patterns are available in PDF format on page SAGITA Final Version. In general terms, a "pattern" refers to a general, reusable solution to a recurring problem. It can be applied in various contexts, from architecture and design to problem-solving in specific fields, such as computer science, psychology, and biology. Christopher Alexander says: *"Each pattern describes a problem that occurs over and over again in our environment, and then describes the core of the solution to that problem, such that you can use this solution a million times, without ever doing it the same way twice"* [16].

Inspired by software patterns, design patterns, and software architecture patterns, we proposed the idea of training patterns [17]. Training patterns are reusable strategies for common problems in the design and execution of software architecture courses to achieve AS competencies. These patterns represent best practices and experiences by the teaching community and provide structured and efficient solutions for specific situations. Each pattern describes a problem that occurs frequently in a given context and presents a general solution that can be adapted and applied to different scenarios. The seven training patterns we propose are:

1. **Mini-Projects-based training**. When students reach their first SA course, they have already seen programming and software development courses. At this level, students have skills in creating simple applications but working only with functional requirements. To develop a SA, the professional must consider quality attributes (scalability, performance, security, etc.) and satisfy functional requirements. Working with mini projects, students can practice architecture patterns and architecture tactics to favor the fulfillment of quality attributes.
2. **Large project-based training**. When students have acquired sufficient software development skills to attack medium to large development projects in complex

domains, the professor could develop a course that connects the theoretical foundations of software architecture with practice through a large project of some complexity. Students learn SA through a complete real project where they can see the results of their architectural design as a product.

3. **Open-source projects-based training**. When recent graduates join the software industry, one of the initial challenges they face is developing software components on existing and usually large projects. Students work with an open-source project to have the unique opportunity to learn attitudes only present in real-world scenarios, which can increase their skills and confidence.
4. **In-house project-based training**. Despite the advantages of confronting students with modifying real systems, working with open-source projects can become too complex for students and professors. Therefore, an alternative is for professors to have their open-source application (In-house project) to teach SA with enough complexity of an industrial system.
5. **Cases-based training**. Making correct architectural decisions while constructing a software system is one of the significant skills a future software architect must develop. Case-based training focuses on designing and analyzing real software projects from companies. Students experience and use the theory and technology of SA design applied to specific projects to improve the teaching effect. Cases are usually taught through the flipped classroom.
6. **Problem-solving-based training.** Making architecture decisions as a team while constructing a new software system is one of the most critical skills a future software architect must develop. The most important decisions are made at the beginning of the creation of an application: technologies to be used, architecture patterns, and trade-offs between quality attributes, among others. After comes the development and maintenance of the application. It is an activity where the goal is to design the architecture of a system close to reality. The activity is usually done in teams, where each group is assigned an exercise to be solved in a given time.
7. **Games-based training**. Teaching SA is complex because the architect's role is multifaceted. The architect requires developing technical, analytical, and communication skills. Most talented architects have acquired extensive knowledge over many years of experience. Professors need fun teaching methods for shortened training time related to SA decision-making. Game-based training is an educational strategy that uses elements of games to foster student engagement, participation, and learning.

The competencies to be achieved by students in the SA field are very broad and complex. In this sense, we propose a list of the minimum competencies that the software industry expects from recent university graduates [18]:

- C01: Clearly identifies the relevant software quality attributes that will drive the architecture of a software system to be built.
- C02: Consistently design the software architecture by defining how components interact with each other.
- C05: Independently evaluates a software architecture to determine functional and non-functional requirements satisfaction.
- C08. Impartially performs a trade-off analysis to evaluate architectures.

- C11: Maintains existing systems and their architecture to achieve the evolution of software systems.
- C12: Redesigns existing architectures for migration to recent technologies and platforms.
- C18: Critically analyzes functional and quality attribute software requirements.
- C19: Understands business and customer needs quickly to ensure that requirements meet these needs.
- C22: Periodically performs reviews of the source code written by the development team.
- C23: Develops reusable software components.
- C28: Designs and implements test procedures considering architectural aspects (component/service types, integration).

4 Collaborative Teaching Strategy

Considering the challenges inherent in teaching SA to university students, professors from two academic institutions, Universidad Nacional de la Plata (Argentina) and Universidad del Cauca (Colombia), joined forces to establish collaborative activities, share resources, and employ joint pedagogical strategies. They initiated a course planning phase, during which we compared the learning objectives, curricula, and teaching techniques and strategies used by both universities to identify convergence points. As a result of this phase, a weekly planning of topics and activities was developed. During this planning, the following decisions were made for both courses:

- Work on a common project called Open Market (similar to the functionalities offered by Mercado Libre), in which the theoretical topics will be applied. The project had two important versions: the first one with a monolithic architecture and the second one a refactoring towards an architecture based on microservices.
- The project was worked on in teams of 4 and 5 students.
- Conferences with guests from the industry were planned to bring architectural design cases to real life.
- For the third part of the courses, a global development experience will be conducted between students from the two institutions.
- Recording and sharing classes between the two institutions.

5 Case Study Design, Execution and Evaluation

Below, we describe the steps we carried out during the study according to Runeson and Host (Runeson 2008).

5.1 Case Study Design

Goal. The objective of this case study was to obtain empirical evidence of the impact on the teacher and students of applying SAGITA and the training patterns to the two AS courses.

Research Questions. The research questions we address are:

- RQ1: What impact did the training patterns have on students' competency development at the end of the courses?
- RQ2: In this case study, how did the professor evaluate the Guide's usefulness and ease of use?
- RQ3: How was the students' satisfaction with the course?

Context of the Case Study. This case study was carried out during the first academic period of 2023, and two institutions participated. The first was the Software Architecture Patterns elective course of the Faculty of Computer Science of the Universidad Nacional de la Plata, Argentina, with 14 students. The second is the Software Engineering II course of the Systems Engineering program of the Universidad del Cauca, with 26 students. The case study is an improvement since it seeks to improve certain aspects of the phenomenon studied, such as students' competencies in AS topics.

The two courses have common objectives:

- Learn to identify early on architecture decisions that, by definition, are costly to modify in the future.
- To understand the challenges and problems that give rise to the evolution of architectural.
- To know the advantages and disadvantages of each of the current architectural styles.
- Learn to contextualize each architectural style to choose the most appropriate one.

5.2 Preparation of Data Collection

The techniques used for data collection were surveys, document analysis, and semi-structured interviews[1]. Still, during the development of the conversation, the order can be decided. The interview questions applied to the professors at the end of the course were:

1. After reading the SA Course Design Guide, describe what changes you made to your course in terms of content, objectives, and methodology?
2. Was the guide useful to you in planning your AS course? Was it worth using? Did it save you time and effort, or, on the contrary, did it add more work?
3. Was the Guide's outline of the steps for designing an SA course easy for us to follow, or did it have complex steps to understand?
4. According to the SA course design Guide, which training patterns did you decide to apply in your course and why?

[1] In a semi-structured interview, the questions are planned, but they are not necessarily developed in the established order [10]

5. Explain how you implemented the training patterns (at what time of the semester, with what human and technical resources).
6. How did these patterns impact your students' skill development at creating, documenting, and evaluating SA?
7. What difficulties did you have applying the training patterns during the course development?
8. Do you consider that the training patterns you used to allow software architecture training to be closer to the real world of the software industry?
9. What needs to be added to the proposed Guide to fulfill its purpose of proposing a set of steps and strategies to support the design and implementation of software architecture courses at the undergraduate level?

5.3 Execution of the Case Study

The case study was carried out during the first academic period of 2023. Initially, course instructors were introduced to the SAGITA Guide. The guide was used to plan the course. In particular, it was used to define the topics to be developed, the resources to be used, the choice and application of the training patterns, and the definition of the class project. Finally, the topics to be taught in the two countries were organized, such as SOLID principles and architectural styles, emphasizing the microservices style.

In terms of human resources, due to the complexity of the course, a group of several professors was organized in each institution. In the case of Argentina, there was one teacher in charge of theory classes and two collaborators for development and deployment. In the case of the Universidad del Cauca, there was one teacher for the theory and another teacher for the laboratories.

Several training patterns were applied. At UNICAUCA, the *Mini-Projects-based training* training pattern was chosen as the central strategy. UNPL applied the *Large Project-based Training* pattern focused on migrating a monolithic application to a microservices-based solution.

The two universities applied the *Cases-based training* pattern through the variant of lectures with invited software architects from the industry. Several lectures were organized throughout the courses, and each guest speaker presented the details of an actual architectural case: the context, the problem, the decisions made, and the results. In this way, the students learned from the experience lived by the architects. The three conferences were:

1. E-sidif project of the Ministry of Economy of Argentina.
2. Case of the chargeback module of the Mercado Libre application, migrating a monolith to microservices.
3. Case of large-scale architecture at Banco Galicia.

In the third part of the course, a *global development* experience was carried out as an integrating activity, merging the work teams of the two educational institutions in a development iteration. The planning made it possible to synchronize the courses in Colombia and Argentina so that they would arrive simultaneously at the third cut with the necessary knowledge and skills.

The two universities worked on the same class project, an E-commerce application similar to Mercado Libre called OpenMarket. However, UNICAUCA students developed a simpler version of the project to adapt it to mini-project development.

One helpful aspect was to record the classes and lectures on a web platform. This recording allowed students and professors in both countries to access the theoretical and practical content anytime.

At the end of the course, an interview was conducted with the professors of the two institutions.

5.4 Results Analysis

We could answer the research questions posed by triangulating the data collected through interviews, surveys, and document analysis.

RQ1: What impact did the training patterns have on students' competency development at the end of the courses?

The Large Project-based Training pattern allowed students to put AS theoretical knowledge into practice by developing a large and complex project. The Open Market project was developed in teams of 4 and 5 students, who performed requirements engineering, proposed system architecture, made design decisions, and communicated effectively for implementation and testing. Although the software did not have real customers, the requirements were inspired by modern e-commerce applications such as Mercado Libre.

Overall, the implementation of this development project had a positive impact on the students. The course development revolved around this project. Relevant aspects of this case study are described below.

- *Practical experience.* Students gained hands-on experience working on this large project, which allowed them to apply the theoretical concepts learned in a practical environment and face real challenges encountered in large-scale software development..
- *Teamwork.* This software project required collaboration among team members. Students learned to work as a team, communicate effectively, and coordinate their efforts to achieve common goals. This skill is crucial in the actual software industry.
- *Communication and collaboration.* This project involved students taking on different roles as developers, designers, architects, testers, and database designers. Students had to communicate and collaborate with their professors and advisors, reflecting the working reality of the industry.
- *Complex problem-solving.* The software project presented complex technical and design challenges. Students addressed problems early in the project and made critical architectural decisions. This situation enhanced their problem-solving and decision-making skills.
- *Planning and management.* The project required careful planning and adequate time and resource management. Students gained skills in time estimation, task allocation, and resource management, which are fundamental to project management in the industry.

- *Understanding architecture.* By working on this significant project, students had the opportunity to experience first-hand how scalable and robust software architectures are designed and built. They saw how components are organized, dependencies are managed, and modularity is ensured.
- *Work with current technologies.* The project involved the use of various current technologies and tools, such as Java EE, Spring Boot, Postman, Docker, etc. Students became familiar with modern development tools and practices used in the industry.
- *Preparation for working with industry.* By facing challenges and situations similar to those they will encounter in their future jobs, students prepare to transition to the software industry after graduation.
- *Personal Portfolio.* These large, complex projects can become valuable additions to students' portfolios, helping them stand out when seeking employment after graduation.
- *Cultural diversity and perspectives.* The global development experience in the final part of the course between UNPL and UNICAUCA students had additional impacts. Working with students from different cultures and academic backgrounds provided students with the opportunity to gain a deeper understanding of cultural diversity and other ways of approaching problems. Students learned to collaborate in teams distributed geographically and across time zones. This situation enhanced their communication and collaboration skills globally, which is increasingly relevant in today's working world. However, the short iteration period made it difficult for students to collaborate with five teams; only one collaborated well and produced an integrated and functional software solution.

Thanks to applying the *Cases-based training* training pattern, it was possible to coordinate three talks with invited software architects from the industry. The students were able to see real cases from the industry. These talks had several positive impacts. Some of them were:

- *Industry linkage.* Industry guest conferences allowed students to connect directly with working professionals and gain a realistic understanding of how SA theoretical concepts are applied in the working world.
- *Practical application.* Learning about real-life software design cases allowed students to see how SA concepts become concrete and applicable solutions in real-world situations.
- *Variety of perspectives.* The guest speakers came from different companies and sectors, exposing students to various approaches. It broadened their perspective on the different ways in which design problems can be addressed.
- *Stories of success and failure.* Guests from the industry shared stories of successful projects and challenges and failures in software design. These stories provided valuable lessons on what works and what doesn't, which helped students make better decisions in their future roles.
- *Direct interaction.* Students could ask direct questions to industry professionals and get answers based on actual, hands-on experience.

Regarding the competencies achieved at the end of the course, each student was asked: *Evaluate to what degree this course helped you achieve each of the following competencies required by the software industry. The following scale will be used for all questions: 1. Not helpful, 2.* The answers can be seen in the Fig. 1. We can see that some competencies such as C05 (*Independently evaluates a software architecture to determine the satisfaction of functional and non-functional requirements*), C08 (*Impartially performs trade-off analysis to evaluate architectures*) and C011 (*Easily maintains existing systems and their architecture to achieve the evolution of software systems*) students state that the course "helped a lot" to develop them in a large proportion. On the other hand, there are competencies that were not developed, such as C22 (*Reviews periodically the source code written by the development team*), since a large percentage of students state that the course "helped a little".

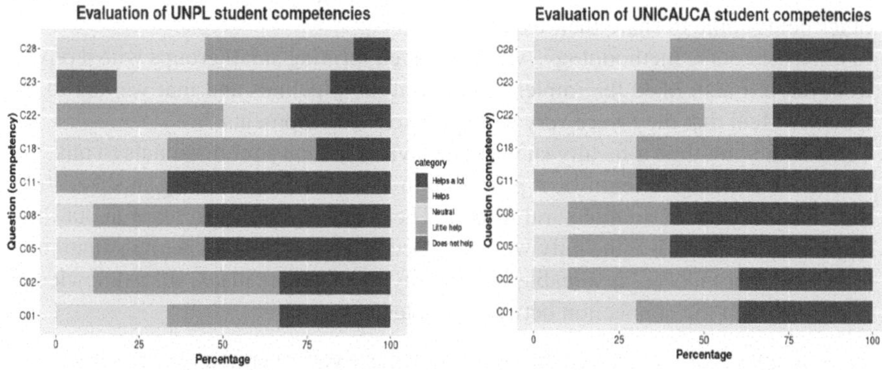

Fig. 1. Responses to the question: Please rate the extent to which you believe the Architectural Patterns course helped to achieve each of the following competencies? [Source: Own elaboration]

The main difficulties encountered in applying training patterns lie in the additional effort and time required by the professor. Each of these patterns entails a specific planning and execution phase. For example, coordinating talks with guests from the industry needed the professor to carry out tasks such as finding the guests, holding prior meetings, and coordinating their availability, among other aspects. Executing a large-scale project involved considerable efforts in drafting, revising, improving, and adjusting the project. In addition, following up and monitoring the students' projects represented a significant challenge. The professors need to be supported by more collaborating instructors who can assist them with issues related to Java technologies, application deployment, and student follow-up.

RQ2: In this case study, how did the professor evaluate the Guide's usefulness and ease of use?

Regarding the perceived usefulness, there were responses such as: "the *guide was handy because it allowed making improvements to the course. Some AS topics were adjusted, the necessary resources were chosen, and the training patterns were chosen to bring the course closer to the industry. The planning made was fulfilled during the execution. The guide provides accurate and relevant information on the design of Software Architecture courses. The concepts and guidelines presented directly apply to my area of study".*

Regarding the ease of use, professors expressed things like: "*The ease of use of the guide is remarkable and has been an overall positive experience. The guide features clear navigation and a well-organized structure. I can easily move between sections and find the information I need without difficulty. The language used in the guide is clear and accessible.*".

RQ3: How was the students' satisfaction with the course?

Valuable comments about the course were captured through surveys. Some of them are described below:

- "It was a great course and a pleasant experience, and I am grateful to my classmates, the professors, and those who came to lecture. It rarely happens that people from other fields come to share their experiences".
- "I liked the course methodology, which involved forming small groups with a project to develop. I also liked the implementation of the pipelines and that we had to use Docker; I feel that they were very useful for real developments.".
- "This is the first time a faculty subject has invited industry professionals to talk.".
- "It was interesting to learn how problems in the industry are being attacked from the point of view of architectural design. These talks allow us to learn about these experiences; otherwise, the only way is to face the problem in an actual situation."
- "I believe that talks are a valuable opportunity to exchange ideas, share knowledge, and strengthen the connection between people."

Several questions were asked through a student survey regarding overall satisfaction with the course. A Likert scale was used, with 1 Not at all satisfied and 5 Very satisfied. Regarding the question, "In general, how satisfied were you with what you learned in the course? The answers in a box plot can be seen in the Fig. 2. The box plots depict the distribution of student satisfaction. The horizontal line in the middle of the box represents the median satisfaction levels. In this case, the median is 4. We can say that most of the responses are in the scores range between 3 and 5, with a median of 4. It suggests that overall satisfaction tends to be high, as most responses are at the high end of the 1 to 5 scale.

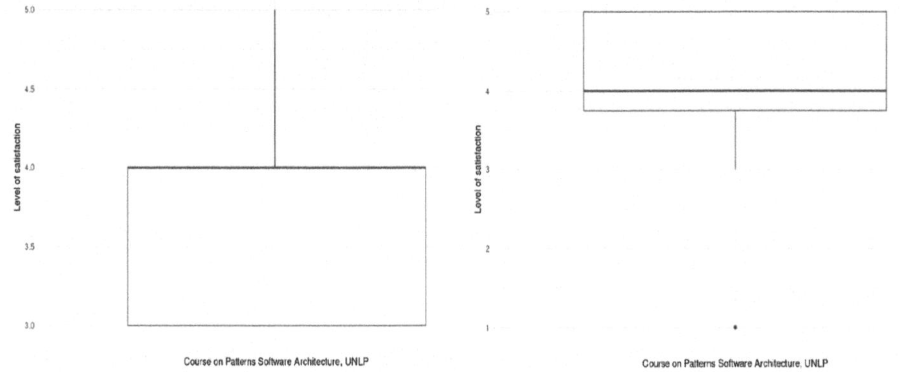

Fig. 2. Box plot of the question: How satisfied were you with what you learned in the course? [Source: Own elaboration]

6 Conclusions

An SA course aligned with industry needs is essential in the systems engineering curricula and related programs. However, training undergraduate students with the AS competencies demanded by industry has many challenges.

This research sought to organize knowledge that would help university professors design and conduct their AS courses in such a way that they would be able to face the difficulties of teaching AS and, on the other hand, align students' competencies with the needs of the industry. To this end, a catalog of seven training patterns was identified, structured, and documented, articulated within a guide that helped professors to design and execute courses at the undergraduate level that developed competencies in the creation, evaluation, and documentation of software architectures in line with the expectations of the software industry. These training patterns solve the problems that professors recurrently have to face, recreate the way of working in the classroom similarly to the environments used by the industry, helping the teacher to make decisions and, on the other hand, organize the architectural knowledge so that class activities can be structured and facilitate incremental learning. The ability to make architectural decisions is fundamental to the training process, but it takes time to develop and is accumulated through multiple project experiences.

Overall, the professor's satisfaction with using and applying SAGITA yielded positive results. In the case study, SAGITA helped professors plan their courses and implement strategies that brought the course closer to the reality of the software industry. In addition, we examined student satisfaction, evaluating through surveys the impact of the proposed strategies on their training. The results were generally satisfactory.

Using software *project-based training patterns* in teams provided UNPL and UNICAUCA students with a unique opportunity to develop practical skills, work in teams, face real challenges, and prepare for careers in the software industry. The pattern that involved bringing industry speakers into the classroom to share real-life software design cases enriched the students' educational experience by providing them with direct knowledge, practical insights, and valuable connections to the working world. The global software project development experience added a dimension of cultural diversity, international communication, and interdisciplinary collaboration, preparing students for an increasingly connected and globalized world of work. However, this activity for future courses should be improved in several aspects, both in time management and in carrying out previous activities to allow students to get to know each other. In addition, at the moment, there is no pattern of training in global software development.

Finally, the catalog of training patterns oriented professors on what and how to teach, developing the most relevant competencies for the current and future industry related to the creation, evaluation and documentation of ES in potential graduates of computer science programs.

Acknowledgments. A third level heading in 9-point font size at the end of the paper is used for general acknowledgments, for example: This study was funded by X (grant number Y).

Disclosure of Interests. t is now necessary to declare any competing interests or to specifically state that thc authors have no competing interests. Please place the statement with a third level heading in 9-point font size beneath the (optional) acknowledgments, for example: The authors have no competing interests to declare that are relevant to the content of this article. Or: Author A has received research grants from Company W. Author B has received a speaker honorarium from Company X and owns stock in Company Y. Author C is a member of committee Z.

References

1. Sherman,S., Unkelos-Shpigel, N.: What do software architects think they (should) do? Research in progress In: Advanced Information Systems Engineering Workshops, pp. 219–225. Springer International Publishing, Cham (2014)
2. Shah, M.A., Ahmed, I., Shafi, M.: Role of software architect: a Pakistani software industry perspective. Res J Recent Sci **3**, 48–52 (2014)
3. Leidig, P.M., Cassel, L.: ACM Taskforce efforts on computing competencies for undergraduate data science curricula. In: Proceedings of the 2020 ACM Conference on Innovation and Technology in Computer Science Education, pp. 519–520 (2020)
4. Moreno Vélez, E.: Arquisoft90 Formación profesional y capacitación (2020). https://www.linkedin.com/showcase/arquisoft90-entrenamiento-den-arquitectura-de-software. Accessed 31 May 2020
5. Lieh Ouh, E., Kok Siew Gan, B., Irawan, Y.: Did our course design on software architecture meet our student's learning expectations? In: 2020 IEEE Frontiers in Education Conference (FIE), pp. 1–9. IEEE, Uppsala, Sweden (2020). https://doi.org/10.1109/FIE44824.2020.9274014
6. Akhriza, T., Ma, Y., Li, J.: Revealing the gap between skills of students and the evolving skills required by the industry of information and communication technology. Int. J. Softw. Eng. Knowl. Eng. **27**, 675–698 (2017). https://doi.org/10.1142/S0218194017500255
7. Ouh, E.L., Irawan, Y.: Applying case-based learning for a postgraduate software architecture course. In: Proceedings of the 2019 ACM Conference on Innovation and Technology in Computer Science Education, in ITiCSE '19, pp. 457–463. Association for Computing Machinery, New York (2019). https://doi.org/10.1145/3304221.3319737
8. Pantoja, W.L., Hurtado, J.A.: Dificultades y retos de la formación de arquitectos de software en programas de pregrado: Causas y efectos. In: Tercer Simposio Doctoral del Doctorado

en Ciencias de la Electrónica, Popayán, Colombia. (2021). https://sites.google.com/view/simposiodoctoral2021/
9. Galster, M., Angelov, S.: What makes teaching software architecture difficult? In: Proceedings - International Conference on Software Engineering, pp. 356–359. Association for Computing Machinery, Austin Texas (2016). https://doi.org/10.1145/2889160.2889187
10. Runeson, P., Höst, M.: Guidelines for conducting and reporting case study research in software engineering. Empir. Softw. Eng. **14**(2), 131–164 (2008). https://doi.org/10.1007/s10664-008-9102-8
11. Giraldo, F.D., et al.: Applying a distributed CSCL activity for teaching software architecture. In: International Conference on Information Society (i-Society 2011), pp. 208–214. IEEE, London (2011). https://doi.org/10.1109/i-Society18435.2011.5978540
12. Garousi, V., Giray, G., Tüzün, E., Catal, C., Felderer, M.: Closing the gap between software engineering education and industrial needs. IEEE Softw. **37**, 68–77 (2020). https://doi.org/10.1109/MS.2018.2880823
13. Niño, M., Anaya, R.: Hacia un enfoque basado en competencias para la enseñanza de la ingeniería de software utilizando investigación-acción. In: Encuentro Internacional de Educación en Ingeniería ACOFI, Cartagena de Indias (21017). https://acofipapers.org/index.php/eiei/article/view/586
14. Kiwelekar, A.W., Wankhede, H.S.: Learning objectives for a course on software architecture. In: European Conference on Software Architecture, pp. 169–180 (2015)
15. Rupakheti, C.R., Chenoweth, S.V.: Teaching software architecture to undergraduate students: an experience report. In: Proceedings - International Conference on Software Engineering, pp. 445–454. IEEE Press, Florence (2015). https://doi.org/10.1109/ICSE.2015.177
16. Alexander, C.: A Pattern Language: Towns, Buildings, Construction. Oxford University Press (1977)
17. Pantoja, W.L., Hurtado, J.A., Bibbó, L.M., Fernández, A., Ajay, B.: Towards a software architecture training pattern language. In: Pattern Languages of Programs Conference PLOP2023, Illinois, USA (2023). https://www.hillside.net/plop/2023/
18. Pantoja, W.L., Solano, A.F., Bandi, A., Hurtado, J.A.: Insights into software architecture competencies integrating industry and academic perspectives. Revista colombiana de tecnologías de avanzada, vol. 1 (2023). https://doi.org/10.24054/rcta.v1i43.2798

A Comprehensive Study on the Importance of Parameters in Neuroevolution Techniques

Rodrigo Benito[1(✉)], Leticia Cagnina[1], and Luis Avila[1,2]

[1] Laboratorio de Investigación y Desarrollo en Inteligencia Computacional (LIDIC), UNSL, Av. Ejército de los Andes 950, 5700HHW San Luis, Argentina
rodrigobenito33@gmail.com, loavila@unsl.edu.ar

[2] Laboratorio de Sistemas Inteligentes (LSI), CONICET-UNSL, Ruta Prov. Nº 55, 5730EKQ San Luis, Argentina

Abstract. Neuroevolution techniques (NE) were developed to address the challenge of subjective definition in the architecture and topology of artificial neural networks. They draw inspiration from the biological process of evolution, iteratively searching for the best solutions among generations of networks. In this work, we performed an exhaustive analysis to evaluate the relevance of the numerous parameters involved in NE models and assess their impact on the performance of the techniques. This study assesses the performance of NEAT and HyperNEAT techniques to determine their capability to develop the required structures for solving a given problem. Specifically, the primary objective is to ascertain whether the topology construction takes place reliably. To ensure comprehensive coverage of the sample space, we employed sampling and statistical inference methods. We obtained independent observations for performing statistical significance tests and analyzing the performance of the NE techniques under study. Results of several experiments show how NEAT tends to employ a smaller number of neurons and links, while HyperNEAT exhibits a notably higher architecture complexity.

Keywords: Neuroevolution · Artificial Neural Networks · Latin Hypercube Sampling · Statistical Inference · Parameter Sensitivity

1 Introduction

With the advancement of computing power and hardware architectures, there has been a resurgence in research on artificial neural networks (ANNs). Nevertheless, ANNs are still often perceived as black boxes, characterized by a high level of ambiguity regarding their architecture. This added to the possible connections and disconnections that can occur during their training, means that the search space is almost infinite in computational terms. Neuroevolution (NE) techniques were designed to partially overcome the problem of subjective definition in the architecture and topology of ANNs. NE is inspired by the biological process of evolution, whereby the best solution is searched iteratively between generations of ANNs.

A first approach to NE techniques is given by the iterative search of synaptic weights for a fixed network topology, an approach known as fixed-topology NE [1]. By employing

V. Agredo-Delgado et al. (Eds.): DECISIONING 2024, CCIS 2369, pp. 16–30, 2025.
https://doi.org/10.1007/978-3-031-91690-8_2

these techniques, the intensity of connection weights is determined by evolution, while the architecture of the ANN remains unchanged across generations. The second is the search for pure architectures where the optimal topology is first searched for and then is trained [2]. Ultimately, a more intriguing approach is to view NE as a strategy for evolving both the topology of the network and the weights of the connections among its neurons. These algorithms are termed as TWEANNs, standing for Topology and Weight Evolving Artificial Neural Network algorithms [3].

Evolutionary algorithms function by operating on a population of genotypes, which are defined by parameters of the network such as its topology or connection weights. In NE, each genotype is associated with an ANN phenotype, which is then assessed on a specific task to determine its fitness. For example, in direct coding schemes, the genotype maps directly to the phenotype. That is, each neuron and connection in the ANN is directly and explicitly specified in the genotype. In contrast, in indirect coding schemes, the genotype indirectly determines how that network should be generated. They can also use direct coding, in which each connection and node of a phenotype is specified in its genotype, or indirect coding, in which genotypes provide rules for constructing phenotypes. As an illustration, NEAT (NE of Augmenting Topologies) and Hyper-NEAT (a variant of NEAT based on Hypercube) are two approaches that evolve both the topology and connection weights of neural networks. NEAT employs a direct encoding method, whereas HyperNEAT utilizes an indirect encoding scheme.

This study assesses the performance of NEAT and HyperNEAT techniques to determine their capability to develop the required structures for solving a given problem. Specifically, the primary objective is to ascertain whether the topology construction takes place reliably. A manner to compare the performance of the algorithms is through a statistical test that allows analyzing the uncertainty, sensitivity and importance of the model parameters. Latin Hypercube Sampling (LHS) [4] is a statistical method for generating a sample of plausible collections of parameter values from multivariate distributions. Sampling serves the objective of acquiring data enabling the estimation of statistical parameters. In this study, the LHS technique is employed to investigate the level of uncertainty and/or sensitivity of the parameters within the models developed by NE techniques. These analyses enable a thorough examination of how the models respond to variations in the input variables. They also allow characterizing the uncertainty of the response and classifying their importance based on the sensitivity. Results of several experiments show significant differences are evident between the solutions generated by each NE technique. NEAT tends to employ a smaller number of neurons and links, while HyperNEAT exhibits a notably higher architecture complexity. In the subsequent sections, we begin by introducing the NEAT and HyperNEAT techniques. Following this, we present a comprehensive experimental study on the involved parameters and assess their sensitivity to changes.

2 Neuroevolution

2.1 Evolutionary Algorithms

Evolutionary Algorithms (EAs), also known as Evolutionary Computation systems, is an engineering method that imitates the mechanism of evolution in organisms and applies this to the creation, synthesis, and selection of data structures. The field traces its origins back to four seminal evolutionary methods: Genetic Algorithms [5], Evolution Strategies [6], Evolutionary Programming [7] and Genetic Programming [8].

EAs encompass operators designed for selection, crossover, and mutation. These operators are responsible for effectively choosing individuals for reproduction, generating new individuals based on the selected individuals, and ultimately determining the composition of the individuals in the population of the following generation. The stochastic crossover operator or recombination, involves exchanging genetic material between two selected individuals. Thus, this operator is in charge of exploiting the search space. The stochastic mutation operator makes random changes to the genes of an individual. This operator is in charge of exploring the search space. The mutation operator is important to guarantee diversity in the population as well as recovering genetic material lost during evolution. This evolutionary process is repeated until a maximum number of generations has been executed. The population in the final generation represents the culmination of exploring and exploiting the search space across multiple generations, and may also embody the global optimum solution.

As a distinctive characteristic, NE employes genetic search to discover an optimal network, mitigating the risk of being stuck in locally optimal solutions, as opposed to backpropagation training. NE represents network link weights as genotypes and uses evolutionary computation to search for the most suitable network. Consequently, the fitness value determines the error in the network output. Moreover, NE can dynamically learn a network structure, adjusting the number of nodes and links to the task. Several NE methods have been applied to the architectural configuration and learning or training of ANNs. In the simplest algorithms, the ANN topology is fixed and only the network's weights evolve [9]. In the NE process, the exploration of the space of connection weights is conducted through evolutionary mechanisms, including crossover of network weight vectors and mutation of individual network weights. Here, the main objective of the NE process is to optimize the weights of connections within a fixed topology. We will concentrate on analyzing the two most prevalent techniques from the family of algorithms based on NE, as they are widely recognized: NEAT and HyperNEAT.

2.2 NEAT

NeuroEvolution of Augmenting Topologies (NEAT) aims to enhance the effectiveness of the NE process by evolving both the topology and connection weights of ANNs. Therefore, the main difference between conventional NE algorithms and NEAT is that NEAT also evolves network topology [10]. NEAT establishes a mapping between genes and the connections within an ANN, allowing for the evolutionary incorporation of new genes that specify additional connections or nodes.

NEAT begins evolution with a population of simple networks and complexifies the network topology into diverse species over generations, leading to an increasingly sophisticated behavior [11]. In Fig. 1 node and connection genes for a simple network structure are shown. NEAT is designed to take advantage of the network structure, trying to minimize the space search dimensionality of weights by evolving the structure from a basic topology to a more complex one. As new genes are introduced through mutations, they are allocated distinctive historical markings. During crossover, genes bearing identical historical markings are combined to generate offspring. The population of networks is partitioned into various species according to the quantity of shared historical markings. Speciation serves to safeguard structural advancements within networks by lessening competition among distinct species. Consequently, the historical markings and speciation mechanisms enable NEAT to construct intricate task-relevant features.

Figure 1 also shows how NEAT produces network phenotypes from genotypes. A genotype consists of two parts: the node information which includes a list of input nodes, hidden nodes, and output nodes; and the link information including a list of the arcs linking pairs of nodes. The link information comprises descriptions of the nodes constituting the starting and ending points of an arc, link weightings, flags indicating whether an arc is enabled or disabled, and ID numbers. For example, in the cited figure there are three input nodes, one hidden node, and one output node. Additionally, it's important to note that while the information linked describes seven arcs, the second arc is disabled and consequently not reflected in the phenotype. In other words, this means the corresponding arc does not exist within the network.

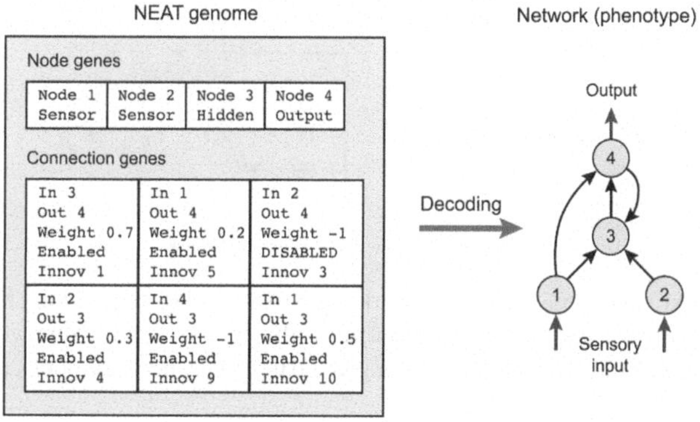

Fig. 1. Genome example used in NEAT to encode the ANN shown on the right (Source [9])

2.3 Hyper-NEAT

NEAT has been extended using a coding method known as composition pattern producing network (CPPN) to create hyperNEAT. Using the HyperNEAT approach, a comparatively compact CPPN network can define a complex task network of any scale and density [9]. CPPN is said to be geometrically aware because each output is a function of the coordinates of the nodes in the corresponding layers of the network, refer to Fig. 2.

Under HyperNEAT, the output of a NEAT-trained network dictates the weights of a secondary network, which is then employed to execute the desired task. In its basic form, this secondary task network is structured with nodes arranged in a two-dimensional space, allowing each node to be identified by its (x, y) coordinates. For example, the HyperNEAT function in Fig. 2 takes four inputs and returns a weight $CPPN(x_1, y_1, x_2, y_2) = w$. The first network, the CPPN, takes four inputs that define the locations of two nodes in the task network, where the first node is located at (x_1, y_1) and the second node is located at (x_2, y_2). The output of the CPPN is the value of the weight that connects these two nodes. Therefore, NEAT can be utilized to evolve a CPPN that guides the "development" of the task network. It's important to note that the task network, rather than the CPPN, undergoes evaluation by the fitness function.

Indirect encoding allows CPPN to describe patterns with regularities like symmetry, repetition, and variation by implementing different activation functions. CPPNs have the capability to encode weights as functions of domain geometry. This results in an Artificial Neural Network (ANN) that inherently incorporates knowledge regarding the geometric relationships within the domain. Particularly, HyperNEAT uses this approach to take advantage of geometric regularities in the network topology [12]. HyperNEAT is an extension of NEAT, moving away from one-to-one encoding between phenotype and genotype. The basic idea of hyperNEAT is to use CPPN to express the links and weights of a neural network at first, and then use NEAT to optimize CPPN.

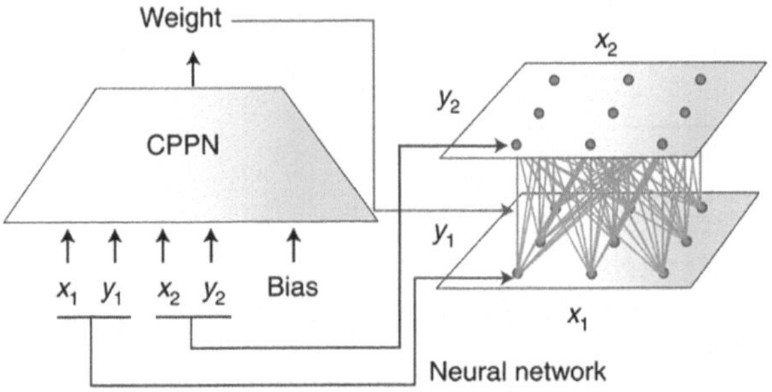

Fig. 2. HyperNEAT encoding. The task network (right) is a two-layered network in which neurons connect between the lower and upper layers, but not within them. The CPPN network (left) defines the connection strengths of the task layer for a given pair of task network nodes (Source [9]).

3 Experimental Study

NE models aim to evolve the structure of the neural networks to improve their performance. Thus, we study how different sets of parameters can influence the neural models in terms of the growth of the structure, removal/addition of weight connections, and changes in the topology. Next, we analyze how these factors impact the performance of the models in terms of efficiency, specifically focusing on the execution time required to find the optimal result while maintaining a minimal architecture, as well as considering consistency. The basic perceptron, as outlined in the 1960s, featured a remarkably straightforward structure consisting of a single layer that received input data, passed through an activation function, and determined the network's output. ANNs were limited to solving linearly separable problems. However, by introducing hidden units to this architecture, a more advanced network known as the Multilayer Perceptron (MLP) was developed. The MLP demonstrated enhanced capabilities, enabling it to effectively solve non-linear functions.

The XOR function has been a classical example of a non-linearly separable function. It has been utilized in the study of ANNs from the early stages due to its simplicity and is often employed to analyze NE methods. Therefore, we incorporated the XOR function into our experiments to examine the various parameters involved in neuroevolutionary models and assess their impact on the performance of the techniques. Given the 4 possible sets of binary inputs (x and y), the output (z) of the XOR function is shown in Table 1.

Table 1. XOR function. x and y are the inputs and z is the corresponding output (Own source)

x	y	z
0	0	0
0	1	1
1	0	1
1	1	0

Classical evolutionary algorithms, such as NE, need to compute a fitness function f. We first define the $error_{MLP}$ (Eq. 1) as the distance of the output of the ANN $output_{MLP}$ from the correct answer z for the four input patterns defined in 1.

$$error_{MLP} = \sum_{i=1}^{4} \left| output_{MLP}(x_i, y_i) - z_i \right| \tag{1}$$

Then, we define the fitness function f in Eq. 2 as the squared error of the difference of 4 and the $error_{MLP}$. When the MLP obtains the correct values for each of the 4 inputs, the error will be 0 therefore $f = (4 - 0)^2 = 16$ (the optimum); f will be a value lower than 16, otherwise.

$$f = (4 - error_{MLP})^2 \tag{2}$$

3.1 Neuroevolution Techniques: Default Parameters

In addition to the typical parameters of EAs, NE introduces several more related to the topology and structure of the ANN being evolved. Below, we describe the main parameters to consider in algorithms implementing NE:

- Population Size: number of simple genomes (individuals) in the initial population.
- Compatibility Threshold: individuals whose genomic distance is lower than this threshold is considered to be in the same species.

- Young-Age Threshold: younger genomes are more likely to be chosen for breeding.
- Species Max Stagnation: the species that have not shown an improvement in the fitness scores in more than this number of generations are considered stagnant and will be extinct.
- Old-Age Threshold: older genomes are more likely to be chosen for extinction.
- Min Species: minimum number of species.
- Max Species: maximum number of species.
- Selection: method used to select the genomes to reproduction.
- Recurrent Probability: of a link becomes recurrent.
- Mutation Rate: probability (overall) that a gene will have some kind of mutation.
- Archive Enforcement: keep an archive of genomes.
- Mutate Weights Probability: to change the weight of a connection by adding a random value.
- Weight Mutation Max Power: standard deviation (zero-centered normal distribution) from which a weight value mutation is set.
- Weight Replacement Max Power: new random value of the weight of a connection.
- Max Weight: of a connection.
- Mutate Add Neuron: probability to add a hidden node to a genome.
- Mutate Add Link: probability to add a link to a genome.
- Mutate Rem Link: probability to remove a link from a genome.
- Activation Function: selected for all nodes.
- Crossover Rate: number of most-fit individuals in each species that will be preserved from one generation to the next.
- MultiPoint Crossover Rate: the chance that genomes swap their genes.
- Survival Rate: fraction for each species allowed to reproduce each generation.
- AllowLoops: are recurrent links allowed?
- AllowClones: allow clones or nearly identical genomes to exist simultaneously in the population?

The abundance of parameters increases the complexity of experiments aimed at identifying the optimal parameter set and extends the execution time of the algorithms. In our analysis, we consider NEAT and HyperNEAT as we described in Sect. 2. Both techniques were used to solve a XOR Neural Network. For simplicity and to facilitate comparison, NEAT and HyperNEAT were configured with the same parameters. We adopted the default parameters proposed in [13], which are shown in the first column of Table 2. The algorithms stop the execution due to success (fitness = 16) or after reaching the maximum number of generations set in 1000.

We run executions of both NE techniques using 30 different seeds and obtained the results as presented below. In Fig. 3 we can observe the obtained optimal fitness distribution, whereas Fig. 4 show the average fitness values distribution obtained with NEAT and HyperNEAT. In turn, Fig. 5 and Fig. 6 show the average number of neurons and links determined as the best MLP architecture found by each method. There is a ramarkable difference between the solutions produced by each NE technique. NEAT tends to utilize fewer neurons, averaging around five, whereas HyperNEAT typically employs twice that amount. In terms of links, the architecture complexity determined by HypeNEAT is notably higher, averaging around 30 links with a maximum of nearly 70.

On the other hand, NEAT tends to use fewer links, averaging around 10 with a maximum of 20. This disparity underscores the distinct approaches taken by both techniques in solving a simple XOR neural network and the varying levels of complexity incorporated into their solutions.

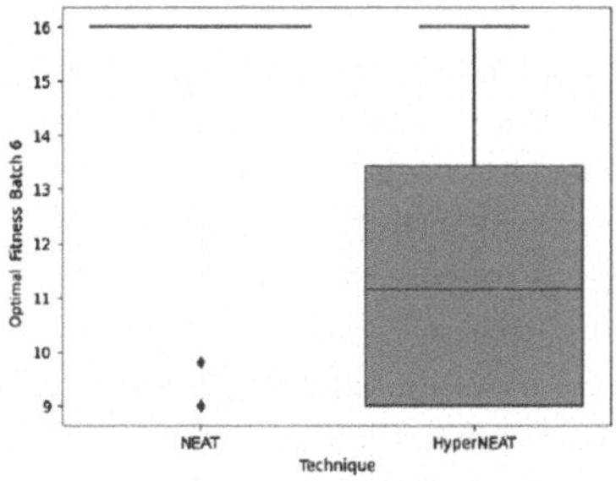

(a) Batch 6

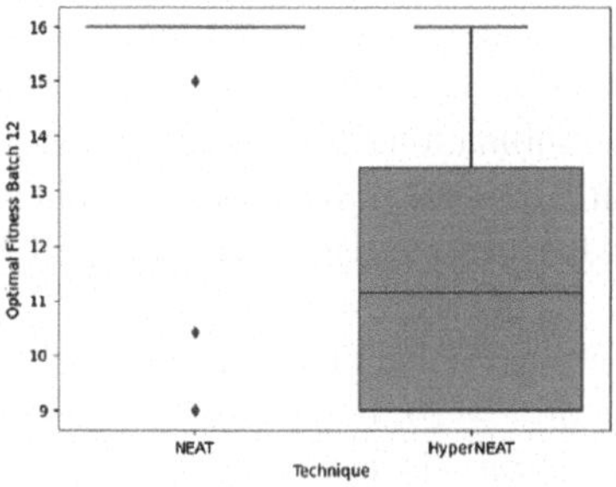

(b) Batch 12

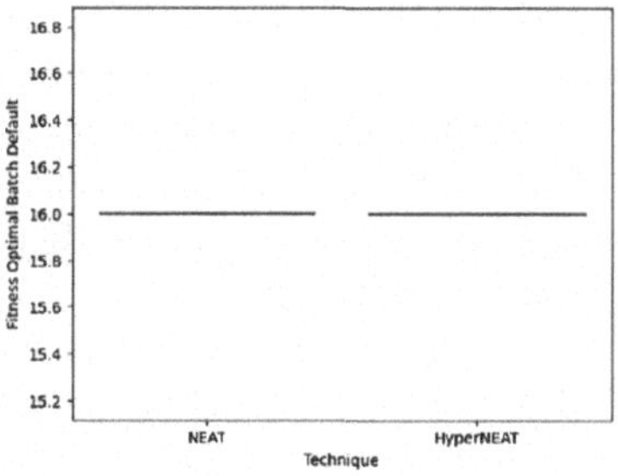

(c) Batch Default

Fig. 3. Optimal Fitness Distribution (Own source)

Nevertheless, although the fitness obtained with both NE techniques are similar, we consider that the performance of both needs to be properly investigated. Thus, at this point we may formulate the following research questions (RQ):

- RQ1: How to select the default parameters?
- RQ2: Does the performance of NEAT and HyperNEAT techniques considerably change with other parameters?
- RQ3: How sensible are the techniques to changes in the values of each parameter?

To answer these questions, a rigorous analysis is performed in the next subsections, describing a detailed design of experiments and statistical significance tests of the results obtained as well as a performance study.

3.2 Design of Experiments and Statistical Significance Test

Primarily, we run additional experiments to evaluate a broader range of parameters beyond those initially proposed [13]. Due to the extensive number of parameters and the wide ranges associated with each, observe Table 2, we have opted to employ an appropriate sampling technique and thus, we answer RQ1.

Let P be the set of parameters of the techniques evaluated in our study, $P = \{X_1, X_2, ..., X_p\}$, , our goal is to generate a set of potential values within the range of each parameter for sampling purposes. To ensure comprehensive coverage of the sample space, we employ the Latin Hypercube Sampling (LHS) method [14]. LHS computes a sample of size N partitioning the range of each parameter X_i into N non-overlapping intervals with probability 1/N. The values are selected at random with respect to the probability density of that interval. The result of the procedure is a set $E = \{E_1, E_2, ..., E_N\}$ of N tuples of size p and each one determines the parameters of the experiments that will be performed for the validation process we want to do. Note that in each E_i-tuple the values are matched at random, that is, N values for parameter X_1 are randomly paired with the N values for X_2, and randomly paired with the N values of X_3, and so on.

In the LHS design for the model validation, we choose $N = 25$, while the number of parameters evaluated is $p = 24$. Then, 25 tuples with different values for the 24 parameters determine the set of experiments E to execute. In Table 2 we can observe the parameters and their corresponding range (as suggested in literature). We conduct each experiment $E_i \in \varepsilon$ a total of 30 times to acquire the fitness values of the NE algorithms corresponding to those parameter combinations. Subsequently, we calculate the mean of these 30 values for each experiment. These mean values serve as independent observations for performing statistical significance tests and analyzing the performance of the algorithms under study.

After conducting the 25 experiments, it is observed that in only 2 of them NEAT and HyperNEAT achieve the optimal fitness value of $f = 16$. It appears that the parameter combinations used in the remaining 23 experiments do not allow for the successful solution of the XOR problem within the specified conditions (a maximum of 1000 iterations).

With this statement we answer RQ2: the performance of NEAT and HyperNEAT techniques considerably changes when different parameters are used, even, for a very easy problem as XOR is, the results are not as expected. Consequently, our analysis will focus on these 2 successful experiments, denoted as *E6* and *E12*. The last two columns of Table 1 display the values of each parameter selected (and utilized) according to the LHS method for each experiment.

For the statistical significance analysis, it is crucial to consider whether the distributional assumptions—namely, independence of observations, normality of sampling distribution, and equality of variances—are met. In this case, the nonparametric Levene's test [15] revealed that the variances obtained in the *Ei* experiments were significantly different. Consequently, the assumption of homogeneity of variance was violated. Subsequently, we employed the non-parametric Wilcoxon signed-rank test [16]. This statistical inference method assesses whether the data provide adequate support for a specific hypothesis. Through hypothesis testing, probabilistic statements about population parameters, such as those observed in the *Ei* experiments, can be made.

The Wilcoxon signed-rank test for matched pairs states that: *Given the same population tested under different circumstances C1 and C2, if there is an improvement in C2, then most of the results recorded in C2 will be greater (better) than those recorded*

Table 2. Parameters of NE: recommended values in literature and selected by our study (Own source)

Parameter	Recommended	Batch 6	Batch 12
Population Size	100	194	143
Compatibility Threshold	2.0	2.471	3.93
Young-Age Threshold	15	32	43
Species Max Stagnation	15	3	48
Old-Age Threshold	35	14	45
Min Species	2	8	11
Max Species	10	29	18
Selection	Random	Roulette	Random
Recurrent Probability	0.0	0.539	0.48
Mutation Rate	1.0	0.508	0.275
Archive Enforcement	False	True	True
Mutate Weights Probability	0.05	0.246	0.938
Weight Mutation Max Power	0.5	0.866	0.65
Weight Replacement	8.0	8.935	16.098
Max Weight	8	13.71	18.956
Mutate Add Neuron	0.001	0.938	0.2
Mutate Add Link	0.3	0.663	0.055
Mutate Rem Link	0.0	0.518	0.849
Activation Function	Sigmoid	Sigmoid	Sigmoid
Crossover Rate	0.0	0.326	0.171
MultiPoint Crossover Rate	0.0	0.488	0.388
Survival Rate	0.2	0.023	0.833
Allow Loops	True	False	True
Allow Clones	True	False	False

in C1, and those that are not greater will be smaller by only a small amount. Here, *C1* and *C2* correspond to *E6* and *E12*, respectively, and the population is determined by the results (fitness) of the XOR problem. The null hypothesis *H0* in the test asserts that *the medians of the two samples E6 and E12 are identical.* That is, *H0* = *The performance of NEAT and HyperNEAT is similar.*

We conducted the test using the 30 medians obtained in the 30 runs for each experiment and considered a significance level $\alpha = 0.05$. The Wilcoxon signed-rank test indicated that there was no significant difference between the medians of the fitness obtained with NEAT and HyperNEAT: z-value $= -1.475$, p-value $= 0.138$ for *E6* and, z-value $= -1.923$, p-value $= 0.055$ for *E12*. As we observe, the critical z-values are in the interval [-1.96, 1.96] then, *H0* is not rejected. Also, the *p*-values are higher than 0.05 (*p*-value $> \alpha$), then, as we stated before, the null hypothesis is not rejected (the results are not significantly different). That means that using different sets of parameters (*E6* and *E12*), Neat and Hyperneat perform similarly for the XOR problem and we can state that both combinations of parameters are equally good to use.

3.3 Result Analysis

In Fig. 4, it is evident that although NEAT achieved better performance by reaching the optimum, it exhibits greater dispersion compared to HyperNEAT. However, NEAT's median is superior, suggesting that despite its lack of robustness, it outperforms HyperNEAT in Batch 6. Regarding Batch 12, depicted in (b), NEAT not only demonstrates superior performance but also HyperNEAT displays greater robustness, showcasing improved maximum, minimum, and median values. Regarding the average distribution of neurons, as depicted in Fig. 5, in (a) for Batch 6, it's evident that HyperNEAT exhibits a more complex neuronal model, surpassing NEAT in every indicator. This difference may be attributed to the parameter MutateAddNeuronProb, which is set to 0.938 for Batch 6 compared to 0.2 for Batch 12. Despite its increased complexity, HyperNEAT demonstrates greater consistency in results across all iterations where Batch 6 parameters were analyzed. Conversely, in (b) for Batch 12, both techniques surpass their counterparts in Batch 6. Notably, NEAT substantially improves both the robustness and the complexity of the neuronal model compared to HyperNEAT.

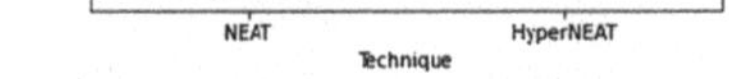

(a) Batch 6

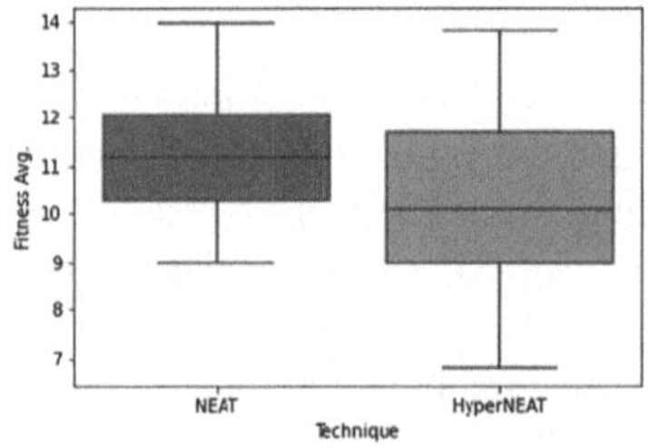

(b) Batch 12

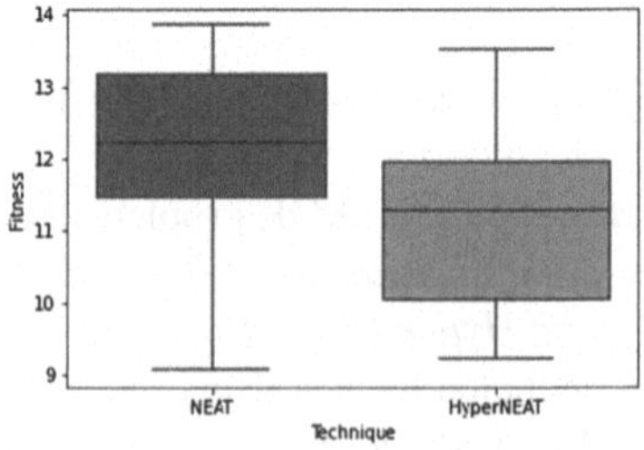

(c) Batch Default

Fig. 4. Average Fitness Distribution (Own source)

In Fig. 6, which represents the average distribution of links, we observe that in (a) the parameters of Batch 6 enabled NEAT to surpass HyperNEAT, resulting in a reduction in the complexity of the neural model obtained in terms of both links and number of nodes, as well as exhibiting less dispersion of the data. However, as an overall comparison, Batch 6 is significantly more complex due to the parameter MutateAddLinkProb, which is set to 0.663 compared to Batch 12, where this parameter is set at 0.055. On the other hand, in (b) for Batch 12, we once again witness a substantial improvement compared to Batch 6. Continuing this trend, NEAT once again outperforms HyperNEAT in all indicators.

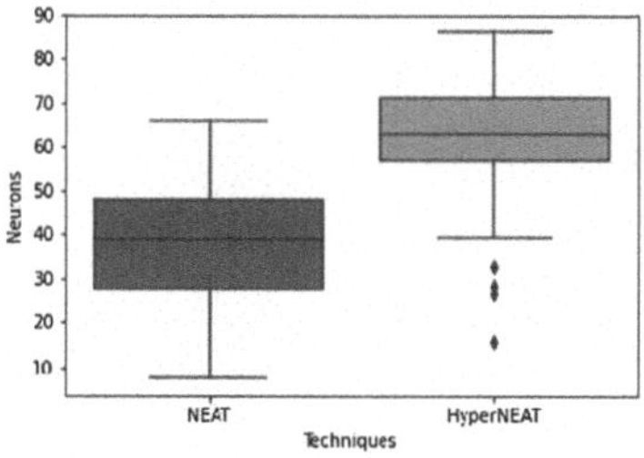

(a) Batch 6

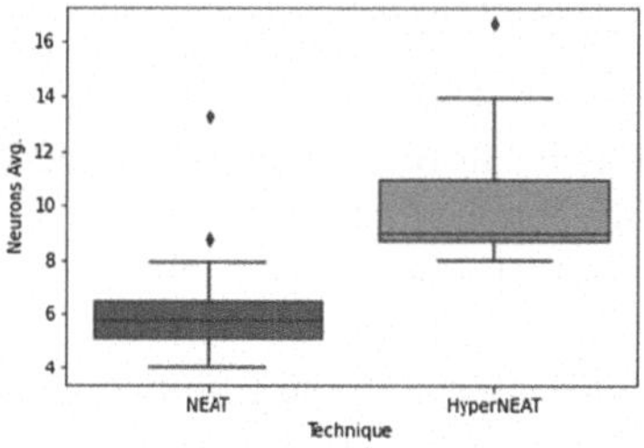

(b) Batch 12

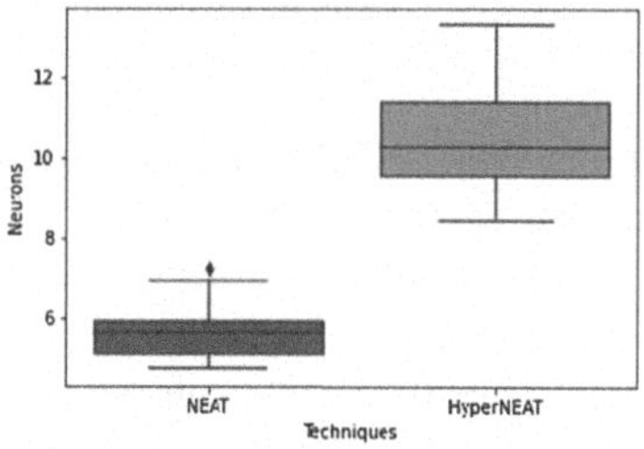

(c) Batch Default

Fig. 5. Average Neurons Distribution (Own source)

In Fig. 7 we see metrics represented throughout the 30 iterations in which the parameters were evaluated, and their corresponding results in Time, measured in ours and their Fitness results. For the parameters of Batch 6, in (a), we can see the high instability of the model in the time results, mainly for NEAT where it varies from 10 h to 48 h and then reaches minimum points of approximately 5 h per iteration. HyperNEAT allows us to see less instability in the time required to complete the iterations, but it remains with values close to 30 h during most of iterations. Its counterpart, in (b) for Batch 12, shows us greater stability for both techniques, but leaving NEAT as the winner, having only some peaks approximately at 3 h. While HyperNEAT, is maintained in most of the iterations in times greater than 2 h. Regarding fitness, it is evident that Batch 12 exhibits superior results compared to Batch 6, both in terms of reducing the time required to reach the optimum and in the maximum fitness level achieved. Although HyperNEAT manages to reach the optimum, it does so only at certain peaks during the total number

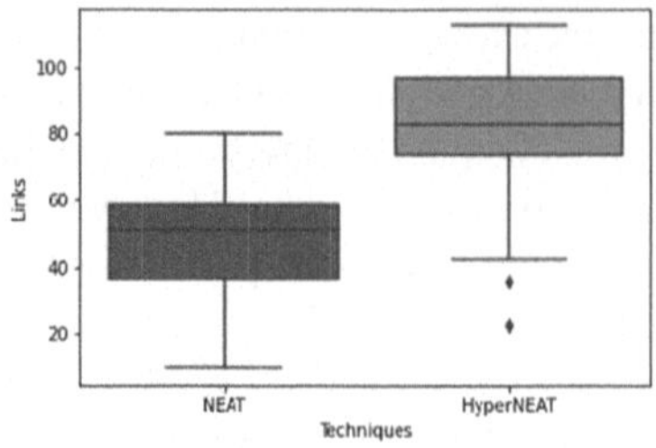

(a) Batch 6

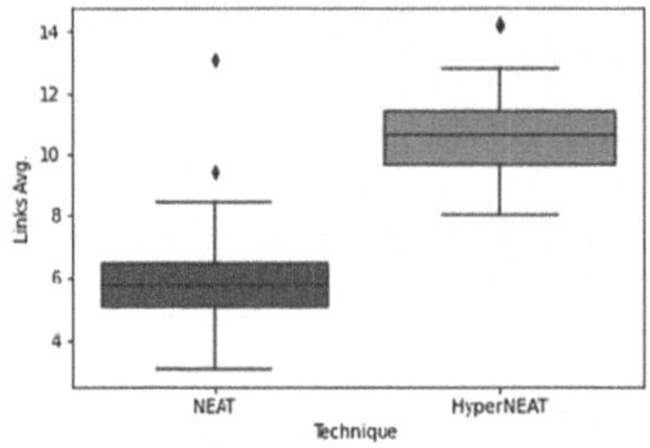

(b) Batch 12

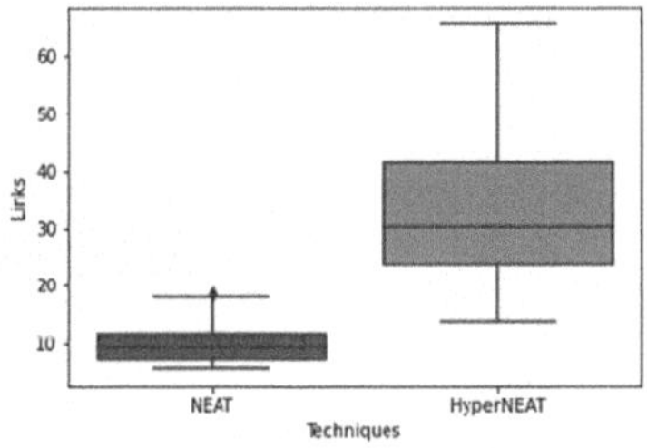

(c) Batch Default

Fig. 6. Average Links Distribution (Own source)

of iterations, while NEAT maintains stable results for three-quarters of the total iterations. In contrast, for Batch 6, NEAT demonstrates commendable performance in terms of fitness, significantly surpassing HyperNEAT in both stability and achieving greater results.

As final conclusion, we can observe many differences in the results obtained by NEAT and HyperNEAT when the same set of parameters are used (Batches 6, 12 and default). These differences are not limited to performance (best fitness, minimum number of neurons and links) but are also seen in the dispersion of results. This demonstrates the sensitivity to the parameters that both techniques exhibit, answering thus the RQ3.

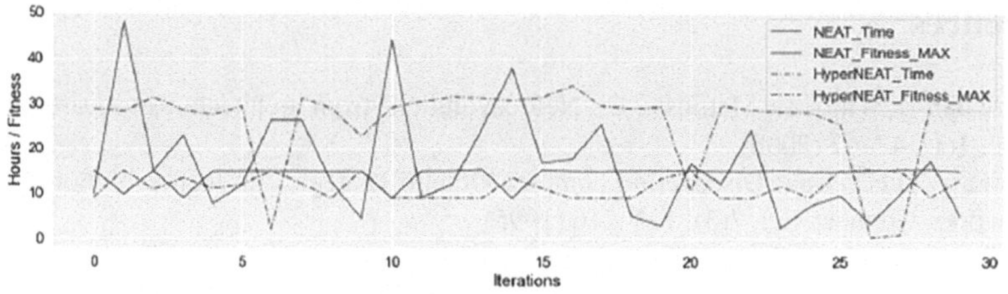

(a) Batch 6

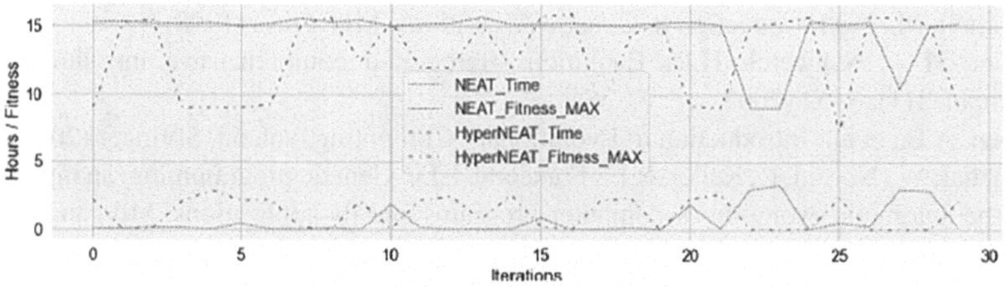

(b) Batch 12

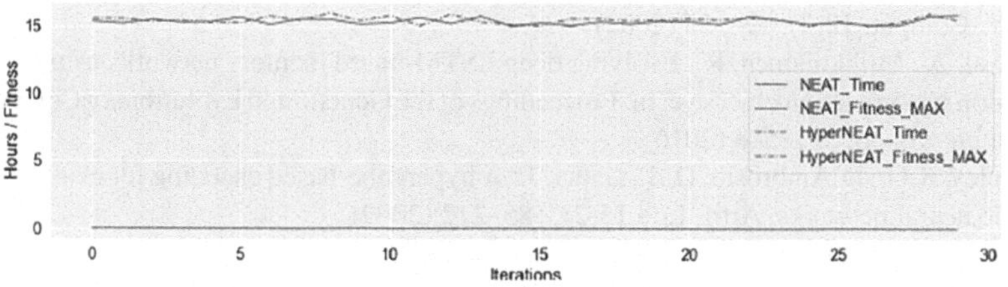

(c) Batch Default

Fig. 7. Time and fitness results (Own source)

4 Conclusions

In this work, we performed an exhaustive analysis to evaluate the relevance of the numerous parameters involved in neuroevolutionary models and assess their impact on the performance of the techniques. Therefore, to ensure comprehensive coverage of the sample space, we employed the Latin Hypercube Sampling (LHS) method. As a result, we obtained independent observations for performing statistical significance tests and analyzing the performance of the NE techniques under study. From that, we can conclude that both techniques offer similar performance for this case of study when fitness is evaluated under similar conditions (parameters).

Nevertheless, we observe a notable difference between the solutions produced by each NE technique when other metrics are considered. In general, NEAT tended to use fewer neurons and links, while the architecture complexity determined by HyperNEAT, especially in terms of links, is notably higher. This disparity underscores the distinct approaches taken by both techniques in solving a simple XOR neural network and highlights the varying levels of complexity incorporated into their solutions.

References

1. Floreano, D., Dürr, P., Mattiussi, C.: Neuroevolution: from architectures to learning. Evol. Intel. **1**(1), 47–62 (2008)
2. Moriarty, D.E., et al.: Discovering complex Othello strategies through evolutionary neural networks. Connect. Sci. **7**(3), 195–210 (1995)
3. Hiraga, M., Ohkura, K.: Topology and weight evolving artificial neural networks in cooperative transport by a robotic swarm. Artif. Life Robot. **27**(2), 324–332 (2022)
4. Koch, P., Bischl, B., Flasch, O., Bartz-Beielstein, T., Weihs, C., Konen, W.: Tuning and evolution of support vector kernels. Evol. Intel. **5**(3), 153–170 (2012)
5. Mitchell, M.: An Introduction to Genetic Algorithms. MIT Press (1998)
6. Beyer, H.G., Schwefel, H.P.: Evolution strategies–a comprehensive introduction. Nat. Comput. **1**(1), 3–52 (2002)
7. Eiben, A.E., et al.: Introduction to Evolutionary Computing, vol. 53. Springer (2003)
8. Banzhaf, W., Nordin, P., Keller, R.E., Francone, F.D.: Genetic programming: an introduction: on the automatic evolution of computer programs and its applications. Morgan Kaufmann Publishers Inc. (1998)
9. Hausknecht, M., Lehman, J., Miikkulainen, R., Stone, P.: A neuroevolution approach to general Atari game playing. IEEE Trans. Comput. Intell. AI Games **6**(4), 355–366 (2014)
10. Stanley, K.O., Miikkulainen, R.: Evolving neural networks through augmenting topologies. Evol. Comput. **10**(2), 99–127 (2002)
11. Rawal, A., Miikkulainen, R.: Evolving deep LSTM-based memory networks using an information maximization objective. In: Proceedings of the Genetic and Evolutionary Computation Conference, pp. 501–508 (2016)
12. Stanley, K.O., D'Ambrosio, D.B., Gauci, J.: A hypercube-based encoding for evolving large-scale neural networks. Artif. Life **15**(2), 185–212 (2009)
13. Chervenski, P.: Portable neuroevolution library (2019)
14. McKay, M.D., Beckman, R.J., Conover, W.J.: A comparison of three methods for selecting values of input variables in the analysis of output from a computer code. Technometrics **21**(2), 239–245 (1979)
15. Nordstokke, D.W., Zumbo, B.D.: A new nonparametric levene test for equal variances. Psicológica **31**(2), 401–430 (2010)
16. Woolson, R.F.: Wilcoxon signed-rank test. Wiley Encycl. Clin. Trials, 1–3 (2007)

A Radar Based on Scientific-Technical Observatories for the Cuban Software Industry

Omar Correa Madrigal[1,2](✉), María Ofelia Calderón[1], Lorena Ibet Rosales González[1], Dunia Naranjo Hernández[1], and Laritza Magdalena Martínez Negrín[1]

[1] Universidad de las Ciencias Informáticas, Havana, Cuba
{ocorrea,ofemar,lirosales,dunia,laritza}@uci.cu
[2] Kazan Federal University, Kazan, Russia

Abstract. This study aims to identify stages and indicators for implementing a technology radar tailored to the Cuban software industry, addressing its unique challenges and opportunities. Through a systematic analysis of specialized literature, including 9 prominent technology radars (e.g., ThoughtWorks Tech Radar, Zalando Tech Radar), the work establishes a framework structured into four quadrants: Business Intelligence, Platforms and Tools, Languages and Frameworks, and Scientific Stage a bilingual (English/Spanish) literature review enabled the identification of global best practices, which were then adapted to Cuba's context. Key results include the radar integrates traditional technical indicators as ISO 9126 for software quality with novel elements like scientometric metrics to balance innovation and practicality. Metrics such as "developer productivity" were redefined to reflect local realities while market growth thresholds were contextualized to Cuba's economic scale. A phased approach was proposed, including adoption ("Adopt"), testing ("Test"), evaluation ("Evaluate"), and sustainability ("Sustain"), aligned with Cuba's infrastructure and skill constraints. The study emphasizes prioritizing open-source solutions and fostering academia-industry collaboration. Comparisons highlighted the need for dynamic updates to the radar, ensuring alignment with Cuba's evolving priorities, such as digital sovereignty and sustainable development.

Keywords: Technological radar · quadrants · indicators applied to technology · scientific indicators

1 Introduction

A radar is a device that emits electromagnetic waves and collects echo resulting from the bouncing of the emissions off nearby targets [1]. The mission of the radar is to detect nearby targets of interest and to discard those that are not relevant to the particular application for which it is designed. Currently there are several types of radars with multiple uses and objectives. To cite some examples, those focused on meteorology with targets (such as clouds) can be considered as targets for certain applications. The oceanographic ones focused on aspects with the seas and its fauna. For military purposes, as jamming signal (aerial exploration) [2] and technological among many others).

V. Agredo-Delgado et al. (Eds.): DECISIONING 2024, CCIS 2369, pp. 31–41, 2025.
https://doi.org/10.1007/978-3-031-91690-8_3

In the study Article: Inspirational Technology Radar Examples, the author [3] presents criteria for the use of technology radar as a technique to continuously monitor and evaluate relevant technologies by means of a set of indicators defined in dependence of the purpose of the radar. The article mentions 9 examples of the most updated and effective radars according to the characteristics and purpose for which they are used. Among those mentioned are the following, but it should be noted that the page is constantly updated with new examples, so the ones present at the time of this study are exemplified. Some of them are: ThoughtWorks Tech Radar, Digitec Galaxus Tech Radar and Zalando Tech Radar; belong to companies that describe greater development and reputation in the technology sector so they acquire greater competitiveness and reputation. Others, such as Software AG's technology radar, are divided into six sections, which, when interpreted, do not allow us to make a more appropriate adaptation to environment. This work, explores the radar approach based in exploratory studies and application in the conception of general radar for Cuban Software Industry.

2 Related Works

A literature search was carried out on the subject of technological radars, scientific observatories and associated indicators with a total of 27,600 results using the Boléan operators (and, or, not) and keyword *Technological Radars, Indicators applied to technology and Scientific Indicators*. The information collected is associated with terms in English (1,678) and Spanish (1,650.4). The search was in the google scholar, a download of 67 articles referring to the thematic and debugging 10 within which it was possible to appreciate the different radars associated to technological observatories that allowed to establish comparisons between 9 radars [4–11].

Technological Radars

1. ThoughtWorks Technology Radar
2. Digitec Galaxus Tech Radar
3. Zalando Tech Radar
4. bbv Technica Radar
5. Software AG Technology Radar
6. Adesso Technology Radar
7. AOE Technology Radar
8. DB Systel Digital Trend Radar
9. My technology radar

ThoughtWorks Tech Radar, Digitec Galaxus Tech Radar and Zalando Tech Radar; belong to companies that describe greater development and reputation in the technology sector so they acquire greater competitiveness and reputation: ThoughtWorks Tech Radar, Digitec Galaxus Tech Radar and Zalando Tech Radar; belong to companies that describe greater development and reputation in the technology sector so they acquire greater competitiveness and reputation. When establishing the comparison, we conclude that to apply and adapt to a integral radar, is necessary take into account the general view about studied radars, since we consider that given its characteristics of presenting 4 quadrants with their respective phases. All radars are part of a leading global technology consultancy that integrates strategy, design and software engineering to enable enterprises and technology descriptors around the world to thrive as modern digital businesses.

3 Radar Based on Scientific-Technical Observatories

Once the analysis of each studied radar is that in one way or another there are similarities between them. Most of them present 4 sessions that coincide in quadrants and rings.

Quadrants

- Programming languages
- Programming tools
- Platforms
- Techniques

Rings Categories

- Adopt
- Test
- Evaluate
- Sustain

Based on the integral analysis the proposed radar, was necessary reorganize the quadrants and add two like Scientific Stage and Business Intelligent (Fig. 1).

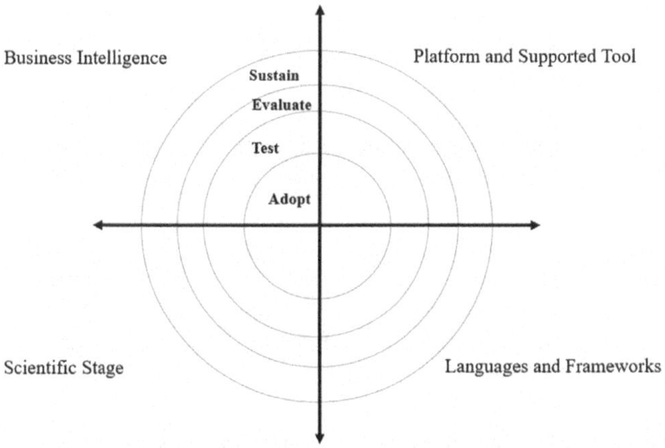

Fig. 1. General design of radar. Source: Own elaboration

The radar shows the 4 quadrants: Business Intelligence, Platform and Supported Tool, Languages and Frameworks and Scientific Stage (scientometric). This point of view permits in a same space to analyses the main components of Software Industry. For the assignment of indicators, the criteria issued by studies associated to the implementation of technological radars were taken into account [12–14]. These indicators were adjusted to a set of stages defined for the implementation of a radar, which are described below. The distribution on each ring- Adopt, Test, Evaluate and Sustain is a working progress (Tables 1, 2, 3 and 4).

Table 1. Indicators for Business Intelligence quadrant

Indicator	Objectives	Measurement criteria	Description
Software Quality	Check by using metrics such as defects per line of code, failure rate in production, correction times, among others	ISO 9126: This framework focuses on software quality and is divided into six quality characteristics: functionality, reliability, usability, efficiency, maintainability and portability	Functionality (if it works) Reliability (no gaps) Usability(handling) Efficiency (performance) Maintainability and portability (it can be Maintenance and portability
Developer's productivity	Measure using metrics, lines of code x hours, number of tasks completed x days, among other factors	High Medium Low	High + 100 Medium-100 Low-50
Impacts on user satisfaction	Measure user satisfaction through surveys	Compliant Nonconforming:	Agrees With dissatisfaction
Software responsiveness	Measure from observation, software response times	Fast Adequate Slow	Fast: Reacts immediately to one click Adequate: > e = 10 s Slow: > to 30 s
Investment in the Market	Annual growth in total net revenues from sales in the IT applications and services market	High Medium Low	High + 100 Medium-50 Low-50
Number of companies linked to technology	To account for the presence of high-tech companies linked to the field of information technology and communications	Counting with the use of formulas	Use of the function: COUNT IF

(*continued*)

Table 1. *(continued)*

Indicator	Objectives	Measurement criteria	Description
Level of access to technology	Census of accessibility to technology based on the increase in the number of users (companies), as well as the use of new technologies	User-device ratio Total ratio of technological devices/person Access to technology per person	Technological census
Data analysis	To measure the organization's effectiveness in data analysis by monitoring new trends and patterns identified in a given period	Efficient Not efficient Insufficient	Efficient: number of determined trends and patterns greater than 100 Low efficient: less than 50-100 Insufficient 50-0
Predictive power:	Measure the accuracy of predictions made in the past and the success rate of measures taken to anticipate future trends	Analyze the market Analyze suppliers	More than 10 companies Reliable suppliers
Use of emerging technologies	The impact of Technology Watch on the implementation of emerging technologies, such as artificial intelligence, augmented/virtual reality, IoT, among others, and its role in the digital transformation of the organization	The number and quality of technological innovations implemented by the organization	Number of patents registered Number of new technologies implemented Percentage of revenues from products and services

Analysis of Technology Placement Based on the Proposed Radar

The proposed technology radar for the cuban software industry, structured into four quadrants (Business Intelligence, Platforms and Tools, Languages and Frameworks, and Scientific Stage), serves as a strategic tool to classify technologies based on their impact, maturity, and alignment with organizational goals. In the Business Intelligence quadrant, technologies that improve software quality, productivity, and user satisfaction are prioritized. For example, tools like React or Jest are positioned here if they reduce

Table 2. Indicators for Platform and Supported Tool quadrant

Indicator	Objectives	Measurement criteria	Description
Typology of language focused platforms (x)	To know the platforms that use the different types of languages that can be used in them	Total number of platforms using the programming language	Out of a total of 20: High: 20-15 Medium: 15-10 Low: less than 10
Most used codes or programs	Distinguish the most commonly used codes or programs for different software	Total number of codes or programs used	Out of a total of 20: High: 20-15 Medium: 15-10 Low: less than 10
Tools with higher performance	Recognize the most effective tools used	Tools with the highest employment scores	Out of a total of 20: High: 20-15 Medium: 15-10 Low: less than 10
The most advanced technologies at a global level	Identify the leading technologies used in the observatories	Numbers of tools leading the search in observatories	Employment impact on observatories (Quality of search)
Tools depending on their effectiveness	Identify tools for a given Objective	Verify if they are feasible or not depending on their objective	If other well-known companies in the industry use them, they are feasible
Most used technology by sector	Identify the latest technologies of greatest employment by sector	Employment impact on sectors	(>number of technologies used, > e = number of recognized technologies, > e = number of recognized technologies
Platform functionalities	Identify platforms by theme	Most popular topics on the platform	Level of access to the topics Download of topics
Level of profitability of the platforms	Number of times they use	Access level	Amount of discharge
Server capacity	Storage number	Appreciate brand, by capacity level	. Identify the weight of the documents Databases, among others
Platform security	Number of restrictions and antivirus	Authorized personnel Updated Antivirus	Antivirus Update License

Table 3. Indicators for Languages and Frameworks quadrant

Indicator	Objectives	Measurement criteria	Description
Legible and elegant	Impossible to write obfuscated code	To be understood	Users understand it
Simple and Powerful	Supports high-level objects and data structures strings, lists, dictionaries, etc Multiple levels of code organization: functions, classes, modules and packages Includes libraries containing a large number of useful classes utility classes	Capacity	Enable large storage volumes
Scripting	You do not have to declare constants and variables before using them	Number of variables	Command behavior
Interoperable Code	Can be used on multiple platforms	Platforms with interoperable codes	Verify code operation
Open Source	Accessible to all	Unrestricted	The platform can be interacted with
General Purpose	Determined end	Justification	That it fulfills its purpose
Functionality	Seeks to measure the contribution of a software standard to the security of access to framework	Accuracy Adequacy Interoperability Security	Show results Corresponding to your objective Handling with the user Not easily accessible
Response time data insertion transaction data insertion	Identify the time it takes for the frameworks	High: 1–6 min Medium:2–4 min Low: 0–1	Locate the time it takes for the frameworks

(*continued*)

Table 3. *(continued)*

Indicator	Objectives	Measurement criteria	Description
Transaction response time update transactions update	Identify the time it takes for the frameworks	High: 1–6 min Medium:2–4 min Low: 0–1	Locate the time it takes for the frameworks
Response time in query transactions data	Identify the time it takes for frameworks to frameworks to list data with a given number	High: 1–6 min Medium:2–4 min Low: 0–1	Locate the time it takes frameworks

Table 4. Indicators for Scientific Stage quadrant

Indicator	Objectives	Measurement criteria	Description
Information Flows and Communication Channels	Observe and analyze the behavior of the information flow and communication channels used	Main directions of information flow and the most used communication channels	Development trends and progress towards technological development. (High impact Medium impact Lower impact)
Most productive authors, companies and institutions	Identify the most productive authors, companies and institutions to analyze behavior	Relevance x productivity of authors, companies and institutions	Position in the international ranking (sites with the greatest technological impact)
Leaders by theme	Study and identify main leaders by topic	(Positioning x identified themes) Identified by different themes: Example: Theme 1: High Hal Low	Level 1: High positioning in the ranking (most cited) Level 2: Medium positioning Level 3: Low positioning (less cited)
Author and institutional collaboration networks	Identify main authorial and institutional collaboration networks	Total platforms that use the programming language	Out of a total of 20: Height: 20–15 Medium: 15 – 10 Low: less than 10

(continued)

Table 4. (*continued*)

Indicator	Objectives	Measurement criteria	Description
Total documents by topic	Identify total documentation by subject	Physical count of documents x topics	Processing x formulas
Authorship Level	Identify the first authors x Articles	Counting using Software tools to create Matrix	Processing using Software tools
Author by genre	Identify articles by number of Authors by female and male sex	Counting using Matrix Software tools	Processing using Software tools
Autorship by Institution	Identify the authors with the greatest number of publications	Counting using software tools to create a matrix	Processing using software tools
Most cited publications	Study the figures of most cited publications for statistical analysis	Number of alerts indicating Most cited publications	All: > e = al 75% between 74 al 50% < del 45%
Most referenced publications	Study more referenced publications	Number of alerts tha indicate reference to the same publication	Positioning table in the referencing of publications in descending order
Publications indexed in top-level journals	Analyze Publication Statistics and recognize those indexed in top-level journals	Physical count of publications in top-level magazines	Formula processing. Counting with conditioning
Information niches Opportunities for impact or novelty	Identify information niches. Opportunities for impact and novelty	Number of information niche alerts. Positioning of development topics of new opportunities and development due to their impact	Relevant: > e = al 75% de _X_ Featured: del 74 al 50% de _X_ Minor relevance: < del 45% de _X_

production defects or optimize response times, validated by metrics such as ISO 9126. However, ambiguous indicators like "High + 100" require adaptation to the local context: in Cuba, a 20% annual revenue increase could define a "high" impact. This quadrant also includes cloud platforms like AWS, but their viability depends on factors such as available infrastructure, suggesting the exploration of open-source alternatives like OpenStack to reduce external dependencies.

In the Platforms and Tools quadrant, technologies like Docker or GitHub Actions are evaluated for their ability to streamline deployments and ensure security. For instance,

Kubernetes could be classified as "Adopt" if it reduces deployment time by 40% in cuban projects. However, criteria such as global adoption ("if other companies use it") must be weighed against local realities. Additionally, metrics like storage capacity require contextual adjustments.

The Languages and Frameworks quadrant prioritizes technologies like Python or FastAPI for their readability, interoperability, and performance. TypeScript, for example, would be positioned here if it reduces type-related errors by 50%, improving code maintainability. However, subjective claims like "impossible to write obfuscated code" should be replaced with objective metrics, such as readability scores from tools like SonarQube. Response times (e.g., < s for financial transactions) must align with use cases, recognizing that acceptable thresholds may differ significantly in healthcare or education.

In the Scientific Stage, emerging technologies like TensorFlow or Qiskit are assessed for their academic backing and disruptive potential. For example, Qiskit would enter the "Evaluate" ring if piloted in collaboration with Cuban universities on quantum computing projects. This quadrant demands bridging research and practice: a technology like OpenCV could be prioritized.

Interaction between quadrants is dynamic. Docker, initially in the Scientific Stage, migrates to Platforms as it becomes standardized, while TypeScript moves from Languages to Business Intelligence by demonstrating error reduction impact. For Cuba, recommendations include contextualizing metrics (e.g., defining "high productivity" as 12+ lines of code/hour), prioritizing open-source tools (PostgreSQL, Nextcloud), and fostering academia-industry alliances. Radar updates, supported by dashboards with current KPIs, will ensure relevance amid technological changes and local needs.

In conclusion, this radar not only classifies technologies but also guides their strategic adoption in Cuba. By integrating global indicators with local realities and fostering a collaborative ecosystem. Cuban software industry can optimize resources, drive innovation, and position itself competitively in the region. The model's flexibility will enable adaptation to emerging trends, from AI to sustainability, ensuring technological growth aligned with national priorities.

4 Conclusion

The comparative analysis of technological radars in the context of the software industry has culminated in a comprehensive radar designed to guide strategic decision-making across three critical dimensions: Business Intelligence, Development Process (encompassing Languages/Frameworks and Platform-Supported Tools), and Scientific Stage. This result adapts global best practices to cuban context, addressing both technical and socio-economic challenges while fostering innovation. By evaluating established radars (e.g., ThoughtWorks and Zalando) and integrating scientometric indicators, the study establishes a structured approach to monitor the industry's state art and prioritize technologies aligned with national objectives. The tests performed show consistency in the quadrant and ring location results as well as in the interrelation between quadrants. While it is true that the number of quadrants per quadrant needs to be optimised, the existing quadrants allow for consistent prediction of the nature of the surveillance target and its possible evolution.

Acknowledgments. This work has been financed by the CITMA-MINCOM projects program of Cuba.

References

1. Arencibia-Jorge, R., Vega-Almeida, R.L., Carrillo-Calvet, H.: Evolución y alcance multidisciplinar de tres técnicas de análisis bibliométrico **10**(1), 102 (2020). https://doi.org/10.24215/18539912e102. ISSN 1853–9912
2. Clavijo García, M.: Análisis de señales de RADAR secundario de vigilancia aeronáutica empleando dispositivo RTL-SDR (2021). http://idus.us.es/
3. Martinez Isaza, D.A., Acevedo Pineda, E.A.: Sistema de Información con Indicadores del uso de recursos para Bibliotecas Universitarias. Caso de estudio Biblioteca Humberto Saldarriaga Carmona del Tecnológico de Antioquía, Institución Universitaria (2023). https://dspace.tdea.edu.co/bitstream/handle/tdea/
4. García-Peñalvo, F.J. EKS Challenges for 2020. Educ. Knowl. Soc. **21**(1) (2020). Disponible en: https://doi.org/10.14201/eks.22203
5. Özerol, G., Arslan Selçuk, S.: Machine learning in the discipline of architecture: A review on the research trends between 2014 and 2020 (2023). Disponible en: https//journals.sagepub.com/
6. Hinings, B., Gegenhuber, T., Greenwood, R.: Digital innovation and transformation: an institutional perspective. Inf. Organ. (2018). https://doi.org/10.1016/j.infoandorg.2018.02.004
7. Jafvert, A., Gustafsson, C.P.: Digital transformation in digitally mature organisations: managers' perspectives on challenges in progressing in digital maturity. Lund University: Master´s Thesis (2019). https://lup.lub.lu.se/luur/
8. Quiroga, J.M., Lugones, M.J., Vera, MNTecnologías tecnologizantes y políticas pendulares: continuidades y rupturas en los sectores nuclear, espacial y radar en Argentina (2003–2019) –.(2022). http://rid.unrn.edu.ar.//
9. Ruiz, A., Delgado, T., Febles, E.A.: Habilitando la transformación digital tomo 2 compilación de autores .colección ciber sociedad , editorial UH, unión de informático de cuba – (2022). https://repositorio.uci.cu/bitstream/123456789/10427/1/tomo1digital.pdf
10. Machado-Fernández, J.R.:de la distribución gamma en matlab para aplicaciones de radar Ciencias Holguín, vol. 22, núm. 4, octubre-diciembre, pp. 1–17. Centro de Información y Gestión Tecnológica de Holguín. Holguín, Cuba (2016). https://www.redalyc.org/pdf/1815/181548029005.pdf
11. Melvin, W.L., Scheer, J.: APrinciples of Modern Radar, Vol III Radar Applications (2014). http://ScitechPublishing/
12. Richards, M.A., Scheer, J.A., Holm, W.A.: Principles of Modern Radar Vol I Basic Principles: Scitech Publishing. (2010). https://citeseerx.ist.psu.edu/
13. Salmela, H., Rousseau, P.: Role of dynamic capabilities for digital transformation: developing dynamic capabilities essential for digital transformation. University of Turku, Turku (2019). https://www.utupub.fi/
14. Yu, Z.: Visualizing artificial intelligence used in education over two decades. J. Inf. Technol. Res. **13**(4), 32–46. (2020). https://doi.org/10.4018/JITR.2020100103

Application of SemIoTica to the Development of a Prototype of an Intelligent System with IoT in Single-Family Aquaponics at the Tecno Academia Popayán

Oscar Santiago López Erazo[1,5](✉), Juliana Delle Ville[2], Giuliana Maltempo[2], Adriana Gómez[3], Juan Camilo Ortega Erazo[4], Luis Freddy Muñoz[5], Julio Ariel Hurtado[1], and Leandro Antonelli[2]

[1] IDIS, Universidad del Cauca, Popayán, Colombia
{santiagolopez94,ahurtado}@unicauca.edu.co

[2] Lifia Facultad de Informática, Universidad Nacional de La Plata, La Plata, Argentina
{jdelleville,gmaltempo,lanto}@lifia.info.unlp.edu.ar

[3] Universidad Tecnológica de Pereira, Pereira, Colombia
adrianagomezr@utp.edu.co

[4] SENA, Servicio Nacional de Aprendizaje, Popayán, Colombia
jcortega@sena.edu.co

[5] Logiciel, Fundación Universitaria de Popayán, Popayán, Colombia
santiago.lopez@docente.fup.edu.co, lfreddyms@fup.edu.co

Abstract. The increasing adoption of Internet of Things (IoT) technologies in agriculture has led to improved decision-making processes. However, deploying IoT devices in agricultural systems raises concerns about security vulnerabilities and potential cyber threats. In this context, SemIoTica emerges as a method to systematically identify and mitigate security risks in IoT solutions for agriculture. This paper presents a case study that applies the methodology to identify the security vulnerabilities of a prototype aquaponics system, a tangible example of IoT application in smart agriculture. SemIoTica comprises four steps: (i) scenarios are described for the intended software, (ii) scenarios with incorrect uses of the system are described, (iii) these scenarios are translated into security scenarios using a set of rules, and (iv) the security scenarios are refined. Therefore, based on SemIoTica's four-step approach, correct and incorrect system use scenarios were systematically analyzed, and security scenarios were derived and refined to address the identified vulnerabilities. This paper presents an empirical application of the methodology in identifying and mitigating security risks in IoT agriculture, providing valuable information for developers and agriculture practitioners. Future approaches from this research may explore further refinement of security analysis methodologies and the development of robust cybersecurity measures tailored to the unique challenges of IoT applications in agriculture.

Keywords: IoT · Security Scenario · Smart Farming · Industry 4.0 · IoT Requirements

V. Agredo-Delgado et al. (Eds.): DECISIONING 2024, CCIS 2369, pp. 42–57, 2025.
https://doi.org/10.1007/978-3-031-91690-8_4

1 Introduction

The quality and quantity of food have increased in recent years due to industrial growth and newer methods in the agricultural field [1]. Such technologies as the Internet of Things (IoT) have been introduced to promote better crop efficiency as well as to address the challenges faced by contemporary agriculture [2–4]. IoT is defined as a network of interconnected objects such as sensors, actuators, devices, and others, which are grouped together for information exchange and collection of context-related data, with the aim of supporting decisions, enhancing processes and offering comprehensive solutions across the virtual and real worlds [3–5].

It is in this context that SemIoTica [6] acquires relevance, since it proposes a method for specifying security scenarios that integrate requirements and architecture elements into IoT agricultural solutions. The method comprises four steps: (i) scenarios for the intended software are described, (ii) scenarios with incorrect uses of the system are described, (iii) these scenarios are translated into security scenarios using a set of rules, and (iv) the security scenarios are improved. Furthermore, the authors present a prototype that uses the algorithm described in the proposal to help strengthen the incorrect use scenario based on the correct use scenarios; afterwards, the expert only needs to complete the information for the analysis and subsequent derivation of the security scenario.

Smart farming improves conventional agricultural practices by introducing technology into the field. This is beneficial; however, the deployment of devices might put agricultural activity at risk. Having devices connected to the internet can expose the system to vulnerabilities and attacks, exposing it at the level of security. Vulnerabilities, risks and threats to equipment and data in modern agriculture can be increased by harsh environmental conditions. Security in IoT has acquired utmost importance as there are more chances that hackers initiate an attack [7]. Another important factor is cybercrime or an unauthorized person accessing the system to cause harm or leak sensitive information [2, 8]. It is therefore crucial that the following items be taken into account when addressing security: (i) undesirable threats, (ii) protection of the surrounding context from damage, (iii) avoidance of physical damage, (iv) access control policies and authorization mechanisms [9–11].

As the previous items are relevant, vulnerabilities become important due to the risk factor associated with them in IoT agriculture systems. Systems like the single-family aquaponics system prototype use low-cost IoT technology [12] for the purpose of allowing users to remotely monitor key aspects of the system and provide an optimal environment for fish and plant growth. The prototype aims to develop a comprehensive IoT-based platform for collecting and analyzing vital data from aquaponic systems in real time. This is an IoT application in smart farming, as it supports the agricultural processes of aquaponics, defined as the union between aquaculture and hydroponics. More precisely, it consists of an agricultural method where fish waste is transformed into essential nutrients for plants. The main purpose of the system is to constantly monitor salinity, temperature, water level, pH, water quality, and sunlight, among others [4].

The SemIoTica approach and the algorithm-generated response can significantly enhance the misuse scenario by providing relevant additional information. This paper reports a preliminary evaluation of the application of the SemIoTica approach in a real project, namely the aquaponics project with the objective of identifying security scenarios for applications in IoT agriculture. This paper is organized as follows: Sect. 2 briefly describes the SemIoTica approach, and Sect. 3 describes related work. Next, Sect. 4 describes how SemIoTica is applied to the prototype. Section 5 presents a discussion. Finally, Sect. 6 presents conclusions and future work.

2 Background

This section describes SemIoTica, the method used to evaluate the security vulnerabilities in agricultural IoT applications. SemIoTica consists of 4 steps [6], summarized in Table 1. The following subsections describe each step-in detail.

Table 1. SemIoTica's approach summarized. Source: Own Elaboration.

➡ Scenarios	1. Description of scenarios with correct use of the intended application	➡	2. Description of scenarios with incorrect use of the intended application	➡	3.Derivation of security scenarios	➡	4. Refinement of the description of the security scenarios	➡	Security Scenarios

2.1 Step 1: Description of Scenarios with Correct Use of the Intended Application

This step entails the description of scenarios that focus on the correct use of the software application regarding security concerns. This step should be executed by a requirements engineer or analyst (or a group of them) who interacts with the experts of the domain (clients, users, and stakeholders in general) to capture the software application's requirements and specify scenarios. They should describe the functionality of the intended software, and they should also consider security concerns. Therefore, the analyst eliciting and defining scenarios should have some background in security non-functional requirements so as to consider this concern in the specification. The result step is a set of scenarios that describe the functionality.

2.2 Step 2: Description of Scenarios with Incorrect Use of the Intended Application and Algorithm

This step consists in analyzing the scenarios described in the previous step to find security issues. Issues that exploit the problems and compromise the security of the software application are described. Ideally, this step should be done by the same requirements engineer (or group of them) that participated in the previous tasks. The requirements engineer describes scenarios of incorrect use of the software application. Basically, they should describe scenarios that exploit possible vulnerabilities. This step is enhanced through the application of an algorithm. The operation of the algorithm can be summarized as follows: first, keywords related to specific attacks are identified in existing scenarios (both correct and incorrect use scenarios). The catalogues are organized as tables, each heading corresponding to a column. Each row of the General Security Aspects catalogue contains information corresponding to one quality attribute (e.g., privacy, confidentiality, etc.). Each row of the Specific Attacks catalogue contains information describing one specific type of related attacks. The catalogues are then searched for the keywords in order to locate the row containing an occurrence of the specific attack. Once the relevant row is identified in both catalogues, the following information is extracted: affected security QA, attack involved, mitigation mechanism, and consequences in the agricultural industry. The algorithm concatenates the information extracted from the catalogues and appends it to a security scenario in a new field labelled 'threats'. The user can use this information to derive more robust and precise security scenarios.

2.3 Step 3: Derivation of Security Scenarios

Is the derivation of security scenario. This step describes a set of rules to map the information contained in an incorrect use scenario so as to obtain a first draft of a scenario describing security concerns. It is worth mentioning that the incorrect use scenario will not provide enough information for a complete security scenario. The rules proposed here use only four attributes from the incorrect use scenario (title, context, actors, and resources) to fill out four attributes of the security scenario (stimulus, environment, source of the stimulus, and artifact). With this information, the following step is to refine the security scenario. In this step a draft scenario is created by filling in some of the fields in a security scenario (Table 2).

Table 2. Mapping rules used in the derivation of security scenarios. Source: Own Elaboration.

Attribute of the incorrect usage scenario	Attribute of the security scenario
Title	Stimulus
Context	Environment + Source of the stimulus
Actors	Sources of stimulus
Resources	Artifact

2.4 Step 4: Refinement of the Description of the Security Scenarios

Some adjustments and improvements should be made to the scenarios derived from the mapping in the previous step. Some new information should be added, and some information should be rephrased. The requirements engineer should use their experience and knowledge to provide further information and paraphrase other based on the elicitation meeting and their expertise in the field as following: (i) an identification must be provided; (ii) the stimulus must be paraphrased; (iii) the environment and source of stimulus must be split into two attributes; (iv) the source of stimulus must be rephrased; (v) the artifact must be rephrased; and finally (vi) the response and the response measure must be completed from scratch. Although the mapping rules do not provide information corresponding to these attributes, the information found in the rest of the scenario provides the necessary context so that the requirements engineers can describe these two last attributes. The requirements engineer should bear in mind that the response measure attribute, in particular, should be described with quantitative measures. The draft is refined on the basis of an expert's expertise. The draft is thus transformed into a security scenario.

3 Related Work

Dorairaju [13] focuses on addressing security vulnerabilities in an IoT remote insect pest monitoring system, which is a critical component for smart agriculture. The objective of their work is to study the impact that digital data produces on the security aspect for an agricultural platform. Their case study investigates security challenges, sensor issues, and IoT devices. Using a case study involving a combination of investigations of IoT modules used in prototype field experiments and a review of related literature, a concrete guide is developed. Their most important contribution is a checklist for reviewing the security requirements of IoT. They also conclude that the people involved in these projects must have training in, and sufficient knowledge of, the principles of cybersecurity. Likewise, Riaz et al. [14] describe an evaluation framework for smart agricultural environments which contains execution scenarios of an agricultural environment with devices and sensors. Storylines are derived from these scenarios by providing real-time environments to expand and incorporate adaptive security frameworks and scenarios in IoT-based agriculture. As future work, they project to create a simulation of the generated scenarios.

A number of studies have considered mitigation for developers with little experience in IoT security [13, 15–17]. It is concluded that requirements engineers as well as software architects require specific and concrete methodologies to identify, understand and limit the risks associated with user privacy/security posed by IoT devices as well as threat scenarios and mitigation efforts. Rutledge and Massey [16] carry out an exploratory case study of the privacy policies of an IoT device (SmartTV), with the objective of characterizing the privacy protections and vulnerabilities associated with this class of devices. Among the most important results, they find that there is a greater risk of suffering damage to privacy due to SmartTVs, and that the user's privacy is further compromised by requiring a connection with the manufacturer background servers.

The work carried out by Demestichas et al. [8] also focuses on the vulnerabilities and threats of IoT agriculture systems. The authors carry out a review of the literature on the use of this technology in the aforementioned domain.

The article by Sicari et al. [18] proposes the use of Node-RED, a flow-supported programming tool specialized in IoT, along with a series of case studies related to different IoT contexts, one of which pertains to Smart Agriculture (an automated greenhouse management application) with the objective of collecting data on soil conditions and consulting a database. Data that contains useful information about the types inside the greenhouse, the data is analyzed by said system, which decides whether to activate one or more actuators of the greenhouse. The authors find that IoT applications suffer from four general problems: (i) scalability, (ii) inter-operability, (iii) security and (iv) privacy. With respect to security and privacy, it is mentioned that complex mechanisms must be integrated into the items mentioned above, policy management systems and tests in order to verify the viability of the proposed approaches [18, 19].

Finally, Wangyal et al. [20] identify risk factors on commercial operations using the risk breakdown structure method, with the objective of expanding the traditional view by including other risks such as physical risks. The authors conclude that applying IoT in different domains brings new challenges such as limitations in resources (energy, memory and computing capacity), and that security remains a high priority aspect for users. This supports the claim by Rettore [21] that conventional protection schemes used in traditional Internet or IoT may not be useful for agricultural systems, a fact that creates additional research opportunities.

4 Method

This paper adopted the method proposed by Wang and Xian [22] to carry out the case study, with the following proposed phases. The necessary resources are shown on Table 3. The rest of the section is organized in the following subsections: (i) Experimental procedures, (ii) Evaluation of the prototype using SemIoTica and the proposed algorithm and (iii) Report of findings (Conceptual Results) and acquired knowledge.

Table 3. Resources needed to carry out the case study. Source: Own Elaboration.

Element	Description
Research Question	Will SemIoTica help to improve experts' ability to identify security scenarios for an Agriculture IoT Prototype?
Instruments	(i) Prototype of an Intelligent System with IoT for the Monitoring of Variables in Single-Family Aquaponics at the Tecnoacademia Popayán: this research project focuses on citizen science through the development of a single-family aquaponics system, using IoT technology that allows users to remotely monitor key aspects of the system, providing an optimal environment for fish and plant growths (ii) A web implementation of SemIoTica called "Requirements Healer": a web application specialized in requirements management and requirements processing
Participants	Four experts in IoT Security are described below (gender, age, culture, experience): (i) Male, 30,Colombian, Software architect, (ii) Female, 25, Argentina, requirements expert, (iii) Female, 26, Argentina, requirements expert and (iv) Female, 32, Colombia, requirements expert

4.1 Experimental Procedures

The prototype called "Desarrollo de un Prototipo de Sistema Inteligente con IoT para el Monitoreo de Variables en Acuaponía Unifamiliar de la Tecnoacademia Popayán" [12] was chosen on the grounds that it applies IoT technologies to agriculture, thus enabling the application of SemIoTica.

To address this section, the definition of the protocol and procedures to follow to execute SemIoTica is carried out. The activities carried out in this phase are the following:

1. The prototype creator explains its design, concepts and operation through an online meeting.
2. Participants take a reasonable amount of time to understand the design and operation of the prototype.
3. The prototype is evaluated with SemIoTica by following the proposal's steps of and algorithm.
4. Findings, acquired knowledge, and results are reported.
5. The results are discussed from a conceptual viewpoint.

The details of phases 3, 4, 5 and 6 are reported below.

4.2 Evaluation of the Prototype Using SemIoTica and the Proposed Algorithm

The results of applying the SemIoTica approach to the aquaponics prototype are shown below. Figures 1, 2 and 3 show the correct usage scenarios generated in step 1. Figures 4, 5 and 6 show the corresponding incorrect usage scenarios generated in step 2.

Element	Description
Scenario Name	Oxygen Sensor
Goal	Measure oxygen in the tank
Context	A tank full of live fish
Resources	Oxygen
Actors	The sensor
Episodes	The sensor takes a measurement of oxygen

Fig. 1. Correct use scenario for oxygen sensor. Source: Own Elaboration.

The output of the algorithm proposed in SemIoTica, which provides information on identified vulnerabilities, can be seen in Table 4.

The output shown in Table 4 will help strengthen the incorrect use scenario that is based on a correct use scenario. After analysis of the output, the expert completes the incorrect use scenarios with additional security information, as shown in Table 5.

Step 3 consists in deriving the draft security scenarios by mapping incorrect scenario fields to security scenario fields as follows: (i) title to stimulus, (ii) context to Environment + Source of stimulus, (iii) Actors to Sources of stimulus, and (iv) resources to artifact. The resulting scenarios are shown in Tables 6, 7 and 8.

Element	Description
Scenario Name	Temperature Sensor
Goal	Measure the tank temperature to ensure the fish
Context	A tank full of live fish
Resources	Temperature
Actors	The sensor
Episodes	The sensor takes a measurement of temperature

Fig. 2. Correct use scenario for temp sensor. Source: Own Elaboration.

Element	Description
Scenario Name	Acidity sensor
Goal	Measure water pH and ensure fish
Context	A tank full of live fish
Resources	Acidity (pH)
Actors	The sensor
Episodes	The sensor takes a measurement of pH

Fig. 3. Correct use scenario for PH sensor. Source: Own Elaboration.

Element	Description
Scenario Name	Intervened/defective oxygen sensor
Goal	Measure oxygen in the tank
Context	A tank full of live fish
Resources	Oxygen
Actors	The sensor
Episodes	The sensor sends a signal to stop the oxygen pump. Fish die from asphyxiation

Fig. 4. Incorrect use scenario for oxygen sensor. Source: Own Elaboration.

Element	Description
Scenario Name	Intervened/defective temperature sensor
Goal	Measure the tank temperature to ensure the fish
Context	A tank full of live fish
Resources	Temperature
Actors	The sensor
Episodes	The sensor sends a warning notification to the dashboard that the water is too cold/warm.

Fig. 5. Incorrect use scenario for temp sensor. Source: Own Elaboration.

Element	Description
Scenario Name	Defective/interfered acidity sensor
Goal	Measure water pH and ensure fish
Context	A tank full of live fish
Resources	Acidity (pH)
Actors	The sensor
Episodes	The sensor sends a warning notification to the dashboard that the water has a low/high pH.

Fig. 6. Incorrect use scenario for PH sensor. Source: Own Elaboration.

Table 4. Result provided by the algorithm proposed in SemIoTica. Source: Own Elaboration.

Element	Description
Affected QA	Privacy, Confidentiality, Authenticity
Affected Layer	Perception Layer, Physical Layer
Layer Details	The first layer is composed of smart IoT sensing devices e.g., smart phones, RFID tags, sensors and actuators, etc. These components are able to automatically sense, collect and measure the various physical parameters e.g., temperature, humidity, location etc. Devices can store collected information inside themselves and sensors can store information into predefined sensor hubs (e.g., a microcontroller unit) to process them. The major functionalities of this layer are data sensing and data acquisition. Standardized plug-and-play mechanisms can be used with the various sensing devices. Furthermore, considering the scale of the number of things in an IoT system, sensing devices may be deployed simultaneously or over time according to the environmental context and practical requirements
Mitigation mechanism:	Two-Factor Authentication. RBAC ensures that only authorized users are given access to certain data or resources. It also supports three well-known security principles: information hiding, least-privilege, and separation of duties
Impact	The collection of information regarding the type and possible usage of devices concerning agriculture projects. These security leaks can be used in order to get access to infrastructure and production standards as well as getting privacy data and compromising the privacy of the system. Theft and vandalism

Finally, on Step 4 some adjustments and improvements should be made to the scenarios derived from the mapping in the previous step. Some new information should be added, and some information should be rephrased. In particular, the following points should be observed:

1. Identification must be provided
2. The stimulus must be rephrased
3. The environment and the source of stimulus must be split in two attributes

Table 5. Incorrect use scenario for oxygen sensor strengthened with information provided by the algorithm. Source: Own Elaboration.

Element	Description
Scenario Name	Intervened/defective oxygen sensor
Goal	Measure oxygen in the tank
Context	A tank full of live fish
Resources	Oxygen
Actors	The sensor
Episodes	The sensor sends a signal to stop the oxygen pump. Fish die from asphyxiation
Threats	The QAs affected are Privacy, Confidentiality, Authenticity. The Layers affected are Perception Layer, Physical Layer. The major functionalities of these layers are data sensing and data acquisition. The suggested mitigation mechanism to correct the affected QAs is Two-Factor Authentication. RBAC ensures that only authorized users are given access to certain data or resources. The impact of not using this mechanism is that these security leaks can be used in order to get access to infrastructure and production standards

Table 6. Security scenario draft for oxygen sensor. Source: Own Elaboration.

Element	Description
Stimulus	Intervened/defective oxygen sensor
Environment + Source of stimulus	The sensor sends a signal to stop the oxygen pump. Fish die from asphyxiation: A tank full of live fish may be compromised because the Layers affected are Perception Layer, Physical Layer. The major functionalities of these layers are data sensing and data acquisition. The QAs affected are Privacy, Confidentiality, Authenticity. These security leaks can be used in order to get access to infrastructure and production standards. The suggested mitigation mechanism to correct the affected QAs is Two-Factor Authentication
Sources of stimulus	The sensor
Artifact	Oxygen

4. The source of stimulus must be rephrased
5. The artifact must be rephrased
6. The response and the response measure must be added

The final results, i.e., the complete security scenarios, are shown in Tables 9, 10 and 11.

Table 7. Security scenario draft for temperature sensor. Source: Own Elaboration.

Element	Description
Stimulus	Intervened/defective temperature sensor
Environment + Source of stimulus	The sensor sends a warning notification to the dashboard that the water is too cold/warm: A tank full of live fish may be compromised because the Layers affected are Perception Layer, Physical Layer. The major functionalities of these layers are data sensing and data acquisition. The QAs affected are Privacy, Confidentiality, Authenticity. These security leaks can be used in order to get access to infrastructure and production standards. The suggested mitigation mechanism to correct the affected QAs is Two-Factor Authentication
Sources of stimulus	The sensor
Artifact	Temperature

Table 8. Security scenario draft for acidity sensor. Source: Own Elaboration.

Element	Description
Stimulus	Intervened/defective acidity sensor
Environment + Source of stimulus	The sensor sends a warning notification to the dashboard that the water has a low/high pH: A tank full of live fish may be compromised because the Layers affected are Perception Layer, Physical Layer. The major functionalities of these layers are data sensing and data acquisition. The QA´s affected are Privacy, Confidenciality, Authencity. These security leaks can be used in order to get access to infrastructure and production standards. The suggested mitigation mechanism to correct the affected QAs is Two-Factor Authentication
Sources of stimulus	The sensor
Artifact	Acidity (pH)

4.3 Report of Findings (Conceptual Results) and Acquired Knowledge

The results found by participants when using the SemIoTica approach are:

1. According to the reported findings, it is found that there is a high possibility of frequently using the SemIoTica proposal because it contributes to the development of security scenarios for smart farming.
2. The proposal was easy to use and did not cause any setbacks because it is not necessary to have an expert to guide its use since the sequence of steps is clear and simple, making it easy for people to quickly use this proposal.

Table 9. Security scenario for oxygen sensor. Source: Own Elaboration.

Element	Description
ID	S-01
Stimulus	Oxygen sensor malfunctioning because it was Intervened/defective
Environment	Fish die from asphyxiation: A tank full of live fish may be compromised because the Layers affected are Perception Layer, Physical Layer. The major functionalities of these layers are data sensing and data acquisition. The QA´s affected are Privacy, Confidentiality, Authenticity. These security leaks can be used in order to get access to infrastructure and production standards. The suggested mitigation mechanism to correct the affected QAs is Two-Factor Authentication
Sources of stimulus	The oxygen sensor of selected prototype makes a measurement
Artifact	Oxygen
Response	The sensor sends a signal to stop the oxygen pump
Response Measure	Ensure the security of the system, it's important that attacks are detected quickly, ideally within 0,5 s

Table 10. Security scenario for temperature sensor. Source: Own Elaboration.

Element	Description
ID	S-02
Stimulus	Temperature sensor malfunctioning because it was Intervened/defective
Environment	The water is too cold/warm: A tank full of live fish may be compromised because the Layers affected are Perception Layer, Physical Layer. The major functionalities of these layers are data sensing and data acquisition. The QAs affected are Privacy, Confidentiality, Authenticity. These security leaks can be used in order to get access to infrastructure and production standards. The suggested mitigation mechanism to correct the affected QAs is Two-Factor Authentication
Sources of stimulus	The temperature sensor of selected prototype makes a measurement
Artifact	Temperature
Response	The sensor sends a warning notification to the dashboard that the water is too cold/warm
Response Measure	Ensure the security of the system, it's important that attacks are detected quickly, ideally within 0,5 s

3. When using SemIoTica, it is observed that the stated steps are well defined, concrete and concise, which makes the proposal provide certainty to anyone who is applying it.

Table 11. Security scenario for acidity sensor. Source: Own Elaboration.

Element	Description
ID	S-03
Stimulus	Acidity sensor malfunctioning because it was Intervened/defective
Environment	The water has a low/high pH: A tank full of live fish may be compromised because the Layers affected are Perception Layer, Physical Layer. The major functionalities of these layers are data sensing and data acquisition. The QAs affected are Privacy, Confidentiality, Authenticity. These security leaks can be used in order to get access to infrastructure and production standards. The suggested mitigation mechanism to correct the affected QAs is Two-Factor Authentication
Sources of stimulus	The acidity sensor of selected prototype makes a measurement
Artifact	Acidity (pH)
Response	The sensor sends a warning notification to the dashboard that the water has a low/high pH
Response Measure	Ensure the security of the system, it's important that attacks are detected quickly, ideally within 0,5 s

4. The information to create the scenarios and associate it with the algorithm must be in English.
5. The response generated by the algorithm was of great help to complement the misuse scenario by associating more information and contributing to improving it.
6. Following the steps of the SemIoTica approach and the algorithm contributes to improving the scenarios, enriching their information and helping the expert in their task of generating security scenarios in IoT Agriculture.
7. The resulting security scenarios have well marked security problems that affect the sensor.
8. The algorithm shows consistency because the information entered in the misuse scenarios of the three sensors have the same associated results.

5 Discussion

The results of SemIoTica's algorithm reflect what kind of vulnerabilities a system may have. In this case, this aquaponics project uses sensors and pumps to maintain the fish—the core of the system. Since the system's well-functioning needs periodical measurements, the sensors are a vital component, and they constitute the physical (or perception) layer. The physical layer plays an important role as it gathers information from the surrounding context in order to act upon said information. This information enables the normal unfolding of correct system behaviors.

Damage to the sensors can result from normal usage over time or due to environmental conditions like erosion. Hence durability must be considered an important variable in the system. Battery durability is another matter of concern as an excess of security algorithms can hasten battery depletion, depriving the system of the necessary equipment to maintain the fish. To extend trust in the sensors, actuators and other devices that make up an IoT system, it is necessary to improve the durability of materials to prevent wrong information, false positives or unwanted behaviors within the application.

Adopting such technology as IoT in agriculture can be advantageous in terms of crop efficiency and support in the crop supply chain. However, the use of this technology can bring some problems because sensors, actuators and other devices are deployed that are connected to the Internet and that can be easily manipulated by third parties in order to cause damage. As the sensors are vital to maintain the fish, some malicious activities are attracted to this equipment. To harm the system, an attacker can intercept the measurements and modify it or store it because it contains sensitive information about the state of the core of the system, the fishes. Another kind of attack can be directly focused on taking the sensors out by accessing them and taking control or attacking them and depleting the energy or faking them. If the fish do not have the right conditions, they can die and therefore the system can no longer function.

It is necessary to keep in mind that if we use IoT in Smart Farming and Aquaponics, we must be extremely careful because the life of a living being such as a fish is involved. Therefore, it is important to mitigate any attempted damage to applications that use this approach, emphasizing the techniques suggested by the literature for IoT security. In order to mitigate those attacks, it's logical to have a two-factor authentication system, because it is difficult for the attackers to get into the device and finally to encrypt the measurements of the sensor to secure the sensitive information and have a hash to ensure the information is in a correct state.

The SemIoTica approach was very useful because it contributes to the security measurements and methods to protect the vital and important equipment and maintain secure the fish. The results are very promising and show effectively what are the vulnerabilities of this real case. In every scenario, it shows what layers are affected, what QAs are involved, what kind of attacks the system is vulnerable to and the countermeasures to deal with them. it contributes to the security measurements and methods to protect the vital and important equipment and maintain secure the fish.

6 Conclusions and Future Work

In this paper we dealt with an application of SemIoTica methodology in a real case of study. We applied a detailed analysis of the case study. Then we applied the SemIoTica approach in order to obtain the security scenarios. And finally, we discussed the results and made a reflection about it. The results obtained are very promising and show how effective is the SemIoTica method. In the resulted scenarios, shows what layers are affected, what QAs are involved, what kind of attacks the system is vulnerable to and the countermeasures to deal with them. Also the application of the algorithm show consistency in every scenario and highlighted the impact if any of this sensor stop working in the system.

SemIoTica helps improve the ability of experts to identify security scenarios of an agricultural IoT prototype because: (i) it helps to build security scenarios in an agile, concise and precise manner with the steps involved given above, (ii) enrich them with information provided by the proposed algorithm prototype and (iii) identify security scenarios effectively in intensive applications in IoT agriculture.

It is intended to continue applying SemIoTica in different agricultural IoT prototypes for the purpose of finding more results that lead to the improvement of the proposal, the algorithm, the designed and identified scenarios. As for the future work a detailed case study is planned about this method. A user perception survey on the prototype is also needed to continue enhancing the method.

References

1. Sinha, B.B., Dhanalakshmi, R.: Recent advancements and challenges of internet of things in smart agriculture: a survey. Futur. Gener. Comput. Syst. **126**, 169–184 (2022). https://doi.org/10.1016/j.future.2021.08.006
2. Yazdinejad, A., et al.: A review on security of smart farming and precision agriculture: Security aspects, attacks, threats and countermeasures. Appl. Sci. **11**(16) (2021). https://doi.org/10.3390/app11167518
3. Sotoudeh, S., Hashemi, S., Garakani, H.G.: Security framework of IoT-based smart home. In: 2020 10th International Symposium on Telecommunications. Smart Communication a Better Life, IST 2020, pp. 251–256 (2020). https://doi.org/10.1109/IST50524.2020.9345886
4. Quy, V.K., et al.: IoT-enabled smart agriculture: architecture, applications, and challenges. Appl. Sci. **12**(7) (2022). https://doi.org/10.3390/app12073396
5. Ojo-Gonzalez, K., Bonilla-Morales, B.: Requerimientos no funcionales para sistemas basados en el Internet de las cosas (IoT): Una revisión," I+D Tecnológico, vol. 17, no. 2 (2021). https://doi.org/10.33412/idt.v17.2.3303
6. Hurtado, J., et al.: Semiotica : An Approach To Model Security Sce- Narios For Iot-Based Agriculture Software Semiotica : Un Enfoque Para Modelar Escenarios De Seguridad Para Software De Agricultura Basado En IoT," Rev. Tecnológicas, vol. 27, p. 23 (2024). https://doi.org/10.22430/22565337.2923
7. Yugha, R., Chithra, S.: A survey on technologies and security protocols: reference for future generation IoT. J. Netw. Comput. Appl. **169**, 102763 (2020). https://doi.org/10.1016/j.jnca.2020.102763
8. Demestichas, K., Peppes, N., Alexakis, T.: Survey on security threats in agricultural IoT and smart farming. Sensors **20**, 17 (2020). https://doi.org/10.1049/et.2012.0601
9. El-Gendy, S., Azer, M.A.: Security framework for Internet of Things (IoT). In: Proceedings of ICCES 2020 - 2020 15th International Conference Computer Engineering System 2020 (2020). https://doi.org/10.1109/ICCES51560.2020.9334589
10. Rizzardi, A., Sicari, S., Coen-Porisini, A.: Towards rapid modeling and prototyping of indoor and outdoor monitoring applications. Sustain. Comput. Informatics Syst., **41**(November 2023), 100951 (2024). https://doi.org/10.1016/j.suscom.2023.100951
11. Liu, J., Xiao, Y., Chen, C.L.P.: Authentication and access control in the Internet of things. In: Proceedings - 32nd IEEE International Conference Distributed Computer System Work. ICDCSW 2012, pp. 588–592 (2012). https://doi.org/10.1109/ICDCSW.2012.23
12. Ortega Erazo, J.C.: Desarrollo de un Prototipo de Sistema Inteligente con IoT para el Monitoreo de Variables en Acuaponía Unifamiliar de la Tecnoacademia Popayán, p. 1. https://cutt.ly/IoT-TecnoacademiaPopayan
13. Dorairaju, G.: Cyber security in modern agriculture. case study: IoT-based insect pest trap system, no. April, p. 81 (2021). http://www.theseus.fi/handle/10024/497436%0Ahttps://www.theseus.fi/bitstream/handle/10024/497436/Thesis_Dorairaju_Ganeas.pdf?sequence=2&isAllowed=y

14. Riaz, A.R., Gilani, S.M.M., Naseer, S., Alshmrany, S., Shafiq, M., Choi, J.G.: Applying adaptive security techniques for risk analysis of internet of things (IoT)-based smart agriculture. Sustain. **14**(17) (2022). https://doi.org/10.3390/su141710964
15. Mauro, D., Melo, L., Lu, H., Damorim, M., Prakash, A.: A study of vulnerability analysis of popular smart devices through their companion apps. In: Proceedings - 2019 IEEE Symposium Security Privacy Work, SPW 2019, pp. 181–186 (2019). https://doi.org/10.1109/SPW.2019.00042
16. Rutledge, R.L., Massey, A.K., Anton, A.I.: Privacy impacts of IoT devices: A SmartTV case study. In: Proceedings - 2016 IEEE 24th International Requirements Engineering Conference Work, REW 2016, pp. 261–270 (2017). https://doi.org/10.1109/REW.2016.40
17. Ye,M., Jiang, N., Yang, H., Yan, Q.: Security analysis of internet-of-things: a case study of august smart lock. In: 2017 IEEE Conference Computer Communications Work, INFOCOM WKSHPS 2017, pp. 499–504 (2017). https://doi.org/10.1109/INFCOMW.2017.8116427
18. Sicari, S., Rizzardi, A., Coen-Porisini, A.: How to evaluate an Internet of Things system: models, case studies, and real developments. Softw. - Pract. Exp. **49**(11), 1663–1685 (2019). https://doi.org/10.1002/spe.2740
19. Miki, M., Yamauchi, T., Kobayashi, S.: Evaluation of effectiveness of MAC systems based on LSM for protecting IoT devices. In: Proceedings - 2023 11th International Symposium on Computing and Networking, CANDAR 2023, pp. 161–167 (2023). https://doi.org/10.1109/CANDAR60563.2023.00029
20. Wangyal, S., Dechen, T., Tanimoto, S., Sato, H., Kanai, A.: A study of multi-viewpoint risk assessment of internet of things (IoT). In: Proceedings - 2020 9th International Congress on Advanced Applied Informatics, IIAI-AAI 2020, pp. 639–644 (2020). https://doi.org/10.1109/IIAI-AAI50415.2020.00131
21. Rettore de Araujo Zanella, A., da Silva, E., Pessoa Albini, L.C.: Security challenges to smart agriculture: current state, key issues, and future directions. Array **8**(December), 100048 (2020). https://doi.org/10.1016/j.array.2020.100048
22. Wang, S., Xian, Y.: A case study on the efficacy of error correction practice by using the automated writing evaluation system WRM 2.0 on Chinese college students' English writing. In: Proceedings - 2011 International Conference Computer Information Science ICCIS 2011, pp. 988–991 (2011). https://doi.org/10.1109/ICCIS.2011.21

Automatic Classification of Petroglyphs: Exploratory Study in the Maule Region of Chile

Cristian Suancha[1(✉)], Marco Suarez[1], Pablo González[2], and Felipe Besoain[3]

[1] Ingeniería de Sistemas y Computación, Universidad Pedagógica y Tecnológica, Sogamoso, Colombia
{Cristian.suancha,Marco.suarez}@uptc.edu.co

[2] Laboratorio de Medios Tecnológicos Mauletec, Faculty of Engineering, Universidad de Talca, Campus Talca, Talca, Chile
pgonzalezb@utalca.cl

[3] Department of Interactive Visualization and Virtual Reality, Faculty of Engineering, Universidad de Talca, Campus Talca, Talca, Chile
fbesoain@utalca.cl

Abstract. This paper explores the utilization of convolutional neural networks (CNNs) in classifying petroglyphs from the Maule Region - Chile. It emphasizes the importance of deep learning approaches for cultural heritage analysis. The methodology encompasses data preparation, network architecture setup, and parameter tuning, utilizing tools tailored for scientific analysis and machine learning. The study analyzes the implemented code and execution to derive meaningful results and performance metrics. The discussion highlights the potential of CNNs in enhancing interpretative precision and addressing challenges in petroglyph classification. Despite achieving promising accuracy, further investigation into model refinement and mitigation of biases is warranted for informed decision-making in classification tasks. The analysis of the petroglyphs of the Maule region not only sheds light on the cultural heritage of the communities, but also raises questions about cultural appropriation and conservation and preservation strategies to enhance it. The conclusions showed the need to improve the model to avoid over-fitting and to obtain better results in the classification of petroglyphs.

Keywords: Deep Learning · Convolutional Neural Network · Cultural Heritage · Petroglyphs · Maule Region

1 Introduction

Rock art constitutes a fundamental component in the processes of social construction of communities, as spaces of integration and as political resources, which transforms it into one of the material practices on which communities and their history are built [1]. It is worth mentioning that these rock engravings are found in various locations around the world, constituting a cultural legacy of great importance for the construction and understanding of modern society [2]. In most cases, petroglyphs have been found carved

V. Agredo-Delgado et al. (Eds.): DECISIONING 2024, CCIS 2369, pp. 58–69, 2025.
https://doi.org/10.1007/978-3-031-91690-8_5

with rudimentary tools on rock surfaces, revealing a diverse range of interpretations [3]. Examples of these representations include human figures, stylized animals, geometric patterns and abstract symbols.

On the other hand, in the South American context, the presence of petroglyphs throughout the millennia is evidence of cultural diversity in countries such as Argentina, Bolivia, Peru and Chile. From the Atacama Desert to Patagonia [4], these rock engravings reveal complex representations associated with cultures with unique iconographies, contributing to the understanding of ritual practices and the relationship with the natural environment of ancient communities [2]. The potential of rock art to expand our knowledge about pre-Hispanic cultures has not been developed to its full extent; one of the aspects that conditions its development has been the archaeological record (dated) and the methods of inquiry [6], which implies the need to complement the results with information from other disciplines [7].

Some of today's perceived approaches to perform image classification, specifically in the field of petroglyphs and rock art, involve the use of neural networks. These methods have gained relevance due to their ability to learn complex patterns and perform accurate classifications on large and varied datasets [5].

Within neural network-based approaches, convolutional neural networks (CNNs) have been highlighted as a powerful tool in classification. These networks are designed to process two-dimensional data, such as images, and are particularly effective in identifying spatial patterns and relevant features in visual representations. CNNs allow the automatic extraction of hierarchical features, which is essential when dealing with the diversity of styles and forms present in petroglyphs from different cultures [5, 8].

Despite the progress made in the application of deep learning techniques to archaeological studies, the study of rock art through these computational methods remains a developing field. One of the main challenges lies in the availability and quality of datasets, as many petroglyph images are found in varying conditions of preservation and lighting, making automatic recognition a complex task. Additionally, rock engravings often present overlapping figures and partial occlusions, requiring robust algorithms capable of distinguishing and classifying individual elements accurately.

Recent works have explored the use of transfer learning and data augmentation techniques to improve the performance of classification models applied to cultural heritage studies [9]. These strategies enhance the adaptability of CNNs to different styles and representations, mitigating the scarcity of labeled datasets. Furthermore, interdisciplinary collaboration between archaeologists and data scientists has proven essential for refining annotation processes and ensuring that computational analyses align with historical and cultural interpretations.

In accordance with the above, this paper shows the feasibility of implementing deep learning-based approaches, such as the use of a convolutional neural network (CNN), to perform classification processes focused on Maule region petroglyphs. Through the application of these computational techniques, the study aims to contribute to the preservation and analysis of rock art, providing new insights into the stylistic and cultural variations present in the region's archaeological record.

2 Methodology

2.1 Data Collection

To develop an automatic classification system based on convolutional neural networks (CNNs), a dataset of petroglyph images was obtained from archaeological sites in the Maule region, Chile. The image acquisition process was conducted using a Canon camera, ensuring high-resolution captures that preserved the intricate details of the engravings. A total of 200 images were collected, covering various petroglyph sites with diverse environmental conditions, including differences in lighting, surface texture, and erosion levels. The dataset aimed to encompass a representative sample of the region's petroglyphs to facilitate a robust classification process.

Following image acquisition, a manual classification process was carried out by an expert in archaeology. This expert assigned labels to each image based on morphological and stylistic characteristics, distinguishing different motifs and engraving techniques. The manual classification step was crucial for establishing a high-quality dataset with reliable annotations, serving as ground truth for subsequent automated classification tasks.

2.2 Materials and Methods for CNN

The research utilized the Google Colab environment for Python execution [10], integrating libraries for data processing. Python's versatility as a high-level language supports specialized machine learning libraries like Scikit-learn, Keras, TensorFlow, and PyTorch.

Scikit-learn offers algorithms for classification, preprocessing, and visualization, while Keras, TensorFlow, and PyTorch are essential for deep learning, providing tools for constructing and training neural networks.

The network architecture starts with an input layer comprising a Convolutional 2D (Conv2D) layer with 32 filters of size 3×3 and a Rectified Linear Unit (ReLU) activation function, aimed at feature extraction from 300×300 pixel RGB images. Following this, two additional pairs of Conv2D and MaxPooling2D layers follow suit. Each pair involves a Conv2D layer with 64 filters, a ReLU activation function, and a MaxPooling2D layer with a pool size of 2×2. To prevent overfitting, a dropout layer with a rate of 0.5 is included post MaxPooling2D.

This pattern repeats for two more pairs of Conv2D, MaxPooling2D, and Dropout layers, with the second pair consisting of a Conv2D layer with 128 filters, while the third pair mirrors the configuration of the second. The feature maps are then flattened into a one-dimensional vector and fed into a fully connected Dense layer with 512 neurons and a ReLU activation function, followed by another dropout layer with a rate of 0.5. The architecture concludes with a single-neuron Dense layer utilizing a sigmoid activation function, outputting the binary classification probability for the input images (see Fig. 1).

In the model compilation phase, the Adam optimizer is employed. Additionally, the binary cross-entropy loss function is utilized as the model's loss function. Binary cross-entropy is commonly used in binary classification tasks, as it measures the difference between the predicted probabilities and the actual binary labels. By minimizing this loss function during training, the model learns to better distinguish between the two classes,

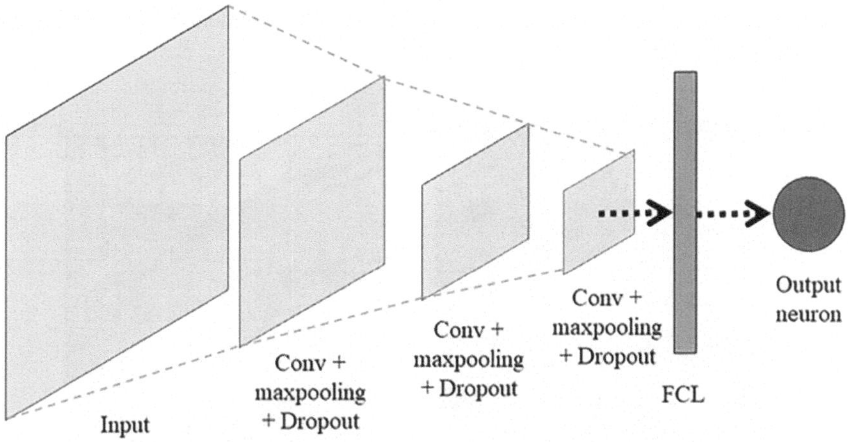

Fig. 1. Convolutional architecture for petroglyphs. Source: authors

maximizing its accuracy on the validation and test datasets. The implemented algorithm can be seen following.

```
model = Sequential()
model.add(Conv2D(32,   kernel_size=(3,3),   activation='relu',
input_shape=(300,300,3)))
model.add(Conv2D(64, (3,3), activation='relu'))
model.add(MaxPooling2D(pool_size=(2,2)))
model.add(Dropout(0.5))
model.add(Conv2D(64, (3,3), activation='relu'))
model.add(MaxPooling2D(pool_size=(2,2)))
model.add(Dropout(0.5))
model.add(Conv2D(128, (3,3), activation='relu'))
model.add(MaxPooling2D(pool_size=(2,2)))
model.add(Dropout(0.5))
model.add(Flatten())
model.add(Dense(64, activation='relu'))
model.add(Dropout(0.5))
model.add(Dense(1, activation='sigmoid'))
model.compile(loss=keras.losses.binary_crossentropy,
optimizer='adam', metrics=['accuracy'])
```

For data augmentation, two image data generators are instantiated. The first, data_generator_train, incorporates transformations to augment the training dataset, including rotation up to 120°, horizontal and vertical flips, and reflection-based filling for missing pixels (fill_mode = ''reflect'). These augmentations help diversify the training data, improving the model's generalization ability by exposing it to a wider range of image variations. The pixel values are also rescaled to a range between 0 and 1 to facilitate model training. Instead, the data_generator_val is used for the validation dataset and only performs pixel rescaling, ensuring consistency with the training data preprocessing without introducing additional variations. Overall, these data generators play enhance the model's robustness and performance by augmenting the training data while maintaining consistency during validation (Fig. 2).

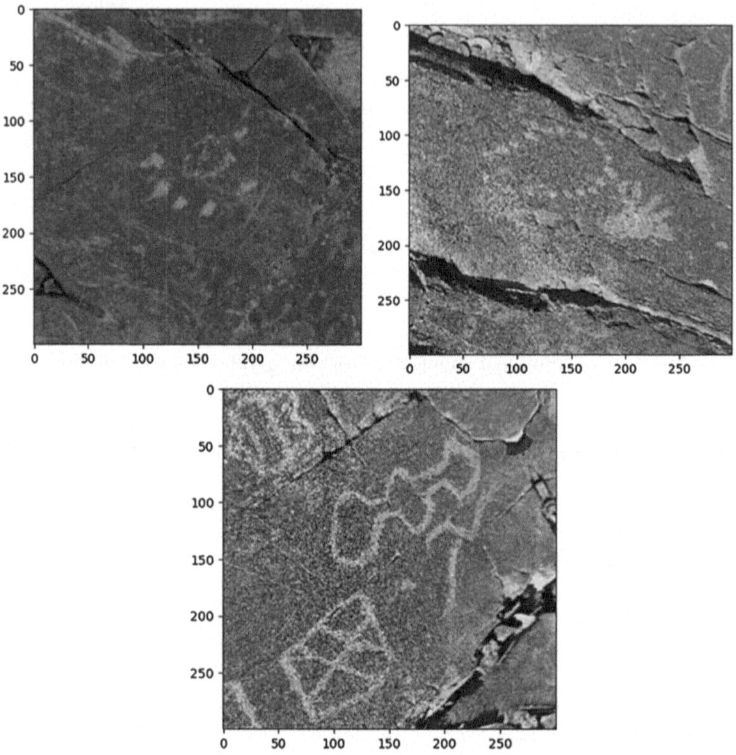

Fig. 2. Example of augmented images. Source: authors

In this case, the classes are labeled as 'BIOMORFOS' and 'GEOMETRICOS', with 'BIOMORFOS' assigned the label 0 and 'GEOMETRICOS' assigned the label 1. This mapping facilitates the training and evaluation processes of the binary classification model, allowing the model to interpret and predict the classes based on their numerical representations. Such a mapping is essential for handling categorical data within machine learning algorithms, enabling seamless integration of class labels into the model's prediction and evaluation pipelines.

In the workflow, the training of the binary classification model is initiated using the fit method, which iterates over the training dataset for a specified number of epochs. The model is trained for 10 epochs, indicating that it will undergo 10 iterations over the entire training dataset. During training, the model adjusts its parameters using the optimization algorithm specified during compilation (in this case, Adam) to minimize the defined loss function (binary cross-entropy). Additionally, the validation dataset is passed to the val_gen generator to monitor the model's performance on unseen data during training, facilitating early detection of overfitting and providing insights into the generalization capabilities of the model.

Finally, it is worth mentioning that the use and choice of these specific tools and approaches had the main purpose of achieving a clear understanding of the topic addressed, where the methodological approach was oriented towards the achievement of the various points of interest identified in the report, with the ultimate goal of deriving relevant conclusions in the context of the study.

3 Results and Discussion

The training accuracy shows a consistent upward trend, indicating that the model is effectively learning patterns from the training data. However, it has not yet reached 1.0, suggesting that there is still room for improvement in optimizing its learning process. The validation accuracy follows a similar trajectory, though it remains slightly lower than the training accuracy. This gap suggests that the model is generalizing well to unseen data while maintaining a reasonable balance between learning and overfitting.

On the other hand, the training loss exhibits some fluctuations, but its overall decreasing trend indicates that the model is progressively minimizing errors during training. The validation loss, however, also fluctuates and appears to have a more positive slope compared to the training loss. This divergence between training and validation loss could be an early sign of overfitting, where the model begins to memorize training data rather than learning generalizable patterns. If this trend continues, it may negatively impact performance on new, unseen data. Further refinements, such as adjusting regularization techniques, optimizing hyperparameters, or expanding the dataset, could help mitigate potential overfitting and improve the model's robustness (see Fig. 3).

These results suggest that the CNN model is effectively learning and performing well in the task of binary image classification. The increasing trend in accuracy indicates that the model is capturing relevant patterns within the data, allowing for meaningful distinctions between the two classes. However, despite this progress, it would be beneficial to extend the training process by increasing the number of epochs. This would provide a clearer understanding of whether the accuracy curves for both training and validation continue to improve and whether the validation loss curve follows a downward trajectory. If the validation loss remains unstable or begins to rise, it could indicate potential overfitting, warranting further investigation into regularization techniques such as dropout, data augmentation, or weight decay.

To further assess the model's classification performance, the Receiver Operating Characteristic (ROC) curve is analyzed (see Fig. 4). The ROC curve is a graphical representation that plots the True Positive Rate (TPR) on the y-axis against the False Positive Rate (FPR) on the x-axis. The TPR, also known as recall, measures the proportion of actual positive instances that were correctly classified by the model. Meanwhile, the FPR represents the proportion of negative instances that were incorrectly labeled as positive. A well-performing model typically has a ROC curve that closely follows the upper-left corner of the plot, indicating a high TPR with a low FPR.

However, in this case, the ROC curve does not adhere closely to the upper-left corner, suggesting suboptimal classification performance. This observation is reinforced by the Area Under the Curve (AUC) score, which summarizes the model's ability to distinguish between positive and negative instances across all possible classification

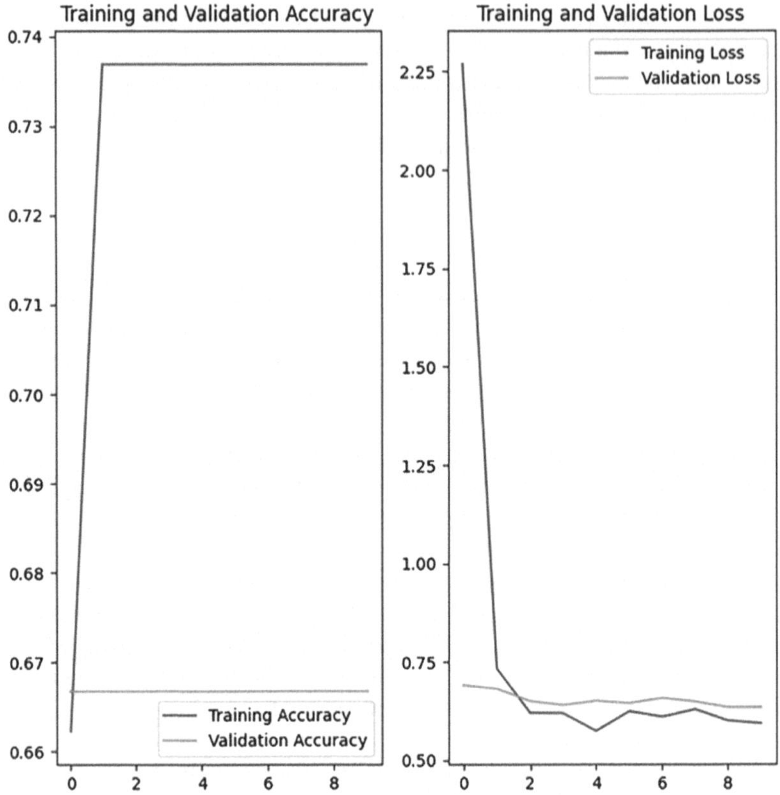

Fig. 3. Accuracy and validation results for petroglyphs. Source: authors

thresholds. An AUC of 1.0 represents a perfect classifier, while an AUC of 0.5 indicates performance equivalent to random guessing. In this study, the model achieves an AUC of 0.36, which falls significantly below the desired threshold for a reliable classification system. This low AUC score suggests that the model struggles to differentiate between the two classes, possibly due to issues such as class imbalance, insufficient feature extraction, or inadequate training data. Addressing these limitations through dataset expansion, improved preprocessing techniques, or architectural modifications may be necessary to enhance the model's ability to make accurate classifications.

The confusion matrix shows that the model predicted a total of 51 instances (see Fig. 5). Out of those, 17 were actual positives (class 0) and the model correctly classified 34 of them (True Positives). There were 34 actual negatives (class 1), out of which the model correctly classified 17 (True Negatives).

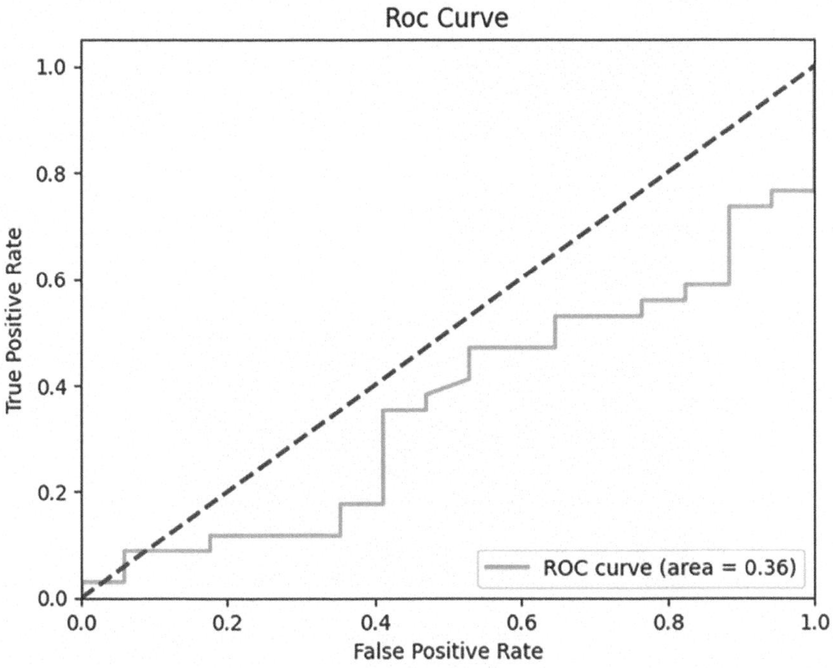

Fig. 4. ROC curve for petroglyphs classification. Source: authors

Based on the outcomes, the algorithm performs as intended, but overfitting can be fixed to increase model effectiveness.

To validate the algorithm, the model was tested using validation data from the same dataset on which it was trained: the petroglyph dataset from the Maule region of Chile. This allowed for a direct evaluation of the model's generalization capacity within the same geographic and cultural context, ensuring consistency in feature recognition and classification.

In addition, to verify the behavior of the algorithm with data from a different location, petroglyphs from the Ex Fundo de San Manuel, Chile, were used. This cross-validation aimed to assess the model's adaptability to new datasets with potentially different artistic styles, environmental conditions, and preservation states. The results from this test provide insights into the model's robustness and its ability to generalize beyond its original training data.

The model's classification results show variability in confidence levels when identifying petroglyphs as "BIOMORFOS." In the left image (see Fig. 6), the model achieves a confidence of 78%, suggesting that the pattern aligns well with its learned features. However, in the right image, confidence drops to 56.25%, indicating greater uncertainty, likely due to variations in texture, erosion, lighting, or shape. This discrepancy highlights the challenges in classification, such as feature recognition issues, possible overfitting to specific patterns, and class ambiguity.

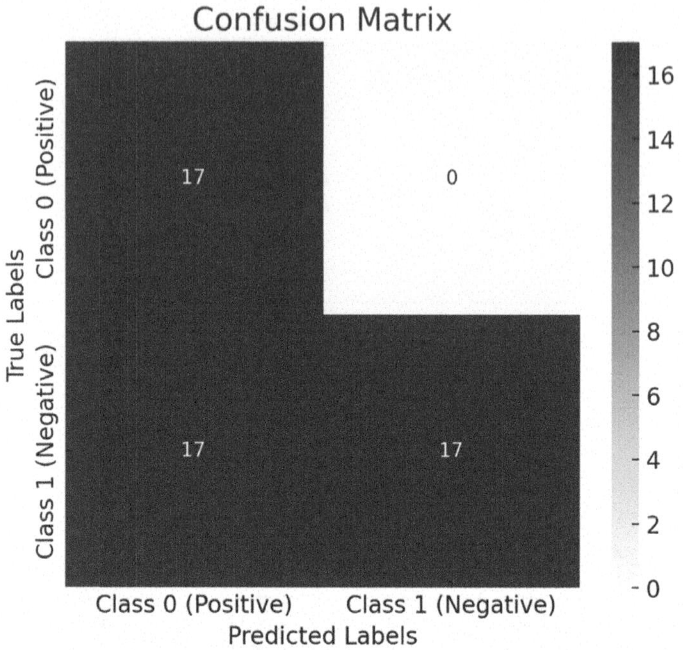

Fig. 5. Confusion matrix for the algorithm implemented. Source: authors

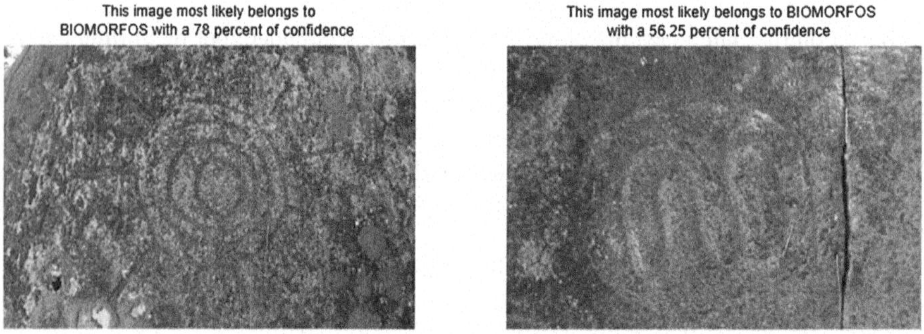

Fig. 6. Model classification with low performance for ex fundo San Manuel petroglyphs. Source: authors

The model demonstrates high confidence in classifying petroglyphs, assigning 99.85% confidence to the "GEOMÉTRICOS" class in the left image and 98.75% to the "BIOMORFOS" class in the right image. These results suggest that the model effectively recognizes and differentiates patterns within these categories, even in the presence of natural elements such as moss and uneven surfaces (see Fig. 7).

Fig. 7. Model classification with high performance for ex fundo San Manuel petroglyphs. Source: authors

4 Conclusions

According to the research carried out, it is possible to determine that the implementation of convolutional neural networks (CNN) is highly relevant in the field of archaeology, particularly in the classification of rock art. The collaboration between disciplines and the integration of advanced machine learning techniques have significantly improved the precision in interpreting these elements, strengthening the analytical capacity of these artistic manifestations.

Furthermore, the efficiency of CNNs in the specific task of petroglyph classification has been demonstrated. This is attributed to the inherent ability of these architectures to learn complex patterns and extract relevant features from images, allowing a more robust distinction and classification compared to traditional methods. The findings suggest that CNNs provide a solid foundation for the automatic classification of rock art, paving the way for further advancements in the field.

The observed training process indicates that the CNN model is learning the task effectively, with an increasing training accuracy and a generally decreasing training loss. However, it may be beneficial to extend the training duration to determine whether validation metrics continue to improve or if the model begins to overfit. A detailed study of the loss curves and validation performance is essential to optimize training strategies.

The analysis of the ROC curve and the low AUC score (0.36) indicate that the model struggles to distinguish between positive and negative cases effectively. This may be attributed to several factors, including class imbalance in the dataset, underfitting, overfitting, or inadequate model architecture. Addressing these issues through data augmentation, improved sampling techniques, and adjustments in model design could lead to better classification performance.

Additionally, the confusion matrix reveals a higher tendency for the model to misclassify positive instances, emphasizing the need for further investigation into the sources of this bias. Possible solutions include refining the dataset, enhancing feature extraction techniques, and fine-tuning hyperparameters to improve overall performance and reduce misclassification rates.

Finally, the results obtained (accuracy of 73.68%) reflect significant progress in the classification of petroglyphs using CNNs. However, there remains a need to further refine the model to achieve higher levels of accuracy. Future work should focus on the implementation of complementary techniques, including hyperparameter tuning, dataset expansion, and the study of overfitting to ensure a more generalizable model. Additionally, a comparative analysis between different classification algorithms, such as Support Vector Machines (SVM), transfer learning approaches, and Kolmogorov Arnold Networks (KAN), should be conducted. This will help evaluate their respective advantages and limitations in the context of petroglyph classification. Understanding the effect of overfitting and implementing strategies to mitigate it will be crucial for improving the reliability and robustness of classification models in archaeological research. Furthermore, future studies could also explore multimodal approaches that integrate additional data sources, such as geological context or spatial distribution patterns, to refine classification accuracy. With these improvements, it will be possible to advance toward the development of a mobile application that leverages these models to classify petroglyph images in real time. This tool would assist researchers by providing contextualized, science-based information, enhancing archaeological analysis and fieldwork efficiency.

Acknowledgments. The author expresses gratitude to the Vice Rectorate for Research at the Universidad Pedagógica y Tecnológica de Colombia (UPTC) for its support and commitment to the development of this research.

References

1. Troncoso, A.: Arte Rupestre, Comunidades e Historia en el Centro Norte de Chile. Socialediciones (2022). ISBN: 9789561912397
2. Martos, L.A., Vitry, C., Cornejo, B., Cornejo, M.: Los petroglifos del sistema huaca yaku, cachi, salta, argentina. Resultados preliminares," Cuadernos del Instituto Nacional de Antropología y Pensamiento Latinoamericano-Series Especiales, vol. 9, pp. 358–371 (2021)
3. Colegial-Gutiérrez, J.D., Moreno-González, M.C., Colegial-Gutiérrez, J.D., Moreno-González, M.C.: Análisis histórico-semioestilístico y geológico de rocas-lienzos con pictogramas y petroglifos Guane en la Mesa de Los Santos (Santander-Colombia). Boletín de Geología **45**(3), 119–136 (2023). https://doi.org/10.18273/REVBOL.V45N3-2023007
4. Carden, N.M., Borella, F., Cardillo, M.: Rock art relatedness and circulation paths in Northeast Patagonia, Argentina. Rock Art Res.: J. Aust. Rock Art Res. Assoc. (AURA) **37**(2), 184–203
5. Horn, C., Ivarsson, O., Lindhé, C., Potter, R., Green, A., Ling, J.: Artificial In- telligence, 3D documentation, and rock art—approaching and reflecting on the automation of identification and classification of rock art images. J. Archaeol. Method Theory **29**(1), 188–213 (2022). https://doi.org/10.1007/S10816-021-09518-6/FIGURES/13
6. Berenguer R.J.: El Arte Rupestre De Taira Dentro De Los Problemas De La Arqueología Atacameña. Chungara: Revista de Antropología Chilena **27**(1), 7–43 (1995). http://www.jstor.org/stable/27802008
7. Alé, A., Maldonado, M., Cisternas, L.: Marcas olvidadas: estudio de las representaciones rupestres históricas del sitio Los Fierros, Andacollo (norte semiárido de Chile). Boletín del Museo Chileno de Arte Precolombino **27**(1), 67–86 (2022). https://doi.org/10.56522/BMCHAP.0050010270002
8. Ćosović, M., Janković, R.: CNN classification of the cultural heritage images. In: 2020 19th International Symposium INFOTEH-JAHORINA (INFOTEH), East Sarajevo, Bosnia and Herzegovina, pp. 1-6 (2020). https://doi.org/10.1109/INFOTEH48170.2020.9066300

9. Matrone, F., Martini, M.: Transfer learning and performance enhancement techniques for deep semantic segmentation of built heritage point clouds. Virtual Archaeol. Rev. **12**(25), 73–84 (2021). https://doi.org/10.4995/VAR.2021.15318
10. Bisong, E.: Google colaboratory. In: Building Machine Learning and Deep Learning Models on Google Cloud Platform: A Comprehensive Guide for Beginners, pp. 59-64. Apress, Berkeley (2019)

Evaluating Information Extraction Approaches in the Construction of a Real Estate Observatory

Luciana Tanevitch[1(✉)], Leandro Antonelli[1,3], and Diego Torres[1,2]

[1] CICPBA-Facultad de Informática, LIFIA, UNLP, La Plata, Argentina
{luciana.tanevitch,leandro.antonelli, diego.torres}@lifia.info.unlp.edu.ar
[2] Departamento de Ciencia y Tecnología, UNQ, Bernal, Argentina
[3] Facultad de Tecnología Informática, CAETI, UAI, Buenos Aires, Argentina

Abstract. A real estate observatory plays a significant role in the aggregation and analysis of real estate market data. The information that lies in real estate advertisements can be leveraged to populate such an observatory. However, this data can present itself in both a structured and an unstructured manner. Unstructured data represents a problem to automatically process and extract information since it lacks a predefined structure. Thus, there's a need for techniques to give structure to unstructured data. Information Extraction (IE) is the process of structuring data from unstructured data. Natural Language Processing techniques enable machines to understand texts, making them particularly significant in the context of IE. This work evaluates both rule-based and machine-learning based IE approaches to extract features from real estate descriptions within advertisements. Those features are relevant in the context of real estate observatory construction.

The performance of each approach is measured using precision, recall and f1-score metrics.

Keywords: Information Extraction · Natural Language Processing · Deep Learning models · Rule-based matching · Real Estate Observatory

1 Introduction

Unstructured data represents 80% of the information on the Web, in the form of text, photos, videos, etc. [12, 14]. This type of data lacks organization so analyzing it implies significant challenges, particularly due to machines' limited understanding of natural language. Structured data is more useful in process automation because of its standardized format, which defines the structure of the elements and how they are related. For example, efficient searching could be performed using contextual information, narrowing the universe of possible results [3].

Natural Language Processing (NLP) is a technique that allows machines to process natural language automatically, enabling human-machine understanding [8]. NLP tools can be used to extract information from unstructured texts. Information Extraction (IE) is the process of analyzing text to extract concepts. Its goal is to discover structured

V. Agredo-Delgado et al. (Eds.): DECISIONING 2024, CCIS 2369, pp. 70–84, 2025.
https://doi.org/10.1007/978-3-031-91690-8_6

information from unstructured or semi-structured text [11, 13]. IE techniques can be divided into machine-learning based and non-machine-learning based.

The early IE systems were rule-based, where patterns based on linguistic features are defined [19]. Rule-based systems are robust if patterns are well-defined, but this requires knowing the format in which the data is written to build effective patterns. The amount of machine learning-based systems is growing exponentially, and they can achieve outstanding results. Named Entity Recognition (NER) is the process of identifying entities within a text. Those entities refer to relevant concepts existent in the real world, such as places, people, organizations, etc. [18]. Although several models are pre-trained to perform NER tasks, they are only able to recognize some limited entities. When the need for a broader detection arises, it becomes necessary to train the model to identify those new entities. NER models are usually trained using supervised learning, which requires to have a big corpus of annotated data.

The leading machine learning-based approach to date is built upon the transformers architecture [20]. Models based on transformers can perform NLP tasks to extract features from text. Within the IE context, Question Answering (QA) is a method that can be used to extract information by asking questions in which the answers are extracted from text. Additionally, generative models can perform more advanced tasks, such as specifying the extraction format or adding instructions. Both QA and generative models leverage the transformers architecture because its attention mechanism allows the model to focus on different parts of the text, thus capturing contextual relationships more effectively.

Several works describe the use of IE techniques to structure information. Ghani et. al. [10] use semi-supervised learning algorithms to extract explicit and implicit attribute-value pairs from product descriptions to augment databases of products.

More [16] uses deep learning methods to extract attribute values from product titles to augment product metadata for e-commerce catalogs. Linková and Gurský [15] present algorithms to extract attributes and their values from product descriptions on e-shops, focusing on three data types: string, boolean and numeric. Those attributes can be useful in deduplication tasks (that is, identifying identical resources). Blandón and Zapata [2] propose a rule-based framework that uses GATE-JAPE patterns to extract attribute values from text to populate an ontology. Sabeh et. al. [17] develop a tool based on QA for attribute verification and enrichment on the e-commerce domain. Wang et. at. [21] propose an approach to extract attribute-value pairs using QA. Their model can classify unanswerable questions based on their context. State-of-the-art works describe both methods and prompt design patterns to perform attribute value extraction from text descriptions using Large-Language-Models [4, 5]. Specifically, Brinkmann et. al. [6] use ChatGPT to extract product attributes and brands from Amazon listings.

Baur et. al. [1] evaluate several machine learning models to valuate real estates based on their textual descriptions.

A Real Estate Observatory (REO) is a tool for analysts to discover trends in the real estate market based on up-to-date information. A Real Estate Observatory (REO) is a powerful tool for both public and private organizations to discover trends in the real estate market, make informed investment decisions, and develop effective urban policies. Hence, the absence of data is a problem because no REO can be built without data. Since real estate listings contain lots of useful information to valuate real estates, Web scrapers can be used as a solution to extract semi-structured features such as bulleted or tabular information. However, Web scrappers tend to struggle with unstructured information, which is why the use of IE techniques can be of help to extract features that are present in text, such as from real estate descriptions provided by advertisers.

The contribution of this work is an analysis of different IE approaches to extract real estate features from unstructured text, specifically real estate descriptions on online listings on Spanish language. Approaches are evaluated with the precision, recall and f1-score metrics with exact matching. The goal is to identify features that are explicitly mentioned in the text, and those that could be inferred by other extracted features. For example, Table 1 presents explicit mentions of features such as address (Soler 700), location (Bahía Blanca), FAR (2.4), and lot dimensions (8.66 × 23 × 19.60). Moreover, the listing doesn't mention if the lot is irregular, but given the lot dimensions, it can be inferred that it actually is.

Table 1. Example of a real estate description on a listing. Source: author's own work.

Lot for sale in an excellent location, with a structure practically ready for demolition. Located at Soler 700, Bahía Blanca. Ideal for construction companies. It boasts 8.66 m of frontage, 23 m on the west side, and 19.60 m on the east side. Zoned as C2 with a FAR of 2.4

This paper is organized as follows. Section 2 describes the different rule-based and machine-learning-based IE approaches that are evaluated in this work, and the process to extract features from real estate descriptions using them. Section 3 describes the evaluation method, the employed metrics and the ground truth construction to evaluate each approach. The results of the evaluation are described in Sect. 4. Section 5 summarizes the application and limitations of each approach for the extraction of features. Finally, Sect. 6 outlines the paper's conclusions and suggests some possible lines of future works.

2 Information Extraction Approaches for Real Estate Text Mining

The selection of target variables is determined by a team of domain experts, who assess their importance to the REO. This study focuses on identifying the most significant variables, although others may also be considered Table 2 enumerates, describes and exemplifies each variable.

Different IE approaches are evaluated in this work, to assess their performance in extracting variables described in Table 2. The following subsections explore different approaches and their application in extracting attribute-value pairs in descriptions of real estate listings.

2.1 Rule-Based Matching

Rule-based matching is a well-known and effective approach to extract information from text. In particular, with NLP, patterns could be defined to extract information according

Table 2. Variables to be extracted. Source: author's own work.

Variable	Description	Type	Example
Address	It describes the address where the property is located at. This field can be useful to enable automatic geocoding	String	Calle 7 n° 4534 Av. 32 y Av. 7 Independencia esq. San Martín Independencia e/ San Martín y Caseros
FOT	FOT is an indicator of the land's potential for vertical construction. It uses to be a single value, but sometimes multiple values can be mentioned	Numeric	FOT 3 FOT 2.5 FOT residencial: 2, FOT comercial: 3
Irregular lot	It indicates if the lot's shape is not rectangular. Irregular lots are typically priced lower than regular ones because they complicate the constructive utilization of real estate products developed on the lot	Boolean	Lote irregular Lote con forma de martillo Lote triangular
Lot dimensions	It shows the lot sizes	String	10 × 40 10 m × 40 m 10 mts × 40 mts 10 metros de frente × 40 metros de fondo
Corner	It indicates if the lot is located in a corner	Boolean	Lote en esquina
Neighborhood	It is the name of the neighborhood	String	Barrio Las Camelias Club de Campo Abril Barrio Privado San Sebastián
Facades	The number of facades of the property. It indicates that the lot faces to more than 1 street	Numeric	2 frentes doble frente salida a tres calles
Swimming pool	It indicates if the lot has swimming pool	Boolean	… con pileta de fibra …

to its linguistic features. Spacy[1] is a library that includes several IE tools within rule-based matching support. Hence, patterns are lists of dictionaries where each dictionary describes the linguistic features that each token should have to make a match. POS tag and dependency tags could be used to indicate which features the tokens should satisfy.

The address can be written in different formats, as shown in Table 2. After analyzing available data, three main format of addresses are detected: *street name and number*

[1] https://spacy.io.

(Calle 7 n° 4534), *street name and street name* (Av. 32 y Av. 7, Independencia esq. San Martín), *street name between streets* (Independencia e/ San Martín y Caseros). In addition, addresses in private neighborhoods tend to be organized as 'lot number' or 'block number', and there are other formats that cannot be generalized by a pattern. Keywords such as 'calle, avenida, diagonal' and their abbreviations can be present or not. That may be matched by the following sequence: [{'LOWER': {'IN': ['calle', 'avenida', 'av', 'diagonal', 'diag']}, 'OP': '?'}]. Since streets can be defined by the number or name, both number and proper nouns should be considered: [{'POS': {'IN': ['PROPN', 'NUM']}, 'OP': ' +'}]. The street number can be exact or not, for example, 'calle Independencia 4555' is an exact address, but 'calle Independencia al 4000' is not because "al" refers to a block or range of addresses around the 4000 mark. This can be supported by making optional the preposition 'al': [{'LOWER': 'al', 'OP': '?'}, {'LIKE_NUM': True}]. Thus, by analyzing the structure of addresses and combining patterns, the different address structures can be covered.

Accordingly, a pattern to detect FOT value could be written as follows: [{'TEXT':'FOT'}, {'LIKE_NUM': True}]. Hence, model will match 'FOT 3' and 'FOT 2.5' but not 'f.o.t 3', 'fot 3', 'F.O.T 3'. As patterns should cover most common written formats, a more adequate pattern could be [{'LOWER':{'IN':['fot', 'f.o.t']}},{'LIKE_NUM': True}], where 'fot', 'FOT', 'f.o.t', 'F.o.t', 'Fot', 'F.O.T' can match. Since FOT can take alternative values, optional tokens can be included to cover this cases: [{'LOWER':{'IN':['fot', 'f.o.t']}},{'LOWER': {'IN': ['res', 'residencial', 'comercial', 'com', 'industrial']}, 'OP': '?'},{'LIKE_NUM': True}].

To detect lot dimensions, a pattern that identifies the format *number x number* is defined (10 × 40). Unit of measure can be present or not (10 mts × 40 mts). Additionally, a pattern to find coincidences based on the structure *number de frente x number de fondo* is defined (10 mts de frente × 40 mts de fondo).

Facades number is usually specified as *number frentes*, but expressions referring to multiple street frontages are also common. So both cases are considered to define adequate patterns.

The neighborhood name can be extracted by a pattern that searches the word 'Barrio' followed by a sequence of one or more proper nouns (Barrio Náutico). As private neighborhoods are also considered, the pattern also covers keywords used to refer to them, such as 'Country', 'Estancia' and 'Club'.

To detect boolean variables, an exact mention of the attribute is considered as a true value. In the case of the shape of the lot, irregularity can be detected by the presence of the word 'irregular' but also by an adjective modifying the word to refer to 'lot' or 'shape' (lote martillo, lote con forma triangular).

2.2 Named Entity Recognition

Named Entity Recognition is an NLP task for information extraction that involves automatically finding and classifying concepts according to defined categories [18]. Since trained NER models have standard categories such as location, person and organization, a new model should be trained to allow the model to use other categories. Training a new NER model requires annotated data, so the first step is to define tags to be used for the annotating process. One tag is defined for each variable on Table 2. Then, a training dataset is created using the field **description** of the REO knowledge base, which is the textual description on the real estate listing extracted by an automatic agent. Afterwards, data must be labeled using pre-defined tags. This requires an effort from a domain expert team to ensure that the process is homogeneous, i.e., all participants annotate data following the same criteria. For example, if dimensions are detected, include the unit measure if present. To make the process easier for people, NER Annotator Tool for Spacy is used to perform the task. This Web application allows users to load a text file and a tags file, and use a graphic interface to annotate each description. The generated file is used to train a Spacy model. In this work, `es_core_news_lg` (corresponding to the large Spanish model) is used.

2.3 Transformers-Based

Transformers is a novel architecture that uses a self-attention mechanism to process data, making it suitable for tasks that require the understanding of context and semantics [20]. Transformers are widely used in NLP tasks, having great results in this application.

Question-Answering

Question-Answering (QA) is an approach that enables machines to extract answers to certain questions given a context. The Transformers[2] library available for Python, provides pre-trained models for QA task, which can be easily manipulated using the pipeline API since it abstracts the implementation. BERT [9] is a state-of-the-art NLP model that is based on transformers architecture and can be used to perform the QA task. Three pre-trained BERT-based Spanish models are selected to compare their performance. The difference lies in optimization techniques. All the models are available on HuggingFace[3] platform.

1. mrm8488/bert-base-spanish-wwm-cased-finetuned-spa-squad2-es
2. timpal0l/mdeberta-v3-base-squad2
3. rvargas93/distill-bert-base-spanish-wwm-cased-finetuned-spa-squad2-es

Since (1) is the base BERT Spanish model, (2) performs disentangled attention and enhanced mask decoder to improve the base model and (3) performs distillation process to compress the model into a smaller and more efficient version. The pipeline API receives a set of questions, one for each attribute, and responds with the mention in the context text that should answer each question. For example, to detect the address attribute a possible question could be "What is the address of the property?" and the model should return the address from the property's description if it's present and abstain if it isn't.

Generative Models

Generative models, which are considered state-of-the-art, have the ability to generate text based on another text. These models are designed to understand the underlying patterns in the data and use this understanding to generate new data, which is useful in diverse applications such as IE. In recent years, there has been an exponential growth in the amount of generative models available. The most popular one is GPT-3 [7], a

[2] https://huggingface.co/docs/transformers/index.

[3] https://huggingface.co/.

huge generative pre-trained model based on the transformers architecture and attention mechanism. This attention mechanism allows the model to focus on the most relevant parts of the input when making predictions, leading to more accurate and contextually aware outputs. Although newer versions of GPT have already been released, GPT-3 still stands out by providing its service free of charge under certain rate limits, with the added of allowing the configuration of prompt instructions.

GPT-3 can perform as a QA model, but it can also follow a task provided in the input. For example, instructions for data extraction and output formatting can be provided. Therefore, prompt engineering significantly affects the outcomes yielded by the model. In order to extract real estate features, the provided instructions are related to the specific attributes that should be retrieved. This includes the type of each variable whether it's a string, a number, or a boolean. The output format is also indicated in the instructions. It's important to note that the model is instructed to respond in a closed manner and not to add any additional information. Finally, it is specified to put a null value if the attribute is not detected in the text. The proposed approach for attribute-value extraction could be extended to newer GPT versions and also to other generative models.

3 Evaluation Method

This section describes the method used to evaluate the performance of each model to automatically detect features in real estate descriptions. In particular, we want to know the capacity of each model to correctly detect variables detailed on Table 2, considering explicit and implicit mentions. To evaluate the performance we use metrics described as follows.

3.1 Metrics

The most widely used metrics to evaluate the performance of machine learning models are precision, recall and f1-score. The following concepts are tightly related to these metrics as they are used to calculate them. True positives (TP) are pairs correctly identified by the model. Exact matching is used to calculate the TP, which means that the predicted and expected pair should be exactly the same. False positives (FP) are those pairs raised by the model that are not present in the ground truth. Another case of FP is when both a predicted and an expected pair exist but they don't match (prediction is wrong). True negatives (TN) occur when no pair is expected and the model doesn't recognize any either. False negatives (FN) occur when the model doesn't recognize any pair, but a pair is expected to be recognized. These concepts play a crucial role in understanding the evaluation metrics. Precision measures the approach's ability to correctly identify the attribute-value pairs. Recall represents the approach's capacity to detect all the existent pairs. Finally, f1-score is a harmonic measure between precision and recall.

3.2 Ground Truth for Real Estate Data Analysis

A ground truth dataset (GT) containing real information was developed to evaluate the IE approaches. The purpose of this dataset is to evaluate the results of the different approaches and to classify them as correct or incorrect. The GT was manually built and curated to ensure its reliability. Real estate listings were manually selected from different websites. Only the listing descriptions that include the desired variables were considered for building de GT. Moreover, the selected listings' descriptions should cover the wide range of written formats of each variable. For example, in the case of lot dimensions, it must have descriptions where the lot dimension is present as 20×10, 20 mts in the front and 10 mts in the back, front: 20 m back: 10 m, etc.

The curation process involves the removal of information that is not related to the property itself (advertiser's contact, information related to the real estate agency, legal disclaimers and auctioneers data). Besides, it implies formatting of the text by adding punctuation marks in line breaks, eliminating non-standard characters, and replacing commas in numbers with dots. This curation process reduces the noise introduced in the advertisements to make them more eye-catching or to include legal disclaimers, keeping the part of the text that describes the property.

Two considerations were taken to be as faithful to reality as possible: not all variables are present in each listing, and variables have an uneven distribution, with varying quantities for each. Each row of GT contains the description, and extracted mentions for each variable of Table 2. Addresses, FOT and neighborhood names are set with exact mentions. Dimensions are set according to the format *number x number*, regardless of how it is mentioned in the description. Boolean variables are set as True if the variable is present on the description. Additionally, the analysis considered those variables that could be deduced from extracted ones to include them in the GT. For example, if lot dimensions are $20 \times 10 \times 30 \times 40$, it is assumed that the lot is irregular, even if it is not explicitly mentioned. The dataset contains 100 rows, corresponding to 100 real estate listing descriptions.

4 Results

This section reports the evaluation results of each IE approach in the task of detecting defined variables.

4.1 Rule-Based Matching

The **address** field was measured considering all possible formats at once. 25 address mentions were correctly found over 53 mentioned addresses. This approach obtained precision: 0.33, recall: 0.89 and f1-score: 0.49. This suggests that the model assigned addresses to a significant portion of the found pairs, but many of these assignments were incorrect, which showed that the model's ability is not optimal to accurately discern addresses from other text elements. **FOT** obtained 0.94 in precision, 0.92 in recall and 0.93 in f1-score. Since 40 FOT mentions were available in text, 35 were correctly detected. This results show a good ability to extract FOT variables. To detect the **dimensions** variable, the model obtained precision: 0.84, recall: 0.56 and f1-score: 0.67. 39 pairs were correctly identified over a total of 74 mentions. The model got precision: 0.61, recall: 0.33 and f1-score: 0.43 on **neighborhood** detection. Only 8 of 28 pairs were correctly extracted. This means that the model performed badly to detect this variable. Detecting the **irregular** shape of the lot obtained precision: 1.0, recall: 0.64 and f1: 0.78. 20 of 31 pairs were detected. Results show that although the model is good at detecting this feature, not all pairs are being detected. 28 over 40 available **facades** mentions were detected, with precision: 0.93, recall: 0.71 and f1-score: 0.81. Since **swimming pool** and **corner** occurrences only appear mentioned in text when they are present in the property, results were good, having f1-score of 1.0 in both cases. Results are summarized on Table 3.

Table 3. Rule based matching performance by variable. Source: author's own work.

Variable	Precision	Recall	F1-Score
address	0.33	0.89	0.49
FOT	0.94	0.92	0.93
irregular	1.0	0.64	0.78
dimensions	0.84	0.56	0.67
corner	1.0	1.0	1.0
neighborhood	0.61	0.33	0.43
facades	0.93	0.71	0.81
pool	1.0	1.0	1.0

4.2 Named Entity Recognition

The **address** field was measured considering all possible formats at once. This approach identified 29 over 53 mentions, with precision: 0.74, recall: 0.61 and f1-score: 0.67. 33 of 40 **FOT** pairs were extracted, giving precision: 1.0, recall: 0.82 and f1-score: 0.9. 41 pairs were correctly detected from a total of 74 in **dimensions** variable. Results were precision: 0.82, recall: 0.6 and f1-score: 0.69. Finding **neighborhood** name obtained 0.53 in precision, 0.32 in recall and 0.4 in f1-score. 8 over 40 pairs were recognized. 18 over 31 pairs were correctly identified for lot **irregularity**, with precision: 1.0, recall: 0.58 and f1-score: 0.73. 26 pairs which referring **facade** amount were detected over 40, with precision: 0.92, recall: 0.66 and f1-score 0.77. To detect **swimming pool** feature, precision was 1.0, recall 0.73 and f1-score 0.85, counting 17 over 23 identified pairs. **Corner** location obtained 1.0 in precision, 0.95 in recall and 0.97 in f1-score, with 19 of 20 pairs extracted. Table 4 summarizes obtained results.

4.3 Transformers-Based

Table 5 shows results obtained by each QA model, for each variable, highlighting the model with reached the higher f1-score for each variable. mDeBERTa model outperforms on most variables compared to the other QA models. In detecting **addresses, dimensions**

Table 4. NER performance by variable. Source: author's own work.

Variable	Precision	Recall	F1-Score
address	0.74	0.61	0.67
FOT	1.0	0.82	0.90
irregular	1.0	0.58	0.73
dimensions	0.82	0.60	0.69
corner	1.0	0.95	0.97
neighborhood	0.53	0.32	0.40
facades	0.92	0.66	0.77
pool	1.0	0.73	0.85

and **neighborhoods** all models had bad results with f1-scores under 0.5. Analyzing the cause of failure, it is associated to a wrong result in most of them. Even modifying the syntax on the question used to extract those variables, performance didn't improve.

Table 5. QA performance by variable. Source: author's own work.

	Address	FOT	Irregular	Dimensions	Corner	Neighborhood	Facades	Pool
Transformers (BETO)	P: 0.13 R: 0.73 F1: 0.22	P: 0.32 R: 0.65 F1: 0.43	P: 1.0 R: 0.35 F1: 0.52	P: 0.34 R: 0.75 F1: 0.47	P: 1.0 R: 0.15 F1: 0.26	P: 0.41 R: 0.17 F1: 0.25	P: 0.60 R: 0.35 F1: 0.45	P: 1.0 R: 0.82 F1: 0.90
Transformers (mDeBERTa)	P: 0.29 R: 0.85 F1: 0.43	P: 0.77 R: 0.80 F1: 0.78	P: 0.90 R: 0.58 F1: 0.70	P: 0.42 R: 0.90 F1: 0.57	P: 1.0 R: 0.55 F1: 0.70	P: 0.52 R: 0.46 F1: 0.48	P: 0.82 R: 0.61 F1: 0.70	P: 1.0 R: 0.82 F1: 0.90
Transformers (BETO + distilled)	P: 0.21 R: 0.85 F1: 0.33	P: 0.20 R: 0.60 F1: 0.30	P: 0.89 R: 0.54 F1: 0.67	P: 0.34 R: 0.76 F1: 0.48	P: 1.0 R: 0.40 F1: 0.57	P: 0.41 R: 0.29 F1: 0.34	P: 0.68 R: 0.51 F1: 0.58	P: 1.0 R: 0.50 F1: 0.68

GPT-3 had great results for almost all variables, considering that it achieved F1-scores above 0.8 in those where it performed well. Most of the observed missings are due to the output format. Since the ground truth dataset is constructed from literal extractions in the descriptions and evaluated with exact matching, pairs containing correct information but not in the format specified by the ground truth may be classified as false. For example, GPT may output 'Melo 836, Lomas del Mirador' while the ground truth states 'Melo 836'. Although the output contains the correct address, it includes additional location data, which results in it being counted as a false positive. All results are shown in Table 6.

Table 6. GPT-3 performance by variable. Source: author's own work.

Variable	Precision	Recall	F1-Score
address	0.45	0.84	0.59
FOT	0.92	0.97	0.94
irregular	0.90	0.96	0.93
dimensions	0.86	0.98	0.92
corner	0.76	1.0	0.86
neighborhood	0.66	0.92	0.77
facades	1.0	1.0	1.0
pool	1.0	1.0	1.0

General Results

Table 7 summarizes all results obtained, highlighting the approach with the best performance for each variable. As observed, the best f1-scores were obtained with GPT-3 in most of variables, followed by NER approach.

Table 7. General results by variable. Source: author's own work.

	Address	FOT	Irregular	Dimensions	Corner	Neighborhood	Facades	Pool
Rule-based matching	P: 0.33 R: 0.89 F1: 0.49	P: 0.94 R: 0.92 F1: 0.93	P: 1.0 R: 0.64 F1: 0.78	P: 0.84 R: 0.56 F1: 0.67	P: 1.0 R: 1.0 F1: 1.0	P: 0.61 R: 0.33 F1: 0.43	P: 0.93 R: 0.71 F1: 0.81	P: 1.0 R: 1.0 F1: 1.0
NER	P: 0.74 R: 0.61 F1: 0.67	P: 1.0 R: 0.82 F1: 0.9	P: 1.0 R: 0.58 F1: 0.73	P: 0.82 R: 0.60 F1: 0.69	P: 1.0 R: 0.95 F1: 0.97	P: 0.53 R: 0.32 F1: 0.40	P: 0.92 R: 0.66 F1: 0.67	P: 1.0 R: 0.73 F1: 0.85

(continued)

Table 7. (*continued*)

	Address	FOT	Irregular	Dimensions	Corner	Neighborhood	Facades	Pool
Transformers (BETO)	P: 0.13 R: 0.73 F1: 0.22	P: 0.32 R: 0.65 F1: 0.43	P: 1.0 R: 0.35 F1: 0.52	P: 0.34 R: 0.75 F1: 0.47	P: 1.0 R: 0.15 F1: 0.26	P: 0.41 R: 0.17 F1: 0.25	P: 0.60 R: 0.35 F1: 0.45	P: 1.0 R: 0.82 F1: 0.90
Transformers (mDeBERTa)	P: 0.29 R: 0.85 F1: 0.43	P: 0.77 R: 0.80 F1: 0.78	P: 0.90 R: 0.58 F1: 0.70	P: 0.42 R: 0.90 F1: 0.57	P: 1.0 R: 0.55 F1: 0.70	P: 0.52 R: 0.46 F1: 0.48	P: 0.82 R: 0.61 F1: 0.70	P: 1.0 R: 0.82 F1: 0.90
Transformers (BETO + distilled)	P: 0.21 R: 0.85 F1: 0.33	P: 0.20 R: 0.60 F1: 0.30	P: 0.89 R: 0.54 F1: 0.67	P: 0.34 R: 0.76 F1: 0.48	P: 1.0 R: 0.40 F1: 0.57	P: 0.41 R: 0.29 F1: 0.34	P: 0.68 R: 0.51 F1: 0.58	P: 1.0 R: 0.50 F1: 0.68
Transformers (GPT3)	P: 0.45 R: 0.84 F1: 0.59	P: 0.92 R: 0.97 F1: 0.94	P: 0.90 R: 0.96 F1: 0.93	P: 0.86 R: 0.98 F1: 0.92	P: 0.76 R: 1.0 F1: 0.86	P: 0.66 R: 0.92 F1: 0.77	P: 1.0 R: 1.0 F1: 1.0	P: 1.0 R: 1.0 F1: 1.0

5 Discussion

Some limitations are being detected in the specific variable extraction along the different evaluation steps. The nature of each variable and the analyzed approach deserve a discussion on use and configuration. In the following, a detailed discussion of the approaches applied to the most relevant variables is presented.

Address detection can enable geocoding. It is desirable to determine the format in which this feature is presented. Due to the high variability in writing formats, it is difficult to create patterns that cover all situations. On the other hand, training a NER to detect each type of address requires a huge amounts of annotated data. GPT-3 tends to include the location in the address, resulting in false positives according to the exact matching proposed. A balanced alternative would be to combine GPT-3 with rule-based matching to extract an answer and then classify it in different formats.

Extracting the dimensions of the lot requires high precision because, as this variable is used to deduce lot irregularity, it must be ensured that the detected value is accurate.

Detecting a neighborhood name is a complex task for machines since it is also difficult for humans to do it. As humans, we expect some keywords to easily detect a name as a neighborhood (Barrio, Country, Club de Campo, Estancia). But if none of those keywords are present, we can't know if the name is a neighborhood, a city, a locality or another place.

A central issue found with QA is interpreting answers when expecting boolean values. One possible approach could be to consider the response generated by the QA system as positive, regardless of its content. This may work when working with datasets that only mention a feature when it is present, which are most of the cases. Given that instances where the feature is mentioned negatively are exceedingly rare but not impossible, identifying certain keywords that indicate the presence of the variable in the obtained responses can enable the interpretation of the truth value (positive or negative) of that variable. In cases where the feature is not mentioned, the model should refrain from responding.

NER encounters similar challenges since it processes input as a sequence labeling problem. Therefore, this approach should also be applied in the presence of negative occurrences. For GPT-3, an adequate prompt offers enough guidance to entrust it with the task of determining the boolean value (or null).

6 Conclusions

This work evaluated different IE approaches to extract features from text, in the context of the construction of a real estate observatory. Both rule-based and machine-learning-based approaches were evaluated over real estate descriptions manually extracted and curated from online advertisements.

GPT-3 obtained the best results in this evaluation with f1-score: 0.87 when averaging every variable. GPT-3 can generate results automatically, which for other approaches would require defining additional rules to derive values based on the extracted information. For instance, if the text mentions that the dimensions of a lot are 10x30x25x40, GPT-3 could identify that the lot is irregular. While it would be possible to define rules for NER-based approaches and rule-based approaches to set the number of sides to 2 if the extraction detects that the lot is in a corner and the facades amount is not specified (but not vice versa), it may also be possible to establish a rule to classify a lot as irregular based on the extracted dimensions (if more than 2 dimensions are specified and it's not rectangular, it's irregular). Another interesting approach is NER, which obtained the second best results even with minimal training with an average f1-score of 0.73. These results could be further improved by training the model on a larger dataset. The third place was obtained by Rule-based Matching with an average f1-score of 0.66, considering that could be improved by writing exhaustively patterns and adding additional rules.

Considering that exact match is the most restrictive evaluation, using partial matching could improve general performance in some variables. For certain variables such as address, dimensions, and neighborhood name, exact matching can be overly restrictive since if the model provides the correct data in a different format, it will be classified as false. Instead, partial matching can be useful to avoid such situations, thereby setting a threshold that is beneficial for obtaining the correct information without losses.

Future works relate to evaluating the performance of the approaches on a massive dataset, considering data augmentation techniques. Moreover, the extracted features should be aligned to existing ones in the real estate observatory, requiring techniques to detect weaknesses in available data.

References

1. Baur, K., Rosenfelder, M., Lutz, B.: Automated real estate valuation with machine learning models using property descriptions. Expert Syst. Appl. **213**, 119147 (2023). https://doi.org/10.1016/j.eswa.2022.119147
2. Blandón Andrade, J.C., Zapata Jaramillo, C.M.: Gate-based rules for extracting attribute values. Computación y Sistemas **25**, 4 (2021). https://doi.org/10.13053/cys-25-4-3493
3. Blumberg, R., Atre, S.: The Problem with Unstructured Data (2003)
4. Brinkmann, A., Baumann, N., Bizer, C.: Using LLMs for the extraction and normalization of product attribute values. In: Tekli, J., Gamper, J., Chbeir, R., and Manolopoulos, Y. (eds.) Advances in Databases and Information Systems, pp. 217–230. Springer Nature Switzerland, Cham (2024). https://doi.org/10.1007/978-3-031-70626-4_15
5. Brinkmann, A., Shraga, R., Bizer, C.: ExtractGPT: exploring the potential of large language models for product attribute value extraction. In: Information Integration and Web Intelligence: 26th International Conference, iiWAS 2024, Bratislava, Slovak Republic, December 2–4, 2024, Proceedings, Part I, pp. 38–52. Springer-Verlag, Berlin, Heidelberg (2024). https://doi.org/10.1007/978-3-031-78090-5_4
6. Brinkmann, A., Shraga, R., Der, R.C., Bizer, C.: Product information extraction using ChatGPT (2023). https://doi.org/10.48550/ARXIV.2306.14921
7. Brown, T.B., et al.: Language models are few-shot learners. In: Larochelle, H., Ranzato, M., Hadsell, R., Balcan, M.-F., and Lin, H.-T. (eds.) Advances in Neural Information Processing Systems 33: Annual Conference on Neural Information Processing Systems 2020, NeurIPS 2020, December 6–12, 2020, virtual (2020)
8. Chowdhury, G.G.: Natural language processing. Annu. Rev. Inf. Sci. Technol. **37**(1), 51–89 (2003). https://doi.org/10.1002/ARIS.1440370103
9. Devlin, J., Chang, M.-W., Lee, K., Toutanova, K.: BERT: pre-training of deep bidirectional transformers for language understanding. In: Burstein, J., Doran, C., and Solorio, T. (eds.) Proceedings of the 2019 Conference of the North American Chapter of the Association for Computational Linguistics: Human Language Technologies, NAACL-HLT 2019, Minneapolis, MN, USA, June 2–7, 2019, Volume 1 (Long and Short Papers), pp. 4171–4186. Association for Computational Linguistics (2019). https://doi.org/10.18653/V1/N19-1423
10. Ghani, R., Probst, K., Liu, Y., Krema, M., Fano, A.E.: Text mining for product attribute extraction. SIGKDD Explor. **8**(1), 41–48 (2006). https://doi.org/10.1145/1147234.1147241
11. Grishman, R.: Information extraction. IEEE Intell. Syst. **30**(5), 8–15 (2015). https://doi.org/10.1109/MIS.2015.68
12. Inmon, W.H., Linstedt, D., Levins, M.: Chapter 4.4 - unstructured data. In: Inmon, W.H., Linstedt, D., and Levins, M. (eds.) Data Architecture (Second Edition), pp. 89–97. Academic Press (2019). https://doi.org/10.1016/B978-0-12-816916-2.00013-9
13. Jiang, J.: Information extraction from text. In: Aggarwal, C.C. and Zhai, C. (eds.) Mining Text Data, pp. 11–41. Springer US, Boston, MA (2012). https://doi.org/10.1007/978-1-4614-3223-4_2
14. Kulkarni, A., Shivananda, A.: Natural Language Processing Recipes: Unlocking Text Data with Machine Learning and Deep Learning using Python. Apress, Berkeley, CA (2019). https://doi.org/10.1007/978-1-4842-4267-4

15. Linková, M., Gurský, P.: Attributes extraction from product descriptions on e-shops. In: Hlavácová, J. (ed.) Proceedings of the 17th Conference on Information Technologies - Applications and Theory (ITAT 2017), Martinské hole, Slovakia, September 22–26, 2017, pp. 23–26. CEUR-WS.org (2017)
16. More, A.: Attribute Extraction from Product Titles in eCommerce (2016). http://arxiv.org/abs/1608.04670
17. Sabeh, K., Kacimi, M., Gamper, J.: CAVE: correcting attribute values in e-commerce profiles. In: Proceedings of the 31st ACM International Conference on Information & Knowledge Management, pp. 4965–4969 ACM, Atlanta GA USA (2022). https://doi.org/10.1145/3511808.3557161
18. Sharnagat, R.: Named Entity Recognition: A Literature Survey
19. Small, S.G., Medsker, L.R.: Review of information extraction technologies and applications. Neural Comput. Appl. **25**(3–4), 533–548 (2014). https://doi.org/10.1007/S00521-013-1516-6
20. Vaswani, A., et al.: Attention is all you need. In: Guyon, I., et al. (eds.) Advances in Neural Information Processing Systems 30: Annual Conference on Neural Information Processing Systems 2017, December 4–9, 2017, Long Beach, CA, USA, pp. 5998–6008 (2017)
21. Wang, Q., et al.: Learning to extract attribute value from product via question answering: a multi-task approach. In: Proceedings of the 26th ACM SIGKDD International Conference on Knowledge Discovery & Data Mining, pp. 47–55. ACM, Virtual Event CA USA (2020). https://doi.org/10.1145/3394486.3403047

Identification of Determinant Factors in Learning Applicable in Virtual Contexts and Measurable with Noninvasive Techniques

Andrés Vargas García(✉) and Julio Cesar Chavarro Porras

UTP, Pereira, Risaralda, Colombia
{avargas,jchavar}@utp.edu.co

Abstract. Since quality education is a pillar of the development of a society and since information and communication technologies (ICT) have permeated the different human activities, including education, it is necessary to evaluate how to achieve quality education in ICT-mediated environments, reducing the identified problems of virtual education, among them the accompaniment, feedback and adaptation to the student's way of learning. Different disciplines ranging from pedagogy to neuroscience have studied human learning. This article presents an early stage in the development of the larger project called "model for the measurement of academic performance based on non-invasive techniques of the determinants of learning" and focuses on showing in a general way the model, which non-invasive techniques are applicable to determine the student's behavior in a virtual learning environment and the possible benefits to all those involved in the teaching/learning process, such as the student, the tutor, the institution and finally the model itself.

Keywords: non-invasive techniques · learning · virtual education

1 Introduction

Education is a fundamental pillar in the development of a society; it is a key factor in the economic, social and cultural progress of a country. For this reason, improving the quality of education is a primary objective for any society, as established by the United Nations when it includes quality education as the fourth goal within the 17 Sustainable Development Goals.

The incorporation of ICT in education has allowed new forms of learning, more interactive, dynamic and collaborative, allowing access to a large amount of information, resources and online tools, enabling autonomous and independent learning [1]. Online education, open educational resources and online learning platforms are some examples of how ICTs are transforming education.

The study of human learning is a subject that has been addressed by several disciplines and areas of knowledge, among them we have: educational psychology, cognitive psychology, cognitive neuroscience, pedagogy, neuroeducation, social psychology. While some seek to understand how the brain works, how it develops or what mechanisms

V. Agredo-Delgado et al. (Eds.): DECISIONING 2024, CCIS 2369, pp. 85–96, 2025.
https://doi.org/10.1007/978-3-031-91690-8_7

underlie the acquisition of knowledge, others, on the other hand, investigate how one learns, what are the most effective methods for learning to take place, what educational models are best suited to students and what forms of teaching are most appropriate.

Our object of study focuses on the identification of factors that affect the learning process and that can be measured non-invasively when this process takes place in virtual learning environments.

2 Theoretical Framework

2.1 The Learning Process

Human learning takes many forms, some easily observable, such as when we perform an action like knitting or embroidery, others a little more subtle, such as when we make logical inferences. People learn for a variety of reasons, for external rewards or for more internal reasons, intrinsic motivation.

The learning process has allowed the human species to have a greater degree of flexibility and adaptation than any other species on the planet, because the instinctive content of our behavior is so small, and there is so much to learn, we are able to benefit from our experience, we know which actions can provoke interesting results and which cannot, and we modify our behavior to achieve them [2].

Psychologists define and conceive learning differently [2].

- Learning is a relatively permanent change in behavior as a result of experience.
- Learning is a relatively permanent change in mental associations or representations as a result of experience.

Here we have two definitions, one observing conduct, behavior, and the other, changes in mental structures or in how we process information. From the psychological point of view, one is behavioral and the other cognitive. In "Machine Learning an Artificial Intelligence Approach", he defines learning as a sequence of events where a system undergoes a modification so that its future behavior is more adequate to achieve the desired results; the result of learning is to make the system capable of carrying out a similar task or tasks more efficiently [3].

The objective of the learning process is to reduce the difference between the level of knowledge that one possesses and the level that one aspires to reach, knowledge can be divided into two types of knowledge, declarative and procedural, while the former can be expressed and used in different occasions, it is considered the "know what" while the procedural knowledge can use and invoke the declarative knowledge to use it in other areas, it is the "know how". Declarative knowledge is static, while procedural knowledge is dynamic.

There is another type of knowledge, used in the field of AI (Artificial Intelligence) and that is heuristic knowledge, which can be formalized as "production rules" acting at the control system level. Heuristic knowledge is empirical knowledge [4], The accumulation of similar but not identical events is necessary for the acquisition of knowledge [5] and in our approach human knowledge is considered an information processing system, where information can be defined as a piece of data that provides knowledge that was not previously known.

2.2 Human Learning

The brain, as a fundamental organ for the learning process, is mainly composed of three elements. The lower brain, which is linked to the spinal cord, is involved in basic physiological processes such as breathing, swallowing, sleeping, and heart rate control. The midbrain which performs tasks associated with vision, hearing, an important part of the midbrain is the reticular formation which is vital for attention and consciousness. And finally, the superior brain located in the frontal and superior zones of the brain, in the superior part of this one, is the cerebral cortex that is divided in two halves or hemispheres and these in turn are divided in lobes. It is in the cortex where activities such as language, attention, reasoning, decision making, learning strategies, long term memory, among others, are performed.

From a physiological point of view, learning occurs when there are inter-connections between neurons, in the strengthening of existing synapses and in the creation of new ones [6–9]. It has also been found that neurogenesis (formation of new neurons, a process thought to occur only in prenatal stages) appears to be stimulated in part by new learning experiences [10]. Learning does not occur in a single part of the brain, but involves multiple systems, so it occurs in different areas of the brain, which is a field of study for neuroscience.

Cognitive processes are the mental operations performed by the brain to process information. These processes enable the acquisition, storage, manipulation and utilization of the information we receive from the environment. Some of the most important cognitive processes include [11]:

- Memory: Includes information retention and retrieval.
- Language: The communication system we use to express and understand ideas and concepts.
- Learning: The process of acquiring knowledge, skills and behaviors through experience, instruction and observation.
- Creativity: The ability to generate new ideas, concepts or solutions to problems.
- Imagination: The ability to create mental representations of objects, situations or events that are not present at the moment.
- Attention: The ability to focus on certain stimuli or information while ignoring others.
- Perception: The interpretation and organization of sensory stimuli to form a mental representation of the environment.
- Motivation and emotion: Influence the way we process information and make decisions.

The integration of neurosciences with education has allowed the generation of fundamental knowledge about the neural bases of the learning process, current research has enabled greater knowledge about the cognitive processes involved in learning through the study of higher and complex brain functions, such as language, memory [12] and attention: language, memory [12] and attention; these are the cognitive processes that are trained through different educational practices for their strengthening [13], taking into account the fundamental role of motivation in this process [14], Motivation, an internal state that encourages us to act, directs us in certain directions and keeps us in some activities, motivation often determines whether and how something is learned, especially if the behaviors and cognitive processes necessary for that learning are voluntary and therefore, under the control of the person. Moreover, once we have learned something, motivation is largely responsible for our continuing to do it [2].

The Memory

Information processing is a process that takes place over a period of time, where data from the environment, in conjunction with internal data, i.e., stored in long-term memory as information and procedures, are processed (in working memory) to produce new data with the status of information; this new information is stored in working memory and can be used in a new process [4].

As we can see memory plays a fundamental role, we can define memory as the brain's capacity to store, retain and retrieve information [15]. It is a fundamental process in cognitive functioning and plays a crucial role in the acquisition of knowledge, decision making and the formation of past experiences. Memory can be subdivided into different types and systems, such as short-term memory, long-term memory, episodic memory, and working memory. These systems work together to process and store information temporarily or permanently, allowing people to recall past events, learn new skills and adapt to their environment.

- Short-term memory is a system of temporary storage of information with a limited capacity and duration, it allows retaining and processing information to carry out a specific cognitive task, in experiments it has been established that it has a capacity of between 5 to 9 elements [16].
- Long-term memory: this is the set of general knowledge stored in the memory.
- Episodic memory: it is a memory located in a specific time and place, it can refer to recent or old memories, it is, together with semantic memory, what some neuroscientists call explicit or declarative memory.
- Working memory: contains knowledge extracted from long-term memory together with recent data produced by short-term processing. The capacity of working memory is limited and its content is regularly renewed during cognitive operations, some authors consider working memory the same as short-term memory [17]. Other authors such as [18] argue that both memories have different characteristics, specifying different functions and neurological substrates [19] states that short-term memory is part of working memory [20] and proposes a two-part model, where working memory is composed of a declarative and a procedural memory.

These are the main types of memory, although neuroscience research continues to explore new aspects and subtypes of memory to better understand how this fundamental cognitive process works.

Motivation

Motivation affects learning in at least four ways [2]:

- Increases the level of energy the individual applies to the performance of the activity.
- Directs the individual toward goals, keeps him focused and allows him to make decisions accordingly.
- It favors the initiation and permanence in certain activities.

- Influences learning strategies, since the student thinks about what he/she is learning and allows cognitive involvement.

Motivation theorists distinguish between intrinsic and extrinsic motivation, intrinsic motivation occurs when the source of motivation resides in the individual and the task, and extrinsic motivation occurs when the source of motivation is outside the individual and the task to be performed.

Intrinsic motivation has greater advantages than extrinsic motivation, since the student: performs the activities on his own initiative, maintains attention on the activity, goes deeper and faces more complicated aspects of the task, learns in a meaningful way, is creative and recursive to solve difficulties, persists in the face of difficulty, among others. Extrinsic motivation such as rewards lose their value once they are obtained, learning is usually not meaningful and students tend to use the minimum effort to achieve the task, although extrinsic motivation is very useful in business environments and in behavior modification. Extrinsic motivation can be to obtain something or to avoid obtaining something, for example, to avoid a punishment or sanction.

Emotions are necessary in the processes of reasoning and decision making, they are the basis of curiosity and attention and are determinant for learning processes. Brain imaging shows that specific regions are activated according to the stimuli, the amygdala in negative stimuli and the hippocampus in positive contexts [21], and as mentioned, the hippocampus is involved in the processes of memory and learning. The brain's reward system allows learning from what catches its attention, what is novel, which is why curiosity is a trigger of emotion, and emotion allows focusing attention on what is necessary for the learning process [22].

Emotions are present in the learning process [23, 24] and one of the challenges of virtual learning environments is to establish mechanisms to generate emotion in the student, it has been emphasized the need to design educational resources that are not only accessible but also attractive and entertaining for students, it is important that students are satisfied with the virtual learning environment.

The characteristics that a virtual learning environment must take into account to make a student feel attracted and enjoy the teaching-learning process are multiple and not all experts reach a consensus, some of the aspects to take into account that a virtual learning environment must have to generate excitement in the student and facilitate the teaching-learning process are [25]:

- Content: is the material made available to the student to facilitate learning.
- Pedagogical facility: functionalities of the environment for teachers, students, teaching and learning process.
- Support: documentation, help, ease of finding solutions to needs and difficulties.
- User interface: the part of the system with which the student comes into contact and interacts to achieve the objectives.
- Communication tools: tools for the management of academic content and communication between students and professors.

The fulfillment of these characteristics by a virtual learning environment does not guarantee that the teaching-learning process will take place in an optimal manner, which is why mechanisms have been studied to evaluate affective aspects, emphasizing emotional aspects.

Most of the tools that have been used are based on questionnaires to determine how users perceive the interaction with the virtual learning environment, these tools have had different methodologies and approaches and measure aspects such as: functionality, usability in aspects such as efficiency, clarity, reliability, as well as aspects of hedonic appearance, pragmatics, emotions and aspects of the user experience such as stimulation, originality and in general the user's perception.

In [26], it provides an updated framework of human factors that influence the effectiveness of Virtual Learning Environments. Here, the methods for sampling emotions are divided into three categories, the first by means of questionnaires that are conducted during the course, this takes snapshots of emotions, the second detects emotions during the learning process through non-intrusive methods such as facial expression detection, gaze detection, analysis of text data generated with the interaction and the third category consists of a questionnaire once the learning process is finished.

The first category has limitations due to the intrusion in the learning process, the third category is limited by the fact that the emotions associated with learning are of short duration and since the emotions are surveyed after the learning process is completed, it does not reflect the real emotions that were experienced during the process.

Many researchers have focused on questionnaire-type tools to measure emotions such as: UEQ [27], AttrakDiff [28], SAM (Self-Assessment Manual) [29], LEM-Tool [30], among others. These questionnaires use emotion scales that can be confusing for the people who participate in the evaluations.

The second category counteracts the limitations of the other two, but it is necessary to solve the problem of how to capture, analyze and correlate facial expressions, body measurements, physical variables and voice characteristics with emotions and these in turn with the effectiveness of the learning process, without using intrusive methods that affect or hinder the learning process.

The Attention

Attention allows us to choose the stimuli we want to prioritize, to control our actions, but, above all, attention is a very limited resource [31]. Cognitive neuroscience is demonstrating that this essential mechanism for learning is not a single brain process, but that there are different attentional networks (alert, orienting and executive) that follow different developmental rhythms and in which specific circuits, regions and neurotransmitters are involved [32]. From an educational perspective, executive attention, associated with self-regulation, is fundamental because it allows the student to focus attention voluntarily by inhibiting irrelevant stimuli [32].

Attention allows us to regulate listening and comprehension behavior, the information processing capacity of our brain is limited and it is attention that regulates the input of information into the mental workspace where we are aware of the information and make decisions based on our goal [33]. But it is necessary to have clear learning intentions and motivation.

2.3 Non-invasive Techniques

In the virtual context, non-invasive techniques are based on the analysis of digital data and behaviors on educational platforms. Some of these techniques include:

- Platform interaction analysis: Use of data such as connection time, clicks, material downloads, browsing patterns, and other LMS interaction data [34].
- Participation in activities: quality and quantity of participation in activities such as chats, forums, surveys and other activities proposed by the OVA during the course [35, 36].
- Online surveys and questionnaires: To collect information on motivation, satisfaction and perception of the course, as well as to collect information on students' perception, satisfaction and motivation [37].
- Analysis of writing patterns: Assessment of participation in writing activities (forums, assignments, essays) to identify levels of engagement and comprehension [38].
- Use of sensors and wearable technology: Use of devices such as smart bracelets or cameras to measure stress levels, attention or physical activity [39].
- Video and audio analysis: Use of recordings of live sessions (lectures, tutorials) to assess participation and behavior, detection of emotions through facial expressions, Analysis of participation in video calls [40].
- Use of Artificial Intelligence: Application of AI algorithms to predict performance, detect learning problems or personalize teaching [41].
- Eye-tracking techniques: technology that records eye movements and points of gaze fixation on a screen. This makes it possible to analyze: where students look, how much time they spend on each element, the order in which they browse the contents, and the order in which they look at the content [42, 43].
- Pupillometry: The study of variations in pupil size, which may be related to: cognitive effort, an increase in pupil size may indicate increased concentration or difficulty in a task, emotional responses, Changes in pupil size may reflect emotions such as stress, interest or fatigue [44].

2.4 Measuring Academic Performance

It is the process of evaluating and quantifying student performance in relation to the learning objectives established in an educational program. This process involves collecting, analyzing, and interpreting data to determine how well students are achieving the expected competencies, skills, and knowledge.

This process not only seeks to know if the expected goals have been achieved, but also to identify areas for improvement, providing valuable feedback to students by informing them of their progress and areas for improvement, to teachers by helping them to adjust their teaching strategies, and to educational institutions to make strategic decisions to improve the quality of education.

In virtual education, academic performance is measured through:

- Grades on activities, exams and projects.
- Participation in forums, chats and video calls.
- Time spent on learning platforms.
- Demonstrated competencies in digital environments.

Academic achievement depends not only on student effort, but also on factors such as:

- Individual: Motivation, self-esteem and cognitive skills, study habits and time management.
- Social: Family and peer support, Relationship with teachers.
- Environmental: Classroom infrastructure or virtual environment, Access to educational resources (books, technology, etc.).
- Pedagogical: Teaching methods and quality of the curriculum, Feedback and support from teachers.

3 Proposed Method

An experimental model is proposed for the measurement of academic performance in virtual learning environment, based on the variables censored with non-invasive methods, which is supported in:

3.1 Preliminary Activities

- Definition of study population
- Definition of sampling type
- Sample size determination
- Definition of inclusion and exclusion criteria

Inclusion criteria: minimum age, grade level, computer equipment, internet access, work environment that meets minimum criteria of: space, lighting, chair, temperature, noise, availability. Students with typical cognitive development, without a diagnosis of mental, cognitive or learning disorders, with the ability to understand and answer the knowledge test autonomously.

Exclusion criteria: students with previous diagnosis of neurodevelopmental disorders (attention deficit hyperactivity disorder, dyslexia, autism, etc.), diagnosed psychiatric disorders (depression, severe anxiety, schizophrenia, etc.), cognitive difficulties affecting information processing or history of significant difficulties in formal learning. Or who do not meet the inclusion criteria.

Determine ethical considerations.

3.2 Measuring Student Behavior in Relation to the Virtual Learning Environment

- Identification of emotions and micro expressions during the interaction of the student with the system.

  Still and moving image capture and processing.
  Machine Learning and Deep Learning model selection
  Selection and classification of images (videos)
  Identification of predominant emotions and changes in emotions during student interaction with the virtual learning environment.

- Study and measurement of pupil size and reactivity to stimuli.

  Preparation and calibration
  Pupillary baseline
  Presentation of cognitive stimuli
  Recording and analysis of the pupillary response to interaction with the virtual learning environment.
  Interpretation of results

- Lexicographic analysis in the virtual learning environment using Natural Language Processing techniques

  Data collection.
  Text preprocessing.
  Lexicographic and emotion analysis.
  Interpretation of results.

- Interaction analytics and activity tracking (clickstream, Navigation)

  Collection of data on student interaction with the virtual learning environment.
  Identification of navigation patterns.
  Identification of click sequences.
  Recording of time of use, frequency.

3.3 Measuring Memory

- Selection of techniques

Determine techniques to assess knowledge retention, retrieval and application (e.g. direct assessment, recognition test, working memory exercises, recall and recognition tasks, spaced repetition technique, etc.) in a virtual learning environment.

- Analysis of learning outcomes

Analyze data captured throughout the process to identify patterns, generate predictions and train the model.

3.4 Feedback

The model proposes feedback to all main actors in a student's learning process as follows:

- Student: personalized recommendations of their study habits, attention times and areas for improvement, resources and techniques to improve their study habits and recommendations of additional material to complement, as well as study techniques applicable according to their type of behavior. Study plan, per-sonalized schedule, content adapted to their abilities and emotional support.

- Tutor: early detection of problems, attention levels of their students, detection of special needs, evaluation of the impact of applied teaching/learning strategies, prediction of results, recommendations for content adaptation.
- Institution: Personalization of learning at scale, optimization of resources, detection of teacher training needs, improvement of student experience, improvement of efficiency and decision making.
- Own system: data for algorithm adaptation and continuous improvement, seeking better predictive outcomes, and adjustments based on learning outcomes. Ability to learn, adapt and continuously improve.

4 Validation

The execution of an experiment with real users is planned, which consists of taking one or several virtual learning objects, which have been validated and meet established quality standards evaluated according to LORI [45], COdA [46] and ECOBA [47] learning object evaluation methodologies. The experiment will be applied to the selected students and the results obtained from the detection system, image processing and prediction of results will be crossed with the results obtained by the students in the learning process, in such a way that the proposed objective can be validated.

5 Final Considerations

The work presented here corresponds to an early stage in the development of the larger project "MODEL FOR THE MEASUREMENT OF ACADEMIC PERFORMANCE USING NON-INVASIVE TECHNIQUES OF THE DETERMINANT FACTORS OF LEARNING" and corresponds to the process of identifying the variables to be measured using non-invasive techniques that are determinant in the learning process.

Therefore, this article addresses the selection of variables with a qualitative approach and focuses on identifying the variables that should be measured in virtual learning environments, during a work session of a student interacting with virtual learning objects through the platform.

Acknowledgments. The project is being developed as part of a doctoral program in Engineering at the Universidad Tecnológica de Pereira, and is not currently being funded by any entity.

Disclosure of Interests. The authors declare that they have no conflict of interest with respect to the research, authorship and publication of this article.

References

1. Karam-Rozo, J.M., et al.: Tecnologías de la información y la comunicación en la educación con enfoque en América Latina. Rev. Electrón. Educ. Pedag. **3**(4), 89–106 (2019)
2. Ormrod, J.E., et al.: Aprendizaje humano, vol. 4. Pearson Educación, Madrid (2005)
3. Michalski, R.S., Carbonell, J.G., Mitchell, T.M.: Machine Learning: An Artificial Intelligence Approach. Springer (2013)

4. Nguyen-Xuan, A.: Cognitive Mechanisms of Learning. Wiley (2020)
5. Herbert, D.M., Burt, J.S.: The effects of different review opportunities on schematisation of knowledge. Learn. Instr. **13**(1), 73–92 (2003)
6. Byrnes, J.P., Fox, N.A.: The educational relevance of research in cognitive neuroscience. Educ. Psychol. Rev. **10**, 297–342 (1998)
7. Greenough, W.T., Black, J.E., Wallace, C.S.: Experience and brain development. Child Dev 539–559 (1987)
8. Merzenich, M.M.: Cortical plasticity contributing to child development. In: Mechanisms of cognitive development, pp. 79–108. Psychology Press (2001)
9. Rosenzweig, M.R., Multiple models of memory. The brain, cognition, and education, 1986: p. 347–371
10. Gould, E., et al.: Learning enhances adult neurogenesis in the hippocampal formation. Nat. Neurosci. **2**(3), 260–265 (1999)
11. Izaguirre, M.: Neuroproceso de la enseñanza y del aprendizaje. Alpha Editorial (2017)
12. Ruiz-Vargas, J.M.: La memoria humana: función y estructura. Alianza (1994)
13. Campos, A.L.: Neuroeducación: uniendo las neurociencias y la educación en la búsqueda del desarrollo humano (2010)
14. Etchepareborda, M.C., Abad-Mas, L.: Memoria de trabajo en los procesos básicos del aprendizaje. Rev. neurología **40**(1), 79–83 (2005)
15. Azcoaga, J.E.: Aprendizaje fisiológico. Psicología. Lenguaje. Aprendizaje (Actas de las Primeras Jornadas Nacionales de APINEP, Rosario, 1986). Ediciones Pedagógicas, Buenos Aires pp. 17–32 (1987)
16. Miller, G.A.: The magical number seven, plus or minus two: some limits on our capacity for processing information. Psychol. Rev. **63**(2), 81 (1956)
17. Richard, J.F.: Les activités mentales: de l'interprétation de l'information à l'action. (No Title) (2005)
18. Cowan, N.: What are the differences between long-term, short-term, and working memory? Prog. Brain Res. **169**, 323–338 (2008)
19. Aben, B., Stapert, S., Blokland, A.: About the distinction between working memory and short-term memory. Front. Psychol. **3**, 301 (2012)
20. Oberauer, K., et al.: Analogous mechanisms of selection and updating in declarative and procedural working memory: experiments and a computational model. Cogn. Psychol. **66**(2), 157–211 (2013)
21. Erk, S., et al.: Emotional context modulates subsequent memory effect. Neuroimage **18**(2), 439–447 (2003)
22. Mora, F.N.: Solo se puede aprender aquello que se ama. Alianza Editorial, Madrid (2013)
23. Pekrun, R., et al.: Academic emotions in students' self-regulated learning and achievement: a program of qualitative and quantitative research. Educ. Psychol. **37**(2), 91–105 (2002)
24. Graesser, A., D'Mello, S.K.: Theoretical perspectives on affect and deep learning, In: New Perspectives on Affect and Learning Technologies, pp. 11–21. Springer (2011)
25. Aballay, L.N., Aciar, S.V., Collazos, C.A.: Emotions for virtual learning environments. IEEE Rev. Iberoamericana Tecnol. Aprendizaje **16**(3), 215–224 (2021)
26. Syed, M., et al.: Implicit and Explicit Emotions in MOOCs. International Educational Data Mining Society (2019)
27. Laugwitz, B., Held, T., Schrepp, M.: Construction and evaluation of a user experience questionnaire. In: HCI and Usability for Education and Work: 4th Symposium of the Workgroup Human-Computer Interaction and Usability Engineering of the Austrian Computer Society, USAB 2008, Graz, Austria, 20–21 November 2008. Proceedings 4. Springer (2008)
28. Hassenzahl, M., Burmester, M., Koller, F.: AttrakDiff: a questionnaire to measure perceived hedonic and pragmatic quality. In: Mensch & Computer. Springer, Heidelberg (2003)

29. Bradley, M.M., Lang, P.J.: Measuring emotion: the self-assessment manikin and the semantic differential. J. Behav. Ther. Exp. Psychiatry **25**(1), 49–59 (1994)
30. Huisman, G., et al.: LEMtool: measuring emotions in visual interfaces. In: Proceedings of the SIGCHI Conference on Human Factors in Computing Systems (2013)
31. Rueda Cuerva, M.D.R.: Educar la atención: con cerebro. Comercial Grupo ANAYA, SA (2021)
32. Posner, M.I., Rothbart, M.K., Voelker, P.: Developing brain networks of attention. Curr. Opin. Pediatr. **28**(6), 720–724 (2016)
33. Rueda Cuerva, M.D.R.: La atención es el corazon de la inteligencia [Video]. In: 2018 Conferencias TED: Conferencias TED (2018)
34. Siemens, G., Long, P.: Penetrating the fog: Analytics in learning and education. EDUCAUSE Rev. **46**(5), 30 (2011)
35. Dawson, S.: 'Seeing'the learning community: an exploration of the development of a resource for monitoring online student networking. Br. J. Edu. Technol. **41**(5), 736–752 (2010)
36. Romero, C., et al.: Handbook of Educational Data Mining. CRC Press (2010)
37. Nulty, D.D.: The adequacy of response rates to online and paper surveys: what can be done? Assess. Eval. High. Educ. **33**(3), 301–314 (2008)
38. Pennebaker, J.W., Chung, C.K.: Expressive writing, emotional upheavals, and health. Found. Health Psychol. 263–284 (2007)
39. Swan, M.: Sensor mania! The internet of things, wearable computing, objective metrics, and the quantified self 2.0. J. Sens. Actuat. Netw. **1**(3), 217–253 (2012)
40. Zeng, Z., et al.: A survey of affect recognition methods: audio, visual and spontaneous expressions. In: Proceedings of the 9th International Conference on Multimodal Interfaces, pp. 126–133 (2007)
41. Baker, R.S., Martin, T., Rossi, L.M.: Educational data mining and learning analytics. In: The Wiley Handbook of Cognition and Assessment: Frameworks, Methodologies, and Applications, pp. 379–396 (2016)
42. Holmqvist, K., et al.: Eye Tracking: A Comprehensive Guide to Methods and Measures. OUP, Oxford (2011)
43. Duchowski, A., Duchowski, A.: Eye tracking techniques. Eye Tracking Methodology: Theory and Practice, pp. 51–59 (2007)
44. Mathôt, S.: Pupillometry: Psychology, physiology, and function. J. Cogn. **1**(1) (2018)
45. Vargo, J., et al.: Learning object evaluation: computer-mediated collaboration and inter-rater reliability. Int. J. Comput. Appl. **25**(3), 198–205 (2003)
46. Fernández, P., Domínguez, R., Armas, R.: Herramienta COdA de evaluación de la calidad de objetos de aprendizaje, desarrollada en el marco de los proyectos de innovación y mejora de la calidad de la docencia (2012). PIMCD 268/2010–2011 y PIMCD 236/2011–2012 financiados por el Vicerrectorado …
47. Ruiz González, R., Muñoz Arteaga, J., Álvarez Rodríguez, F.: Formato para la determinación de la Calidad en los Objetos de Aprendizaje. In: Primera Conferencia Latinoamericana de Objetos de Aprendizaje, LACLO. Coordinan: Repositorio de Conocimiento Europeo (ARIADNE), Corporación Latinoamericana de Redes Avanzadas (CLARA), Guayaquil, Ecuador (2006)

Incrementally Updating Concept Lattices in Arbitrarily Distributed Formal Contexts

Nicolás Leutwyler[1,2,3,4], Mario Lezoche[1], Hervé Panetto[1], and Diego Torres[2,3](✉)

[1] University of Lorraine, CNRS, CRAN, 54000 Nancy, France
{nicolas.leutwyler,mario.lezoche,herve.panetto}@univ-lorraine.fr
[2] LIFIA, CICPBA-Facultad de Informática, UNLP, La Plata, 1900 Buenos Aires, Argentina
diego.torres@lifia.info.unlp.edu.ar
[3] Dto. CyT, UNQ, Bernal, 1876 Buenos Aires, Argentina
[4] SNMSF, 38240 Meylan, France

Abstract. Decision-making can be significantly enhanced by knowledge extraction techniques such as Formal Concept Analysis (FCA), which provides a structured way to analyze and organize data. However, in distributed environments, information is often fragmented, arriving in streams rather than as a complete dataset. Consulting the entire dataset at once is not always feasible due to time and resource constraints. While an existing batch algorithm allows concept lattice computation without requiring full attribute knowledge, batch processing is inherently unsuitable for dynamic, continuously evolving data. In this article, we propose an incremental algorithm for concept lattice computation in arbitrarily distributed formal contexts, which can efficiently update the lattice as new information becomes available. Our method ensures that knowledge extraction remains computationally feasible even when data is incomplete, distributed, or evolving over time. We further analyze the complexity of our approach in comparison to the existing batch-based distributed algorithm, highlighting its advantages in stream processing scenarios. By addressing the limitations of batch computation and enabling real-time lattice updates, our work contributes to enhancing FCA's applicability in distributed and dynamic knowledge systems. The proposed incremental approach paves the way for more adaptive, efficient, and scalable knowledge extraction methods, particularly in fields requiring real-time decision-making and pattern discovery.

Keywords: Decision-making systems · Incremental algorithm · Formal Concept Analysis · Algorithm Complexity

1 Introduction

Introduced by Wille in [1], Formal Concept Analysis (FCA) is a mathematical framework that provides a systematic approach to analyzing complex decision-making systems by modeling relationships between concepts and attributes. At its core, FCA explores

V. Agredo-Delgado et al. (Eds.): DECISIONING 2024, CCIS 2369, pp. 97–108, 2025.
https://doi.org/10.1007/978-3-031-91690-8_8

the inherent structure of data through the identification of *formal concepts*, which represent sets of objects sharing common properties. These concepts are organized into a lattice structure, often referred to as *concept lattice*, where each concept represents a combination of attributes that define a particular decision criterion or classification rule. By leveraging the principles of lattice theory and order theory, FCA facilitates the exploration of decision spaces, enabling decision-makers to identify relevant patterns, dependencies, and decision rules within their datasets.

FCA has found applications in various domains, including data mining [2, 3], knowledge representation [4, 5], and information retrieval [6], due to its ability to uncover hidden relationships and structures in data. In decision-making systems, FCA serves as a powerful tool for knowledge extraction and decision support, allowing decision-makers to derive actionable insights from complex datasets. By formalizing the relationships between concepts and attributes, FCA enables decision-makers to analyze decision criteria, evaluate alternatives, and identify optimal courses of action. Moreover, FCA provides a principled framework for handling uncertainty and ambiguity in decision-making processes, making it a valuable asset for organizations seeking to improve their decision-making capabilities.

Several algorithms exist to compute the concept lattice of a formal context (i.e., objects and their attributes). These algorithms are usually categorized into two categories: *batch* and *incremental*. The first one comprises algorithms that have full knowledge of the whole input (i.e., the formal context), and compute the concept lattice with it [7, 8]. The latter includes algorithms that do not know the whole set of objects in advance, and update the current lattice as they arrive [9]. Moreover, contrary to batch algorithms, incremental algorithms have the advantage that they can be used in stream processing applications, because they do not need to recompute everything from scratch every time a new object is added to the context. However, incremental algorithms consider that the set of all attributes is known from the beginning, which might not be the case in all scenarios.

Goel and Chaudary in [10] present an algorithm to compute a concept lattice in a distributed environment, where the formal context is arbitrarily distributed. In other words, since there are no constraints in how the formal context (i.e., object, attributes, and the incidence relationship) is distributed across nodes, not only all objects are unknown in advance, but neither the attributes are. Additionally, the algorithm leverages the advantages of the Apache Spark[1] batch streams, making it suitable to analyze *static* snapshots of the stream. Therefore, the algorithm they present falls into the batch category, even if the batch comes from a data stream. Nevertheless, an algorithm that takes advantage of the concept lattice already being computed would be necessary to aid the flexibility and usability of FCA.

Since to the best of our knowledge, no algorithm exists to *incrementally* compute a concept lattice from *arbitrarily distributed formal contexts*, in this article an algorithm to do so is presented. Moreover, its computational complexity bound is studied. In addition, a discussion on different approaches to address the problematic is provided.

This work is structured as follows, Sect. 2 presents necessary notation and concepts to understand the contents of the article. Moreover, it presents the algorithm of Goel and

[1] https://spark.apache.org/.

Chaudhary as the only related know to the best of our knowledge. Then, Sect. 3 presents the AddPair incremental algorithm for lattice construction coming from an arbitrarily distributed formal context. Furthermore, Sect. 4 carries on with a discussion on the big O complexity bound of both algorithms. And finally, in Sect. 5, the conclusions and future work are presented.

2 Preliminaries and Related Works

In this section, preliminary notation will be given so that the rest of the article is easier to follow. Furthermore, the related work [10] is presented in detail.

2.1 Formal Concept Analysis

Firstly, let us define the core formalities of FCA,

Definition 1. *A* ***formal context*** *K is a triple* $<G, M, I>$, *where G is a set of objects, M is a set of attributes, and I is an incidence matrix where iIj if* $g_i \in G$ *has the attribute* $m_j \in M$, *and iIj otherwise.*

Let $'$ be the derivation operation on a set of objects $X \subseteq G$ (dually, on a set of attributes $Y \subseteq M$) given by

$$X' = \{m \in M | \forall g \in X, gIm\} \tag{1}$$

$$Y' = \{g \in G | \forall m \in Y, gIm\} \tag{2}$$

A *formal concept* is a pair $C = < X, Y >$ where $X \subseteq G, Y \subseteq M, X' = Y$, and $Y' = X$. X is called the extent and Y the intent. In other words, if we add any attribute to Y, then $(Y \cup \{m\})' \subset X$ for $m \in M \wedge m \notin Y$, and analogously, if we add any object to X, $X \cup \{g\} \subset Y$ for $g \in G \wedge g \notin X$. With these definitions, the set of all formal concepts, typically noted with the letter C, and the relation of inclusion of extents ($\leq$) form the so-called *concept lattice*, which is a partially ordered set, and is usually noted with the letter $\mathcal{L} = <\mathrm{C}, \leq>$.

2.2 Goel and Chaudhary's Algorithm

Multiple algorithms exist to mine formal concepts from a given data-set on standalone and single threaded systems. However, these algorithms are restricted in applicability as the size of the context increases. One of the reasons why this happens is that lattice construction algorithms are inherently exponential in the worst case: the amount of formal concepts is bound by $2^{O(|G|+|M|)}$. Consequently, interest in finding distributed solutions that would reduce the time for mining as well as enable distributed storage using low-cost networked computing nodes has been spurred by these limitations.

For instance, it has been successfully used in a distributed environment in [11], but in conjunction with the extensions called Fuzzy Formal Concept Analysis (i.e., an extension of FCA [12] where the incidence matrix is a relation $I \subseteq G \times M \rightarrow$ [0,1]) and Temporal Concept Analysis [13]. This work takes advantage of the fuzzy and temporal characteristics of the extensions in order to deal with the exponential growth of the fuzzy lattice. In addition, numerous works have been conducted to address the problem of scalability by leveraging the MapReduce paradigm. However, these algorithms encounter constraints that hinder their scalability the larger the formal context size gets. One of these constraints involves the necessity to store the entire context on every node, while the other is weighed down by significant communication overhead at the conclusion of each iteration. In practical scenarios, we encounter extensive datasets that exceed the storage capacity of a single machine. For instance, consider a dataset comprising emails sent by customers to a company, which may be utilized to identify correlations among customers. Another illustration could be an e-commerce platform that provides a diverse array of products to its customers, aiming to categorize customers based on their specific product browsing behaviors.

In the light of this context, in [10], the authors present an algorithm for computing concept lattices from an unconstrained (i.e., arbitrarily distributed) formal context. The algorithm utilizes the Apache Spark MapReduce framework and leverages its core abstraction called Resilient Distributed Dataset (RDD). In their approach, the formal context is only used at the beginning of the algorithm to generate a distributed collection of key-value pairs (object-attribute if $|G| < |M|$, , or attribute-object otherwise). Then, they generate a new key-value pair from an existing one representing the formal concepts of size k, with $k \in \mathbb{N}$. The process is repeated until $k = |G|$ and, as a result, all formal contexts have been generated.

Going more in depth, we will first set a common ground on what MapReduce is. Generally, we can think of it as a computational model where two operations can be performed: *map* and *reduce*. Map refers to a function applied to every element of the input, and reduce is the combination of the results performed by the map step. Typically, the map is the operation that is expected to leverage concurrency, while reduce is the one that "combines" the results computed in several nodes. In Fig. 1, a basic example is given, where a driver node first performs a $map(*2)$ which makes each node to multiply every value (assuming they are all numbers) by two. Then, it performs a reduce (+) which combine the results of the map, returning the sum of the results performed in each of the nodes.

More precisely, the algorithm proposed in [10] can be summarised as follows,

Input: A key-value pair P of object-attribute or attribute-object, i.e., $<g, m>$ such that $g \in |G| \wedge m \in |M|$ if $|G| < |M|$, $<g, m>$ otherwise.

Output: An RDD C with pairs $< k, v >$ where k is an extent (or intent if $|M| < |G|$), v an intent (or extent), and $< k, v > \in C$ iff $< k, v >$ is a formal concept from the underlying formal context $K =< \{\pi_1(p)|\forall p \in P\}, \{\pi_2(p)|\forall p \in P\}, P >$.

Procedure: Since mining concepts on a formal context or its transpose yields the same result, the authors chose to aggregate data by objects or by attributes, depending on which one has the lower count. To make this decision, they utilize the countApproximate function present in Apache Spark, that does not need to actually count *all* the elements on each dimension. Once the dimension is chosen, and assuming for simplicity that the objects are more than the attributes, the idea of the algorithm relies on generating candidate formal concepts by key size (i.e., attributes in this case).

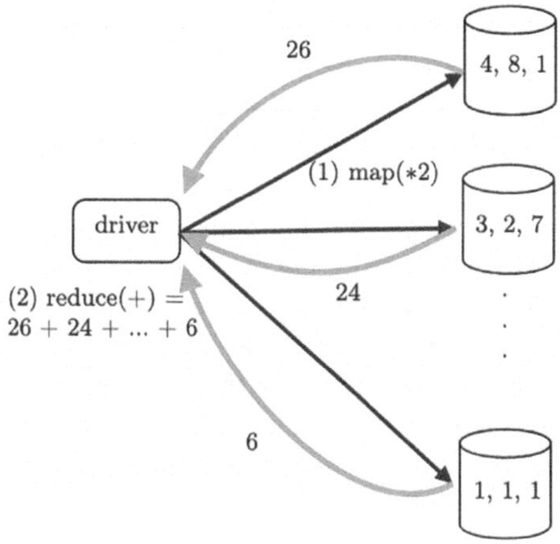

Fig. 1. Basic Map Reduce example. (created by Leutwyler and al.)

The generation of candidate formal concepts of size 1 (referred as CC_1) is performed by aggregating pairs on the key as an *id* in the following way,

$$CC_1 = \{<g, M>|g \in G \wedge M = \{m|<g, m> \in P\}\} \tag{3}$$

Then, an iterative process is defined based on the candidate set of formal concepts CC_N consisting of key-value pairs (as defined in Eq. 3) $<K_N, V>$ of keys with size N. First, let us define K_{N+1} by considering K_N to be lexicographically ordered, i.e., $k_i \leq k_{i+1} \forall i \in [1, l) for K_N = \{k_1, k_2, \ldots, k_l\}$. Given two keys of size N with their first N elements in common, $P_N = \{e_1, e_2, \ldots, e_{n-1}, a\}$ and $Q_N = \{e_1, e_2, \ldots, e_{n-1}, b\}$, a new key of size $N + 1$ would be generated as follows:

$$K_{N+1} = e_1, e_2, \ldots, e_{n-1}, a, b \tag{4}$$

Then, C_{N+1} is defined by combining all possible combinations of lexicographically ordered keys in CC_N ($\frac{l(l-1)}{2}$ combinations where $|CC_N| = l$) by using the formula Eq. 4. And finally, given $P_N = \{e_1, e_2, \ldots, e_{n-1}, a\}$ and $Q_N = \{e_1, e_2, \ldots, e_{n-1}, b\}$ two keys of size N, and V_1, V_2 their values, then, the set of pairs of the form $<e_1, e_2, \ldots, e_{n-1}, a, b, V_1 \cap V_2>$ defines CC_{N+1}.

Now, the set of valid formal concepts of size N are defined using CC_N and CC_{N+1}. Let $V_X = \{\pi_2(p)|p \in CC_{N+1}\}$ be the set of values of CC_{N+1}. Then, the set of valid formal concepts of size N is

$$VC_N = \{< K_N, V > |< K_N, V > \in CC_N and V \notin V_X\} \tag{5}$$

The final result is given by all the valid formal concepts VC_i with $i \in \mathbb{N}$ *and* $1 \leq i <$ $|M|$ (or $|G|$ if there were more attributes than objects). The bottom and top concepts are computed separately.

2.3 Additional Relevant Methods

In the literature, at least three other related methods have been found that seek to make the FCA computation more flexible, considering constraints such as not having the entire input in memory. Firstly, Valtchev and Missaoui in [14] generalized the theory regarding incremental algorithms, by proposing an algorithm that can add several objects in one incremental step. To do so, they used the notion of *subposition*, i.e., the assembly of contexts sharing the same attributes, or in other words, adding objects with certain non-new attributes to a context. Secondly, in [15] the idea of assembling *partial* lattices to construct a global one is introduced using both subposition and apposition (i.e., the horizontal concatenation of contexts sharing the same set of objects [16]). This is done with the goal of allowing FCA algorithms to compute lattices beyond what fits in memory. Finally, in [17], the problem of knowledge loss while maintaining a bounded-sized lattice in data stream processing is introduced, and the merging (assembling) of lattices is proposed as a solution. However, although they certainly contribute to the application of FCA to data streams, they are still not enough to consider *arbitrarily* distributed formal contexts incrementally.

3 AddPair Algorithm

In the last section, we presented an algorithm that performs a distributed batch algorithm to compute the set of formal concepts from an arbitrarily distributed formal context. In this section, we present an *incremental* algorithm to compute a set of formal concepts and its line diagram.

In order to incrementally add pairs $<g, m>$ to a lattice $\mathcal{L}$, we need to first clarify certain aspects. First, all incremental algorithms to the best of our knowledge consider that either M or G is known in advance, and then the incremental steps happen on the elements that are unknown. Second, an incremental update is usually considered between $\mathcal{L}_i$ and $\mathcal{L}_{i+1}$ where the difference between the two lattices is that g is being added to $\mathcal{L}_i$ with all attributes g', and additionally $g \notin G_i$. Third, the techniques these algorithms use in order to efficiently traverse the lattice and avoid doing unnecessary computations usually rely on having the line diagram ($\leq$ lower and upper neighbors in [16]) updated after each incremental step. Moreover, in this type of algorithm, given an update from the lattice $\mathcal{L}_i$ to $\mathcal{L}_{i+1}$, they typically separate the concepts into the categories.

AI.1 *New*: a concept $<C, D> \in \mathcal{L}_{i+1}$ where D is not an intent in $\mathcal{L}_i$.

AI.2 *Modified*: a concept $<A, B> \in \mathcal{L}_i$ such that $B \subseteq g'$ since g has to be added to its extent in $\mathcal{L}_{i+1}$.

AI.3 *Generator*: a concept $<A, B> \in \mathcal{L}_i$ such that given a *new* concept $<C, D> \in \mathcal{L}_{i+1}$, $D = B \cap g' \neq B$. And.

AI.4 *old*: any other concept.

The primary challenge of incremental construction lies in the identification of all modified concepts and the determination of all canonical generators for new concepts (to ensure each new concept is generated precisely once). Efficient algorithms aim to minimize the effort spent on searching through unmodified and non-canonical generators. Some algorithms such as AddIntent, defined in [9], address this challenge by recursively traversing the diagram graph of $\mathcal{L}$.

For the purpose of this conception of 'incrementally adding pairs", we will define new versions of the concepts categories,

AP.1 New: a concept $< C, D > \in \mathcal{L}_{i+1}$ where D is not an intent in $\mathcal{L}_i$ and C is not an extent in $\mathcal{L}_i$.
AP.2 Modified: a concept $< A, B > \in \mathcal{L}_i$ such that $B \subseteq g'$ since g has to be added to its extent in $\mathcal{L}_{i+1}$ or $A \subseteq m'$ since m has to be added to its intent in $\mathcal{L}_{i+1}$.
AP.3 Generator: a concept $< A, B > \in \mathcal{L}_i$ such that given a *new* concept $< C, D > \in \mathcal{L}_{i+1}$, $D = B \cap g' \neq B$ or $C = A \cap m' \neq A$ (these second ones will be referred to as generator concept $^{-1}$). And.
AP.4 old: the rest.

So, let us firstly identify what are the different scenarios when adding g, m to $\mathcal{L}_i$ where g might or might not be in G_i, m might or might not be in M_i, and $< g, m > \notin I_i$.

First, let us consider the case where $g \notin G_i$, and $m \notin M_i$. In this case, the only concepts $< A, B > \in_i$ that could be *modified* are the bottom and the top. In fact, if $\bot_i = <\varnothing, M_i>$, then, it is a modified concept and its new version would be $\bot_{i+1} = <\varnothing, M_i \cup \{m\}>$. Analogously, if $\top_i = <G_i, \varnothing>$, its modified version would be $\top_{i+1} = < G_i \cup \{g\}, \varnothing >$. However, if $\bot_i = <X, M_i>, X \neq \varnothing$, then it is the canonical generator of the *new* concept $\bot_{i+1}$. Similarly, if the intent of $\top_i$ is not empty, then it will be the canonical generator $^{-1}$ of the *new* concept $\top_{i+1} = <G_i \cup \{g\}, \varnothing>$.

Second, if $g \notin G_i$, but $m \in M_i$ the cases are, in fact, exactly the same as in AddIntent (AI.1-AI.4). Analogously, if $m \notin M_i$, but $g \in G_i$, the dual version of the AddIntent algorithm (e.g., we can call it "AddExtent") would suffice, hence, the cases are also dual (see the additions of AP.1-AP.4 with respect to AI.1-AI.4).

Finally, let us consider the case when $g \in G_i$ and $m \in M_i$. As we can see in Fig. 2, in $\mathcal{L}_i$, assuming that b is the generator concept $^{-1}$ of g, whereas d is the generator concept of m, we can see in **red**all concepts containing g in their extents, and in **light-blue**, all concepts containing m. Moreover, concepts *below b* might or might not contain m in their intent, whilst concepts *above d* might or might not contain g in their extent. For instance, in this particular scenario, w contains m in its intent because it is a sub-concept of d. What we know, from a procedural point of view, is that the **red**concepts *may be* modified because their intent now might include m, and **light-blue**concepts *may be* modified analogously because their extent might have to include g now.

Considering that finding one generator can be done in $O(|G|^2|M|)^2$, while, dually, finding a generator $^{-1}$, in $O(|G||M|^2)$, we could argue that an algorithm to find the generator of m and the generator $^{-1}$ of g would cost $O(|G|^2|M| + |G||M|^2)$, or its simplified version $O(max(|G|^2|M|, |G||M|^2))$. Additionally, in the worst case, either above the generator $^{-1}$ of g or below the generator of m, there could be $|\mathcal{L}_i|$ concepts.

---

[2] This bound depends on several aspects, notably, the worst case happens when the algorithm start traversing the lattice from the $\bot$ (or dually from the $${\top }$$). However, this can be considerably faster if we start from higher in the hierarchy (or lower in the case of generator $^{-1}$).

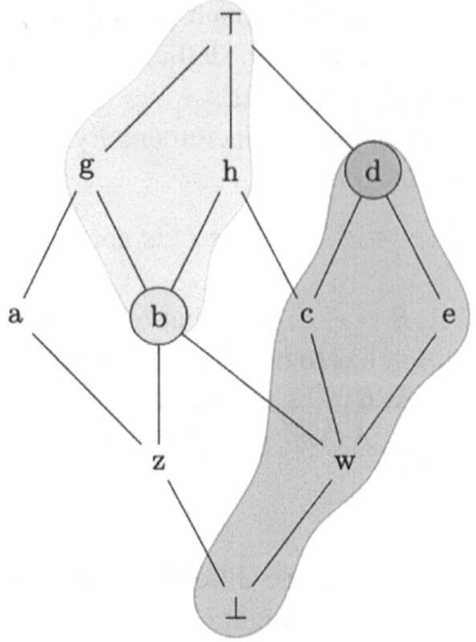

Fig. 2. Concept categories during an AddPair incremental step in a concept lattice. (created by Leutwyler and al.)

In the light of that, we propose Algorithm 1 to incrementally add a pair $< g, m >$ to a lattice $\mathcal{L}_i$ such that both g and m may or may not be present in G_i and M_i respectively. The algorithm consists in the combination of two other incremental algorithms: AddIntent [9] and DeleteInstance [18]. Basically, if $g \in \mathcal{L}_i$, between lines 1–5 the algorithm sets a variable *old_intent* with the value of g' (i.e., in $\mathcal{L}_i$, thus it does not include m yet), then, it deletes the object g (i.e., equivalent to deleting the row in which that instance appears in the formal context), and finally, it sets a variable *new_intent* as $g' \cup \{m\}$. Otherwise, *new_intent* $= \{m\}$, since g is new in $\mathcal{L}_{i+1}$ and its only related attribute is m (line 6). Then, at line 7, *new_intent* $= g'$ regardless of whether $g \in G_i$ or not. Continuing, in line 8, in case $m \notin M_i$, the algorithm updates the bottom using Algorithm 2, which simply creates a new bottom containing all attributes (as it should be) when there exists at least an object in $\bot$, or it updates the existing one otherwise. Then, we are in the case in which $m \in M$, and $g \notin G$, hence, we can use AddIntent given that we also have g' in the *new_intent* variable (line 11). Finally, the resulting is returned which corresponds to $\mathcal{L}_{i+1}$.

Algorithm 1 Algorithm to incrementally add the attribute *m* to the object *g* in the lattice L

```
1: if g ∈ L.G then
2:     old_intent ← g'
3:     delete_instance(g, L)
4:     new_intent ← old_intent ∪ {m}
5: else
6:     new_intent ← {m}
7: end if
8: if m ∉ L.M then
9:     update_bottom(m, L)
10: end if
11: add_intent(g, m, L)
12: return L
```

Algorithm 2 Algorithm to update the ⊥ concept in L considering that $m \notin M$

```
1: L.M ← L.M ∪ {m}
2: if L.⊥.E = ∅ then
3:     L.⊥.I ← L.M
4: else
5:     new_bottom ← ⟨L.⊥.E, L.M⟩
6:     set_link(L.⊥, new_bottom)
7:     L.⊥ ← new_bottom
8: end if
9: return L
```

4 Discussion

As stated before, one of the challenges of incremental construction algorithms is efficiently identifying the *modified* concepts. Furthermore, for each of the modified concepts, it would be necessary to find its generator (or dually, its generator $^{-1}$), because by adding g to its extent (or m to its intent), it is possible that a concept with that extent (or intent) already exists in $\mathcal{L}_i$. Since the amount of modified concepts in the worst case is $|\mathcal{L}_i|$, and finding the generator $^{-1}$ of g and the generator of m would cost O $(max(|G|^2|M|, |G||M|^2))$, the best we could hope for is bounded[3] by,

$$\begin{aligned} O(|\mathcal{L}|max(|G|^2|M|, |G||M|^2)) &= O(|\mathcal{L}|(|G|^2|M| + |G||M|^2)) \\ &= O(|\mathcal{L}||G||M|(|G| + |M|)) \\ &= O(|\mathcal{L}||G||M|max(|G|, |M|)) \end{aligned} \tag{6}$$

Then, if we analyze Algorithm 1, the complexity between the lines 1–7 is the complexity of DeleteInstance, i.e., O $(|\mathcal{L}||G||M|^2)$ [18]. Then, the complexity between the lines 8–12 is the maximum between Algorithm 2 and AddIntent. Since the complexity of

[3] Notice that O is an *upper* bound.

Algorithm 2 is negligible compared to that of AddIntent, the complexity between these lines ends up being$O(|\mathcal{L}||G|^2|M|)$[4] ([9]). Further, the total complexity of Algorithm 1 is

$$\begin{aligned} O((|\mathcal{L}||G|^2|M| + |G||M|^2)) &= O(|\mathcal{L}||G||M|(|G| + |M|)) \\ &= O(|\mathcal{L}||G||M|max(|G|, |M|)) \end{aligned} \quad (7)$$

Then, it is noticeable that Eq. 7 is exactly the same bound as Eq. 6, which in turn is the best we can hope for when updating every modified object exactly once.

Finally, let us give an asymptotic bound for the Goel and Chaudhary's Algorithm. Recalling Eq. 3, which in their implementation is performed with a *reduceByKey* function on the distributed pairs. This first step does not play a considerable role in the complexity of the algorithm, and for that reason, we will leave it aside. The most crucial part of this algorithm for the asymptotic behavior is the calculation of C_{N+1} from C_N, since it generates $O(|C_N|^2)$ (or more precisely $\frac{C_N(C_N-1)}{2}$, which is quadratic nonetheless) new candidate concepts. This is repeated for every C_N with $1 \leq N < max(|g'|)$ (or $max(|m'|)$). Since in the worst case $max(|g'|) = |M|$, and considering that $|C_1| \leq |M|$ (or $|G|$ when there are more attributes than objects), a big O bound for these steps would be

$$O\left(\sum_{i=1}^{|M|-1} |M|^{2^i}\right) \quad (8)$$

Although $|\mathcal{L}| = O(2^{max(|G|,|M|)})$ in the worst case, in practical scenarios, when there is highly correlated data, the amount of concepts could be much smaller than its exponential bound. However, Eq. 8 reveals that the complexity of Goel and Chaudhary's Algorithm, although scalable and parallelizable, suffers from the *exponential* generation of candidate concepts, *regardless* of the sparsity of the formal context, e.g., if only one object in the formal context has its $g' \approx |M|$, then the algorithm would necessarily compute Eq. 8 candidate concepts up to $|M|$.

5 Conclusions and Future Work

In this article, a novel algorithm for incrementally updating a lattice $\mathcal{L}$ with a complexity of $O(|\mathcal{L}||G||M|\, max(|G|, |M|))$ has been presented. Furthermore, the results of the theoretical analysis suggest that Algorithm 1 should be a better fit than the algorithm of Goel and Chaudhary complexitywise, when the formal context is *sparse* (which is often the case in practice). However, both algorithms have several differences that make the comparison very hard to perform. Firstly, being *batch* vs *incremental*, and secondly, being parallel vs single threaded. The existing batch algorithm have the upper hand in scalability regarding the fact that it is an inherently distributed algorithm, or in other words, if needed, more nodes can be added to the used cluster in order to compute the lattice faster. Furthermore, when it comes to flexibility, Algorithm 1 is preferable

[4] With certain optimizations, a tighter bound is $O(|\mathcal{L}||G|^2 max(|g'|))$ where $$max(|g\text{'}|)$$ is the maximum amount of attributes related to an object. However, to simplify the math, we will use the simpler version of the two.

because it does not require to restart the computation when new objects or attributes are added. Yet, ideally, a fully distributed solution to the incremental computation of arbitrarily distributed formal context must be explored.

Acknowledgments. This work has been funded with the help of the French National Agency for Research and Technology (ANRT) and French National Syndicate of Ski Teachers (SNMSF).

Disclosure of Interests. The authors have no competing interests to declare that are relevant to the content of this article.

References

1. Wille, R.: Restructuring lattice theory: an approach based on hierarchies of concepts. In: Rival, I. (ed.) Ordered Sets. NATO Advanced Study Institutes Series, pp. 445–470. Springer, Dordrecht (1982). https://doi.org/10.1007/978-94-009-7798-3_15
2. Seid, D., Mehrotra, S.: Efficient relationship pattern mining using multirelational iceberg-cubes. In: Fourth IEEE International Conference on Data Mining (ICDM 2004), pp. 515–518 (2004). https://doi.org/10.1109/ICDM.2004.10059
3. Dolques, X., Le Ber, F., Huchard, M., Grac, C.: Performance-friendly rule extraction in large water data-sets with AOC posets and relational concept analysis. Int. J. Gener. Syst. **45**(2), 187–210 (2016). https://doi.org/10.1080/03081079.2015.1072927
4. Fu, G.: FCA based ontology development for data integration. Inf. Process. Manage.**52**(5), 765–782 (2016). https://doi.org/10.1016/j.ipm.2016.02.003, https://www.sciencedirect.com/science/article/pii/S030645731630019X
5. Wang, P., Lu, W., Meng, Z., Wei, J., Fogelman-Soulié, F.: Towards knowledge structuring of sensor data based on FCA and ontology, p. 1 (2013)
6. Anoop, V. S., Asharaf, S.: Extracting conceptual relationships and inducing concept lattices from unstructured text. J. Intell. Syst. **28** (2017). https://doi.org/10.1515/jisys-2017-0225
7. Andrews, S.: In-close, a fast algorithm for computing formal concepts, p. 15. Moscow (2009)
8. Nourine, L., Raynaud, O.: A fast algorithm for building lattices. Inf. Process. Lett. **71**(5–6), 199–204 (1999). https://doi.org/10.1016/S0020-0190(99)00108-8, https://hal.archives-ouvertes.fr/hal-01765512
9. van der Merwe, D., Obiedkov, S., Kourie, D.: AddIntent: a new incremental algorithm for constructing concept lattices. In: Eklund, P. (ed.) Concept Lattices. Lecture Notes in Computer Science, pp. 372–385. Springer, Heidelberg (2004). https://doi.org/10.1007/978-3-540-24651-0_31
10. Goel, V., Chaudhary, B.D.: Concept discovery from un-constrained distributed context. In: Proceedings of the 4th International Conference on Big Data Analytics, BDA 2015, vol. 9498, pp. 151–164. Springer, Heidelberg (2015). https://doi.org/10.1007/978-3-319-27057-9_11
11. De Maio, C., Fenza, G., Loia, V., Orciuoli, F.: Distributed online temporal fuzzy concept analysis for stream processing in smart cities. J. Parallel Distrib. Comput. **110**, 31–41 (2017). https://doi.org/10.1016/j.jpdc.2017.02.002, https://www.sciencedirect.com/science/article/pii/S0743731517300503
12. Majidian, A., Martin, T., Cintra, M.: Fuzzy formal concept analysis and algorithm, pp. 1–7 (2011)
13. Wolff, K.E.: Temporal concept analysis. In: ICCS-2001 International Workshop on Concept Lattices-Based Theory, Methods and Tools for Knowledge Discovery in Databases, Stanford University, Palo Alto, CA, pp. 91–107 (2001)

14. Valtchev, P., Missaoui, R.: Building concept (galois) lattices from parts: generalizing the incremental methods. In: Delugach, H.S., Stumme, G. (eds.) Conceptual Structures: Broadening the Base. Lecture Notes in Computer Science, pp. 290–303. Springer, Heidelberg (2001). https://doi.org/10.1007/3-540-44583-8_21
15. Valtchev, P., Missaoui, R., Lebrun, P.: A partition-based approach towards constructing Galois (concept) lattices. Discrete Math. **256**(3), 801–829 (2002). https://doi.org/10.1016/S0012-365X(02)00349-7, https://www.sciencedirect.com/science/article/pii/S0012365X02003497
16. Ganter, B., Wille, R.: Formal Concept Analysis: Mathematical Foundations. Springer, Heidelberg (1999). https://doi.org/10.1007/978-3-642-59830-2
17. Leutwyler, N., Lezoche, M., Torres, D., Panetto, H.: Towards a flexible and scalable data stream algorithm in FCA. In: Ojeda-Aciego, M., Sauerwald, K., Jäschke, R. (eds.) Graph-Based Representation and Reasoning. Lecture Notes in Computer Science, pp. 104–117. Springer, Cham (2023). https://doi.org/10.1007/978-3-031-40960-8_9
18. Zou, L., Zhang, Z., Long, J., Zhang, H.: A fast incremental algorithm for deleting objects from a concept lattice. Knowl.-Based Syst. **89**, 411–419 (2015). https://doi.org/10.1016/j.knosys.2015.07.022, https://www.sciencedirect.com/science/article/pii/S0950705115002762

Indicator Visualization System for Technology Watch in Software Development

Sandy Valiente Rodríguez[1] and Omar Correa Madrigal[1,2](✉)

[1] Universidad de las Ciencias Informáticas, 19370 Havana, Cuba
ocorrea@uci.cu

[2] Institute of Information Technologies and Intelligent Systems, Kazan Federal University, Kazan, Russia

Abstract. Technological surveillance and competitive intelligence are concepts that mark an organization's experience in adapting to changes in the environment. Monitoring and its visual expression in instruments such as dashboards presuppose important processes of data retrieval and analysis for its presentation as information for decision making. The objective of the research is to develop a system that allows the monitoring of information on research topics through the use of indicators that support decision making. Business intelligence elements, such as dashboards, are used to model this system with functionalities that enable data analysis and visualization. For this purpose, an automated visualization tool is used. This paper presents the results in the indicator visualization cycle for the analysis of software development technologies such as programming languages, frameworks and databases, using indicators that expose the popularity of the technology over a period of time. In this way, a first step towards system scalability and flexibility is taken.

Keywords: dashboard · data analysis · decision making · technological surveillance · visualization of the information

1 Introduction

It is often said that "a picture is worth a thousand words". Today, in the age of big data, when companies are inundated with information from various types of data coming from cloud-based sources, sifting through information to understand what matters and what doesn't is becoming increasingly difficult. Images make analysis much easier and faster, and offer the ability to see what matters. What's more, most people respond much better to images than to text: 90% of the information the brain receives is visual, and it processes images 60,000 times faster than text. These points make a compelling case for the use of data visualization in the analysis and transmission of information [1].

According to the UNE 166006:2018 R&D&I management standard, technology watch is an organized, selective and permanent process of capturing information from outside and from the organization itself on science and technology, selecting it, analyzing it, disseminating it and communicating it, in order to convert it into knowledge to

V. Agredo-Delgado et al. (Eds.): DECISIONING 2024, CCIS 2369, pp. 109–119, 2025.
https://doi.org/10.1007/978-3-031-91690-8_9

make decisions with less risk and to be able to anticipate changes [2]. Technological surveillance contributes to competitive intelligence, which is vital for any organization. Competitive intelligence is understood as the systematic collection and analysis of information from multiple sources and through a programmer. By supporting the strategic processes of an organization, as a sensor that shows managers whether the organization is advancing or not, whether it is competitive or not, technology watch becomes a strategic process and a fundamental tool for the development of the organization [3].

In Cuba, different companies have been interested in the processes of technology watch, and have tried to make inroads into them. Most of the systems developed at that time were simple search engines, which in a way constitute a stage of technology watch. In recent years, more concrete progress has been made in the foundation of platforms developed specifically for technology watch.

In Cuba, Technology Surveillance Systems (TSS) stand out in the Higher Education sector and in the business sector, where the importance and impact they have in the framework of R&D&I management systems is demonstrated. Governmental support for a greater introduction of the results of science, and thus achieve technological, organizational and social innovation, has led to the promotion of the practice of technology watch, supported by observatories. In the country there are institutions that support this process of greater impact of science and technology, such as: the Institute of Scientific and Technological Information of CITMA, the INFOMED Company of MINSAP, ETI of Biocubafarma, and the Network of Observatories of the MES. In this context, important scientific events have taken place, such as the International Information Congress and the InfoPolos International Workshop at the International Convention on Science, Technology and Innovation. Both have allowed to position and discuss important aspects of the development of technology watch in the country and the world [4]. On the other hand, technology watch in the country has generated ecosystems of applications and D'TIC platforms [5] and VIGITEL, a platform supported by Hontza and belonging to Biocubafarma's ETI company.

On the other hand, international projects of relevance to this context are being developed at national level, such as the ELINF project, part of the VLIR-UOS programmer "NETWORK University Cooperation: Strengthening of the ICT role in Cuban Universities for the development of the society". ELINF aims to develop a network where actors in Cuban education and research can search for virtual services necessary for their professional tasks, access information for scientific research, exchange publications and data and work together in an integrated environment that supports open science. The project promotes, within the member universities and the Ministry of Higher Education, an ecosystem of applications derived from the implementation of the project that constitute important references to nurture technological surveillance in ICT [6].

The Universidad de las Ciencias Informáticas, in order to favor the development of technological sovereignty for surveillance and to support the development of the software industry in Cuba, is working on the development of a computational ecosystem for technological surveillance. The systems that make up this technological ecosystem carry out specialized searches through the internet using multiple sources of information such as search engines, repositories, libraries and academic databases. In this sense, tools are implemented that allow specialists to carry out searches on a given topic, as well as to manage the results for technology watch analysis. The system for monitoring indicators and trends is essential to provide the graphical information necessary for decision-making. This paper shows a web-based system for monitoring indicators and trends for decision making for the use of technologies in the software industry.

2 Main Concepts

A *technological observatory* is related to a set of organized actions with the purpose of interpreting realities, objects, actors, reconstructing situations, variables, indicators in order to process and generate information and data that support decision-making. The observatories are a structured and organized system in permanent search of quality information, validating its origin, analyzing the environment, monitoring it, building a new one, motivating its use in the design of strategies for another [7]. In this context, technology watch activity is fundamental. According to UNE 166006, *technology watch* is an organized, selective and permanent process of capturing information from outside and from the organization itself on science and technology, in order to convert it into knowledge to make decisions with less risk and to be able to anticipate changes [2].

The evolution of computer technologies to support these processes has resulted in increasingly autonomous tools for information retrieval, analysis and visualization. Among the trends in visualization are *dashboards*, which according to Stephen Few, is the visualization of the most important information needed to achieve one or more objectives; consolidated and organized on a single screen so that the information can be monitored at a glance [8]. The design of such a tool not only presupposes an adequate distribution of content from the user interface, but also the definition of *key performance indicators (KPIs)*. These are the critical quantifiable (key) indicators of progress towards an expected result. KPIs provide a focus for strategic and operational improvement, create an analytical basis for decision-making and help focus attention on what matters most [9].

3 Materials and Methods

3.1 Visualization Tool

Grafana's open source software allows you to query, visualize, alert and explore your metrics, logs and traces wherever they are stored. Grafana OSS provides tools to convert time series database (TSDB) data into insightful graphs and visualizations. The Grafana OSS add-on framework also allows connecting other data sources such as NoSQL/SQL databases, ticketing tools like Jira or ServiceNow, and CI/CD tools like GitLab [10].

Grafana has the following characteristics:

- Explore metrics, logs and traces: Grafana allows you to explore data through queries and dynamic drill-down. It splits the view and compares different time ranges, queries and data sources in parallel.
- Dashboard: A Grafana dashboard consists of panels that display data in graphs, charts and other visualizations. These dashboards are created using components that transform raw data from a data source into visualizations. The process involves passing data through three gates: a plug-in, a query and an optional transformation.

- Data sources: A data source refers to any entity consisting of data. It can be a SQL database, Grafana Loki, Grafana Mimir or a JSON-based API. It can even be a basic CSV file. The first step in creating a dashboard visualization is to select the data source that contains the data you need.
- Plugins: A Grafana plugin is software that adds new capabilities to Grafana. They come in many types, such as dashboards and data feeds.
- Panel: After the data is retrieved, queried and transformed, it goes to a dashboard, which is the final gateway in the journey to a Grafana visualization final gateway on the journey to a Grafana visualization. A dashboard is a container that displays the visualization and provides various controls to manipulate it.
- Panel variables: Template variables allow you to create panels that can be reused for many different use cases different use cases. The values are not hard-coded with these templates, so, for example, if you have both a production server and a test server, you can use the same template.
- Import/export panels: Grafana offers multiple ways to import and export panels, either from the user interface, using JSON files or through the API. This flexibility allows efficient sharing of dashboard configurations between different environments and collaborators.
- Authentication: Authentication in Grafana can be achieved through various methods, such as username and password, OAuth, LDAP, Auth Proxy and authentication tokens. The choice of the appropriate method depends on the security needs and preferences of the organization.
- Permissions: Allows you to set privileges on panels and users. These privileges establish the permissions that users have over the data panels and Grafana in general. The tool categorizes users into three roles: viewer, editor and administrator. Each of them has default permissions on Grafana.

The advantages of Grafana as a visualization tool lie in the following:

- Flexibility and variety of visualizations: Grafana offers a wide range of visualization options, from line and bar charts to maps, tables and gauges. It also allows advanced customization and configuration of visualizations, giving you the flexibility to represent data in the most appropriate way for your specific needs.
- Easy integration with various data sources: Grafana has an extensive list of connectors that allow integration with many popular data sources. This allows real-time data to be obtained and visualized in a centralized interface without having to switch tools or query multiple systems.
- Interactivity and data exploration: Allows users to explore and analyze data by selecting and filtering series, zooming, comparing and much more. This facilitates understanding and in-depth analysis of the visualized data.
- Customizable dashboards: Grafana allows you to create and customize dashboards according to your needs and objectives. You can combine multiple visualizations in a single dashboard, organize them in customized layouts, add annotations, alerts and make use of variables to facilitate interactivity and adaptation to different scenarios.
- Active community and add-on ecosystem: Grafana has an active community that develops and shares add-ons and extensions. This further extends Grafana's capabilities and provides access to a wide variety of add-ons and pre-defined templates that

you can use to enrich visualizations and customize them according to your specific needs.

- Free and open source: Grafana is an open source software tool distributed under the Apache 2.0 license. This means that it can be used free of charge and have access to the source code, which gives the freedom to modify and customize the tool as needed.
- Webapp: Grafana belongs to the web application domain, so this tool can be accessed from a PC connected to the network through a browser. It is guaranteed to use a web application as the rest of the modules that belong to the project's ecosystem also belong to the webapp domain.

3.2 Programming Language

Python is a powerful and easy-to-learn programming language. It has efficient high-level data structures and a simple but effective object-oriented programming system. Python's elegant syntax and dynamic typing, coupled with its interpreted nature, make it an ideal language for scripting and rapid application development in many areas, for most platforms. Python is available on Windows, macOS and Unix operating systems [11].

Python has developed a large and active data analysis and scientific computing community. Over the past 20 years, Python has grown from a cutting-edge computer science language to one of the most important languages for data science, machine learning and general software development, both academically and within the industry. For data analytics, interactive computing and data visualization, Python inevitably draws comparisons with other widely used open source and commercial programming languages and tools, such as R, MATLAB, SAS, Stata. In recent years, Python's enhanced open source libraries (such as pandas and scikitlearn) have made it the standard choice for data analysis tasks. Combined with the overall robustness of Python for generic software engineering, it is an excellent alternative as a core language for creating data applications [12].

Pandas is an open source, BSD-licensed library that provides high-performance, easy-to-use data structures and data analysis tools for the Python programming language. [13].

3.3 Data Storage

CSV stands for Comma Separated Values. A CSV file is a plain text file that stores tables and spreadsheet information. The contents are often a table of text, numbers, or dates. CSV files can be easily imported and exported using programs that store data in tables. Usually, the first line in a CSV file contains the table column labels. Each of the subsequent lines represent a row of the table. Commas separate each cell in the row, which is where the name comes from [14].

3.4 Sources of Information

The system draws on information obtained from the collection and analysis of multiple sources of information, some of which are listed below.

The vast majority of the information comes from other websites and projects, including:

- Github: github.com
- Gitlab: gitlab.com
- Stackoverflow Insights: insights.stackoverflow.com
- AWS Amazon: aws.amazon.com
- Google Cloud: cloud.google.com
- Jupyter: jupyter.org
- Linkedin: linkedin.com
- Reddit: reddit.com
- PYPL PopularitY of Programming Language: pypl.github.io
- TIOBE Index: tiobe.com
- Twitter: twitter.com
- Ubuntu: ubuntu.com
- Wikipedia: wikipedia.org

3.5 Indicators

These indicators are selected because they provide value to measure the quality of the technology in question. Therefore, the associated indicators are presented below.

- Name: name of the technology to be analyzed.
- Type: subjective category of technology where this entity fits. For example: application, programming language, programming library, programming framework, database, code editor, operating system.
- Number of books: count of books on the technology in question.
- Number of articles: count of articles on the technology in question.
- Number of users: estimate of the number of users using this technology.
- Number of projects: estimate of the number of projects that exist on this technology.
- Number of repositories: number of repositories reported by Github on this technology.
- Total: sum of all the previous indicators. Indispensable to establish the popularity ranking.
- Count of searches for tutorials on Google (taken from PYPL): count of searches for tutorials on the programming language on Google.
- Download page search count on Google (taken from PYPL): search count of download pages about the IDE on Google.
- Count of searches for the name in Google (taken from PYPL): count of searches for the name of the database in Google.
- Count of searches for the name in multiple search engines (taken from TIOBE): count of searches for the name of the programming language in various search engines.

4 Analysis and Design of a Visualization System of Indicators for Technology Watch

4.1 Description of the Proposed Solution

The proposed solution is based on the mastering of a web application software, also known as a webapp. The purpose of this indicator visualization system for technology watch is to enable researchers to graphically analyze data on metrics associated with research topics in order to analyze trends, establish strategies and make decisions. The system will be implemented using Grafana, a monitoring tool for data visualization. Scientific-technological KPIs are used to measure the behavior of software development technologies, such as programming languages and databases. The system draws on multiple sources of information from the web. The data extracted from these sources is processed and then stored for visualization in the tool. It bases its visualizations on ranking systems, where indexes are calculated from the stored data. It has a system of authentication and roles, which define the access and permissions of users to the system.

4.2 Architectural Pattern

The Model View Controller (MVC) architecture pattern separates an application into three main component groups: models, views and controllers. This pattern allows the separation of interests to be achieved. With this pattern, user requests are routed to a controller that is responsible for working with the model to perform user actions or retrieve query results. The controller chooses the view to display to the user and provides any necessary model data [15].

The following diagram shows the three main components and which one refers to the others (Fig. 1).

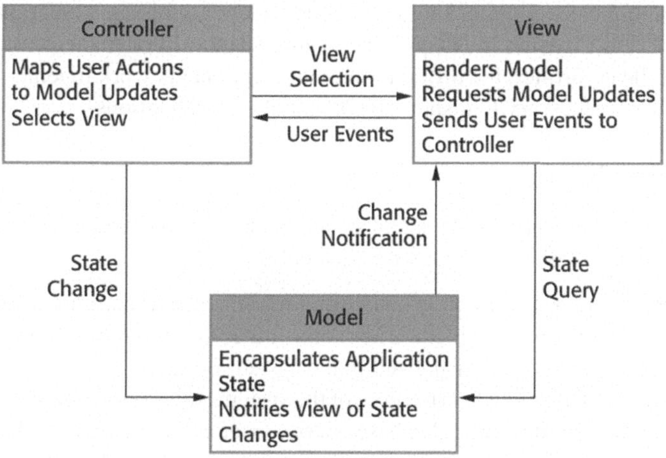

Fig. 1. The organization of the MVC. Source: Sommerville, Ian. Software engineering 9th Edition (2011).

The model in an MVC application represents the state of the application and any business logic or operations it must perform. The business logic must be encapsulated in the model, along with any implementation logic to preserve the state of the application [15].

Views are responsible for presenting content through the user interface. There should be minimal logic between views and any logic in them should be related to the presentation of content [15].

Controllers are the components that control user interaction, work with the model, and ultimately select a view to represent. In an MVC application, the view only displays information; the controller controls and responds to the interaction and data entered by users. In the MVC pattern, the controller is the initial entry point that is responsible for selecting which types of model to work with and which views to represent (hence its name, since it controls how the application responds to a given request) [15].

The visualization system follows the Model-View-Controller (MVC) architecture pattern.

- Model: The model mainly represents the data access and data management layer. It integrates with different data sources, such as databases, web services or real-time metrics services. These data sources act as the model, providing the data used in dashboards and visualizations. The system allows you to configure and query these data sources to obtain the data needed for the visualization.
- View: The view is what users see and interact with. An intuitive and flexible graphical user interface (GUI) is provided to create and customize dashboards and visualizations. Dashboards are composed of various visual components, such as graphs, charts, tables and status panels, which are combined to form the final view. Users can customize the appearance and layout of the visualizations.
- Controller: The controller is responsible for managing user interactions and coordinating the flow of data between the model and the view. Components such as visualization panels, plugins and data queries interact with each other and with the model and view to obtain and display the required data. Although there is no clear separation of the controller, the different internal components work together to perform the operations necessary to display the data in the visualizations.

4.3 Main Modules

The system's modules are fundamental to understanding its functionality. The main modules that make up the system are detailed below.

- Information sources: information sources refer to the materials, sources or resources from which data are obtained. They constitute the referents from which the information processed and visualized in the system is taken.
- Grafana Server: This module is the core of the system and is responsible for managing and serving the user interface, database queries, user authentication, and general system configuration. The Grafana server is the central component that allows interaction with the application through a web browser.
- User interface: The user interface is the visible and accessible component of the system that allows users to interact with the system. It includes data visualization panels, customizable dashboards, query tools and a variety of options for configuring and customizing visualizations.
- Data connectors: supports a wide range of data connectors, which facilitate integration with various data sources, such as time series databases (e.g. InfluxDB, Prometheus), relational databases (e.g. MySQL, PostgreSQL), monitoring systems (e.g. Zabbix), and many other data sources.

- Dashboards and visualizations: these modules allow the creation and visualization of different types of data through customizable dashboards. The system offers a wide range of visualizations, including line graphs, bar charts, gauges, heat maps, tables, and other formats that can be configured and combined in a dashboard to intuitively and effectively represent information.

These modules form the basis of the system and provide a wide range of capabilities for data visualization and analysis.

4.4 Information Flow

The following explains how these modules interact and produce the flow of information in the system.

- Data collection: First, data is collected from various sources of information.
- Data processing: Secondly, the extracted data is processed by applying data analysis methods and techniques. In this step, the Python language and its libraries are used to process the information.
- Data storage: After processing, data sources are defined for data storage. CSV files are used.
- Connecting to data sources: Once data is stored, it connects to these sources to extract information. It uses connectors and plugins specific to each type of data source, allowing it to obtain the data needed for visualization.
- Creating dashboards and graphs: Users can then use the interface to create custom dashboards and graphs. They can select the data of interest and choose how they want to visualize it, whether through line graphs, bar charts, scatter plots, maps, tables or other types of visualizations.
- Distribution of dashboards: Finally, the dashboards and charts created are distributed to relevant users or teams. These dashboards can be embedded in other systems or simply shared via links, allowing users to access the information easily and clearly.

In conclusion, the flow of information in the system involves collecting, processing and storing data, connecting it to specific sources, creating customized visualizations and distributing these dashboards for consumption (see Fig. 2).

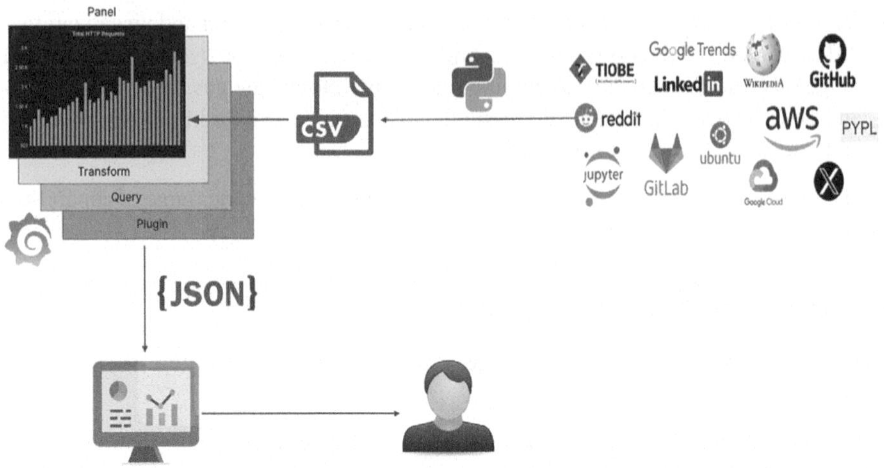

Fig. 2. Information flow of the proposed solution. Source: Own elaboration.

5 Conclusions

This work has succeeded in designing and implementing a visualization system using Grafana that enables the effective presentation of a wide range of indicators relevant to technology watch. Through the implementation of this system, an effective visual representation of trends and patterns in technology watch indicators has been achieved. This is essential for identifying opportunities, threats and possible turning points in the technology landscape. The potential of this system was identified to influence the agility of strategic decision making, as well as to improve the organization's ability to identify trends, opportunities and threats in the technological environment such as the use of programming languages and their ecosystems.

The technological integration achieved provides the functionalities for data visualization and analysis, as well as the creation of customized control panels to monitor systems and applications.

The modules form the basis of the system and provide a wide range of capabilities for data visualization and analysis, as well as the creation of customized dashboards for monitoring systems and applications. Modularity and flexibility allows it to adapt to a wide variety of environments and use cases, making it a powerful tool for data visualization and monitoring. It offers flexibility in the way data can be visualized and analyzed. This is crucial in a technology watch environment, where data requirements and sources can vary widely. Users can interact with the data and customize visualizations to their specific needs. This is critical for adapting to different use cases in technology surveillance.

Through the development and deployment of this system, an understanding of the importance of data visualization in the technology watch process has been deepened, highlighting its value for decision making.

Acknowledgments. This paper has been supported by the Kazan Federal University Strategic Academic Leadership Program ("PRIORITY-2030").

References

1. Oracle España. https://www.oracle.com/es/business-analytics/what-is-data-visualization/. Accessed 20 Sept 2023
2. UNE 166006:2018 Gestión de la I+D+i. https://www.une.org/encuentra-tu-norma/busca-tu-norma/norma?c=N0059973. Accessed 22 Oct 2023
3. Du Toit, A.S.A.: Competitive intelligence research: an investigation of trends in the literature. J. Intell. Stud. Bus. **5**(2), 14–21 (2015). https://doi.org/10.37380/jisib.v5i2.127
4. Red de Observatorios de Ciencia, Tecnología e Innovación. La Habana, Cuba (2022)
5. Juan, Y.I.S., Rodríguez, F.I.R.: Modelos y herramientas para la vigilancia tecnológica. Ciencias Inform. **47**(2), 11–18 (2016)
6. San Juan, Y., Romero, F.: Management, extraction and storing sources for technological watch and competitive intelligence. VIII Congreso Internacional de Tecnologías y Contenidos Multimedia, pp. 19–23. La Habana, Cuba (2018)
7. Martínez Albarracín, C.E., Bolívar Salgado, W.E., Gutiérrez Salgado, N.M.: Information source observatories: concepts and theoretical review. J. Bus. Entrep. Stud. **5**(3) (2021). https://doi.org/10.37956/jbes.v5i3.187
8. Few, S.: Information Dashboard Design: The Effective Visual Communication of Data. O'Reilly Media Inc., Sebastopol (2006)
9. KPI.org. https://www.kpi.org/kpi-basics/. Accessed 22 Oct 2023
10. Grafana documentation. https://grafana.com/docs/grafana/latest/. Accessed 15 Sept 2023
11. Python.org. https://www.python.org/doc/. Accessed 15 Sept 2023
12. McKinney, W.: Python for Data Analysis: Data Wrangling with Pandas, NumPy, and IPython. O'Reilly Media Inc., Sebastopol (2012)
13. Pandas documentation. https://pandas.pydata.org/docs/. Accessed 15 Sept 2023
14. freeCodeCamp.org. https://www.freecodecamp.org/news/what-is-a-csv-file-and-how-to-open-the-csv-file-format/. Accessed 15 Sept 2023
15. Microsoft Learn. https://learn.microsoft.com/es/aspnet/core/mvc/overview?view=aspnetcore-7.0. Accessed 21 Sept 2023

Initial Explorations for Document Clustering Tasks in Latin Elegiac Poets

Carlos Javier Nusch[1(✉)], Gimena del Rio Riande[2], Leticia Cecilia Cagnina[3], Marcelo Luis Errecalde[3], and Leandro Antonelli[4,5]

[1] PREBI, SEDICI, Universidad Nacional de La Plata, La Plata, Argentina
carlosnusch@prebi.unlp.edu.ar
[2] IIBICRIT, Consejo Nacional de Investigaciones Científicas y Técnicas, Buenos Aires, Argentina
gdelrio@conicet.gov.ar
[3] LIDIC, Facultad de Ciencias Físico Matemáticas y Naturales, Universidad Nacional de San Luis, San Luis, Argentina
{lcagnina,merreca}@email.unsl.edu.ar
[4] LIFIA, Facultad de Informática, Universidad Nacional de La Plata, La Plata, Argentina
lanto@lifia.info.unlp.edu.ar
[5] CAETI, Facultad de Tecnología Informática, Universidad Abierta Interamericana, Buenos Aires, Argentina

Abstract. This article describes various Automatic Text Analysis tasks applying Natural Language Processing techniques on a corpus of Latin texts from the 1st century BC and 1st century AD. The motivation behind this work is to delve into and understand a historical literary trend revolving around the themes of love, spanning from antiquity through to the medieval period. The analyzed authors include Gaius Valerius Catullus, Albius Tibullus, and Sextus Propertius, who represent the literary movement of the neoterics, as a group of poets to be identified, and Publius Vergilius Maro and Marcus Annaeus Lucanus, epic poets with remarkably distinct styles, as control samples. The purpose of this preliminary and exploratory study is to investigate the potential and best features for document clustering. The clustering tasks were carried out using fixed ranges of character n-grams and word n-grams. For the clustering tasks, the K-Means method and the Silhouette Index were used for determining the optimal cluster sizes. Using optimal clusters as labels, decision trees were trained for each range of n-grams, aiming to identify features with the highest Information Gain and Information Gain Ratio. The trees were trained based on the criterion of Entropy, and calculations of Feature Importance were performed. Results show variations based on text preprocessing techniques: simple filtering of stopwords in the corpus yields better Silhouette scores, with one or two features showing potential classification value for the decision trees. The application of TF-IDF weighting results in Silhouette indices closer to zero, albeit with a more balanced distribution of Importance among different features.

Keywords: Latin Elegiac Poets · Document Clustering · K Means · Silhouette Coefficient · Decision Trees · Feature Importance · Information Gain Ratio

V. Agredo-Delgado et al. (Eds.): DECISIONING 2024, CCIS 2369, pp. 120–134, 2025.
https://doi.org/10.1007/978-3-031-91690-8_10

1 Introduction

This study builds upon issues previously addressed in individual bachelor's and master's thesis works [19] considerations made by C. S. Lewis [12] on the influence of Courtly love and Occitan literature on the love imaginary of the 20th century. It was timely noted that there were some remarkable similarities between love themes, the treatment of the beloved, and certain terms derived from the political and military fields in erotic poems, both in Occitan and Latin literature of the 1st century BC. The overarching framework of this doctoral thesis is centered on attempting to identify textual patterns that could shed light on a potential literary tradition of love themes originating in antiquity and culminating in the development of the imagery of the "Religion of Love" by medieval Occitan poets. To narrow down the analysis corpus and circumvent the challenges inherent in working with vernacular languages, the research focused on texts from the Latin literary tradition. The comparative approach will be conducted by combining traditional close reading techniques with the capabilities of distant reading tools provided by computational methods [16, 23]. In the initial stages of the research, various document clustering techniques are being analyzed to uncover features that allow profiling and identifying poetry with love themes. For this specific article, various clustering techniques were evaluated to differentiate elegiac poems from other types of Latin poetry and to discover lexical features that could prove useful in document classification tasks. This study contributes to the field by testing the efficacy of clustering algorithms on a specific corpus of Latin poetry.

2 State of the Art

In the field of ancient text studies, several authors have applied clustering techniques to ancient texts, including Bracco et al. [2] worked on the automatic detection of literary genres in cuneiform texts using the K-means algorithm to group texts based on grammatical, graphemic, and other stylistic features. Regarding specifically Latin texts, Martins et al. [14] used the k-Nearest Neighbors (k-NN) approach in a multi-author classification task of the *Historia Augusta.* Cantaluppi and Passarotti [5] conducted an in-depth investigation of the corpus of Seneca's *opera omnia* using hierarchical cluster analysis and latent semantic analysis, comparing it with the corpora of Cicero's *orationes*, Jerome's Latin New Testament (*Vulgata*), and Thomas Aquinas's *opera maiora.* The authors demonstrated that a lexical-based approach is successful in classifying texts across different authors, genres, and eras. About the authors studied in this work, B. Nagy [18] used clustering and multivariate analysis to examine the conscious use of rhyme in twelve classical Latin poets (including Catullus, Propertius, and Tibullus), identifying stylistic differences between genres and authors. Forstall et al. [8, 9] have compared lexical and rhythmic characteristics at the level of character and word n-grams with other poets from the 1st century BC and later.

3 Problem Definition and Contributions

The primary aim of this work was to explore clustering techniques capable of distinguishing elegiac poems from other types of poetry and to determine which lexical characteristics might be useful in document classification tasks. The K-means algorithm [13] was selected for this purpose, and the optimal number of clusters was evaluated using the Silhouette Index [24], which evaluates the cohesion of each grouping and its distinctiveness from the other clusters. Given that the K-means method is based on Euclidean distance and, apart from identifying the points or documents closest to the centroid, does not allow for the extraction of detailed information about the features of the documents that comprise each cluster, it was decided to complement this approach with decision trees [22]. This combination allowed for the indirect extraction of the features/In this way, an effort was made to indirectly obtain the features with the greatest classification potential using metrics of Importance, Information Gain, and Information Gain Ratio [26].

4 Research Methodology and Approach

4.1 Analysis Corpus and Used Editions

The working corpus includes the complete Works of Gaius Valerius Catullus [15], Albius Tibullus [21], and Sextus Propertius [17] as the authors of love-themed poetry whose particular characteristics are sought to be identified. The various cantos from the epic poems *Aeneid* by Publius Vergilius Maro [10] and *Pharsalia* by Marcus Annaeus Lucanus [28] were used as control samples since their themes focus on political, historical, and martial matters. The analysis of the works of five Latin authors reveals differences in their use of words and verse structure. catullus, with a total of 2,289 verses[1] and 12,887 words, has an average of 110.15 words per poem and 5,821 unique words. Tibullus wrote 1,930 verses and 12,705 words, with a rather high average of 343.38 words per poem and 5,328 unique words. propertius, with 4,008 verses and 25,320 words, maintains an average of 241.14 words per poem and a repertoire of 9,021 unique words. Lucan stands out with 8,061 verses and 51,065 words, with an average of 5,106.50 words per canto and 14,766 unique words. Finally, Virgil leads in volume with 9,896 verses and 63,719 words, and an average of 5,309.92 words per canto, in addition to the widest variety of unique words, totaling 16,619.

To construct the analysis corpus, resources from the Perseus Project digital library [6, 29] at the Department of Classics at Tufts University were utilized. The library also houses 2,412 works in 3,192 editions and translations (1,639 in Greek and 636 in Latin) and 69.7 million words: 32.1 million in Greek, 16.3 million in Latin, and the remainder

[1] In the Merrill edition of *Catullus*, the canonical total of 2296 verses is proposed by the editor, who notably includes 7 missing verses (vv. 79-82 and 112-114) in *Carmen* 61. I would also like to express my gratitude to Professor Benjamin Nagy of the Institute of Polish Language, Polish Academy of Sciences (IJP PAN), Kraków, Poland, for his invaluable advice and assistance in correcting the verse count in line with the authoritative editions of the studied authors. His expertise greatly contributed to ensuring accuracy in this text mining endeavor.

in English translations and sources in other languages. The texts are carefully curated by specialists, and shared under a CC BY SA 3.0 (US) license, with the texts being available in XML format for download. Additionally, the project offers additional resources, including a model for grammatical tagging or Parts of Speech Tagging (PoS Tagging) and stopwords for Latin. The poems that constitute the corpus were harvested for previous Automatic Text Analysis tasks through web scraping procedures. The software used for performing the scraping was R. On the other hand, for the text analysis and mining, particular libraries of Python were used. R was utilized as the software for the scraping, while Python libraries were employed for text analysis and mining purposes.

In this study, we explored the characteristics of n-grams at different levels, including character n-grams (ranging from 2 to 7) and word n-grams (from 1 to 5). For our analysis, we employed the traditional Bag of Words (BOW)[25] method. We generated three types of matrices: the first matrix was created using Scikit-learn's module CountVectorizer, which tallies the frequency of simple terms and enables filtering common words or 'stopwords'. The second matrix used the TF-IDF (Term Frequency-Inverse Document Frequency) [27] weighting technique, which highlights important words by weighing their frequency relative to their rarity across the entire dataset. Finally, the third matrix combined TF-IDF weighting with 'stopwords' filtering, providing a more refined approach by excluding less significant terms while highlighting the importance of the remaining terms.

The difference between a matrix generated with CountVectorizer and one with TF-IDF is that the former simply counts the frequency of each word's occurrence in the documents, resulting in a direct numerical representation of the terms, whereas the latter considers not only the frequency of words but also their relative importance across the document set. TF-IDF weights common words that appear in many documents so that they have less impact, highlighting terms that are more unique to each document and therefore, potentially more significant for analysis.

4.2 Text Preprocessing Tasks

Before proceeding with the text analysis, cleaning and text preprocessing tasks were carried out. Consecutive empty lines and combinations of new lines and spaces in different sequences ("\n \n\n\n' and variants) that did not provide information were removed, as they were the remnants of scraping tasks. Furthermore, signs often used by editors to denote illegible gaps in the original codices ("†") were also removed due to the problems these signs caused. Spanish double ("") and single ('') quotation marks were replaced with English ones ("", '') to ensure compatibility with tools developed for english, thus preventing potential processing errors.

For working with character n-grams, punctuation marks were removed since they are an addition by the editors of the ancient texts and it is not possible to ascertain the original punctuation of the authors, given that modern punctuation did not exist in the 1st century BC.

Regarding stopwords, the package designed for Latin from Stopwords ISO [31], a project compiling a collection of stopwords in various languages, was used. The interest in using these particular stopwords over others like the Perseus Project [30] was motivated by the fact that they do not remove some words previously identified as important within the elegiac style, such as *ego*, thus allowing for the exploration of the prevalence of personal pronouns among the most significant features of the documents, a phenomenon already noted in previous works [19, 20].

5 Evaluation: Silhouette and Optimal Number of Clusters

5.1 Clustering with K Means and Silhouette Index

To conduct document clustering, the K-means method was used, enabling the partitioning of a dataset consisting of *n* observations into K different groups based on feature similarity. One of the limitations of the algorithm lies in its prerequisite knowledge of the number of K groups which the corpus will be distributed into. To reduce/mitigate bias in determining the K groups, the Silhouette calculation was used as it allows evaluating two important parameters: firstly, the cohesion within each cluster, i.e., the average distance of all the points that make it up among themselves, and secondly, the separation between the different clusters according to the distance of one point to all other points in the nearest cluster. The optimal k for clusters was determined by testing a range from 2 to 20 clusters and the k groups exhibiting the best coefficient were selected.

5.2 Character N-grams and Word N-grams

Tests were conducted utilizing different fixed ranges of character n-grams (from 2 to 7) and word n-grams (from 1 to 5). For each of these ranges, the Silhouette coefficient was calculated for k groups ranging from 2 to 20. This endeavor aimed to discern the optimal range of character and word n-grams for clustering tasks. The goal was to find not only the best k for clusters but also the most effective n-gram ranges for optimizing the grouping process.

5.3 TF-IDF Weighting

Term Frequency-Inverse Document Frequency (TF-IDF) [27] a statistical technique, was used to evaluate the importance of a word in a document relative to a collection of documents or corpus. This technique weights a term's frequency of appearance in a specific document relative to the total number of terms in the document and the term's significance across the entire corpus. The calculation within the corpus helps to mitigate the impact of terms ubiquitous across multiple documents and are therefore not useful for classification tasks.

5.4 Decision Trees and Key Corpus Features

With data labeled by clusters, decision trees were trained using the entropy criterion to analyze the importance of different features across various n-gram levels. The importance of features was calculated, and additionally, Information Gain (IG) and Information Gain Ratio (IGR) were determined.

The importance of a feature reflects the extent to which that specific feature contributes to the improvement of the model's predictive capacity, based on its efficacy to help reduce impurity or disorder in the data set. Entropy measures the impurity or disorder in a dataset, calculated as the sum of the products of the probabilities of the labels and their logarithms. Information Gain is obtained by reducing the total entropy with the entropy weighted by the presence or absence of each feature. The Information Gain Ratio (IGR) is calculated on the entropy of the labels corresponding to each feature where the feature is present, obtaining the information gain by subtracting the feature's entropy from the total entropy.

6 Preliminary or Intermediate Results

Regarding the calculation of the optimal number of clusters, there were no major differences between using the two types of stopwords. It should be noted that a better performance in terms of the Silhouette index was observed when using the frequency matrix and simple stopwords filtering (CountVectorizer with Stopwords). The matrix resulting from the TF-IDF weighting shows Silhouette scores close to zero, indicating inadequate cluster separation and potential overlap.. In the case of 5-character n-grams, the negative value even suggests the likelihood of misassigned elements in the clusters (Table 1).

Table 1. Optimal clusters and corresponding Silhouette values for different ranges of n-grams. Source: author's own work.

Optimal Clusters (Stopwords ISO)				
N-gram Type	CountVec with Stopwords: Clusters	Score	TF-IDF: Clusters	Score
Char 2-g	**2**	**0.94**	**2**	**0.16**
Char 3-g	2	0.91	2	0.12
Char 4-g	2	0.88	2	0.029
Char 5-g	2	0.81	17	−0.00026
Char 6-g	3	0.76	14	0.004
Char 7-g	2	0.72	16	0.0025
Word 1-g	**3**	**0.77**	**3**	**0.012**
Word 2-g	2	0.704	17	0.0013
Word 3-g	2	0.69	15	0.0075
Word 4-g	2	0.69	17	0.0076
Word 5-g	2	0.69	19	0.0074

Regarding the features deemed most crucial for classifying different types of clusters, the results obtained may suggest that it might be necessary to reevaluate the methodology and resources used. Although the Silhouette scores were high using the frequency matrix, when calculating the different metrics to evaluate the importance of the features, a very uneven distribution appears (Tables 2 and 3). In almost all cases, one or two attributes concentrate all the importance. Applying the TF-IDF technique, on the other hand, while the Silhouette scores had been close to zero, a greater number of features contributing information for the classification task can be observed (Tables 4 and 5).

Table 2. Most important features at the level of character n-grams according to Importance, Information Gain, Information Gain Ratio using the frequency matrix method and Stopwords filtering. Source: author's own work.

CountVectorizer with Stopwords. Char n-grams (2, 2)					
Feature	Importance	Feature	IG	Feature	IGR
“a “	1	“gm”	0.206	“dh”	0.503
“us”	0	“dh”	0.1928	“gm”	0.4631
“ep”	0	“ze”	0.178	“dg”	0.4498
“ea”	0	“rh”	0.1738	“ x”	0.4182
“eb”	0	“dv”	0.1686	“ae”	0.4182
“ec”	0	“yc”	0.166	“oï”	0.402
“ed”	0	“df”	0.1651	“sn”	0.392
“ee”	0	“lm”	0.1636	“ze”	0.39
“ef”	0	“ya”	0.1614	“mf”	0.3883
“eg”	0	“uq”	0.1614	“gg”	0.3873

Table 3. Most important features at the level of word n-grams according to Importance, Information Gain, Information Gain Ratio using the frequency matrix method and Stopwords filtering. Source: author's own work.

CountVectorizer with Stopwords. Word n-grams (1,1)					
Feature	Importance	Feature	IG	Feature	IGR
“iam”	0.8358	“fatis”	0.2599	“mundo”	0.6931
“omnipotens”	0.1642	“late”	0.2397	“bellorum”	0.6931
“flava”	0	“hos”	0.2285	“aeneas”	0.6931
“flammigeros”	0	“fatur”	0.2174	“teucrum”	0.6931
“flammis”	0	“metu”	0.2151	“divom”	0.6418
“flammisque”	0	“iamque”	0.2151	“teucros”	0.6418
“flamma”	0	“cursu”	0.2144	“civile”	0.6366
“flare”	0	“haud”	0.2127	“coelo”	0.6366

(*continued*)

Table 3. (*continued*)

CountVectorizer with Stopwords. Word n-grams (1,1)					
Feature	Importance	Feature	IG	Feature	IGR
"flatibus"	0	"urbem"	0.2089	"caussa"	0.6366
"flatu"	0	"vires"	0.2082	"nocentes"	0.6366

Table 4. Most important features at the level of character n-grams ranked by Importance, Information Gain, Information Gain Ratio using the TF-IDF matrix method. Source: author's own work.

TF-IDF. Char n-grams (2, 2)					
Feature	Importance	Feature	IG	Feature	IGR
"a "	0.4611	"rm"	0.2306	"bh"	0.3652
"s "	0.1504	"fu"	0.2019	"rm"	0.2311
"ri"	0.0608	" t"	0.1904	"ta"	0.2306
" e"	0.0456	"fo"	0.1802	"ct"	0.229
"xi"	0.0441	"ct"	0.1801	"fu"	0.2231
"st"	0.0432	"aq"	0.179	"co"	0.2224
"lu"	0.0419	"e"	0.1786	"to"	0.2215
"or"	0.0374	"go"	0.1738	"ro"	0.2079
"m "	0.0338	"ph"	0.1729	"e"	0.203
"mu"	0.0243	"rb"	0.1723	"no"	0.2018

Regarding a qualitative reading of the results, assessing the relevance of specific character n-grams for text classification proves challenging. This analysis would require a more detailed stylistic study of the preferences of each author.

Table 5. Most important features at the level of character n-grams according to Importance, Information Gain, Information Gain Ratio using the TF-IDF matrix method. Source: author's own work.

TF-IDF. Word n-grams (1, 1)					
Feature	Importance	Feature	IG	Feature	IGR
"et"	0.4448	"hic"	0.1912	"spes"	0.3198
"opus"	0.1748	"ab"	0.1818	"belli"	0.3042
"ille"	0.0894	"signa"	0.1744	"acies"	0.299
"per"	0.0797	"manus"	0.1736	"labor"	0.2938
"liquor"	0.0476	"per"	0.1698	"fatis"	0.2938
"turpis"	0.0433	"ad"	0.1637	"marte"	0.2886
"iam"	0.0407	"arma"	0.1586	"late"	0.2886
"altera"	0.0322	"tellus"	0.1548	"tellus"	0.2855
"fugaci"	0.0269	"ubi"	0.1526	"gentis"	0.2834
"classe"	0.0207	"spes"	0.1496	"iuventus"	0.2834

Concluding with the findings, although at the level of features the techniques used did not yield terms predominantly typical of the elegiac love repertoire, the division of documents into clusters seems to have shown efficacy in certain instances. With the Bag of Words technique and frequency counting at the level of 2 character n-grams, the 2 resulting clusters separate the elegiac poets from the epic poets (Figs. 1 and 2).

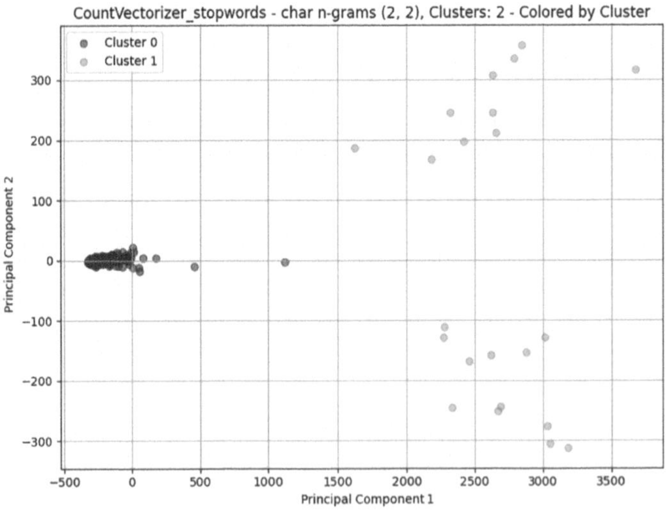

Fig. 1. Scatter plot of clustering by K Means using a frequency matrix of 2 character n-grams indicating the clusters with different colors. Source: author's own work.

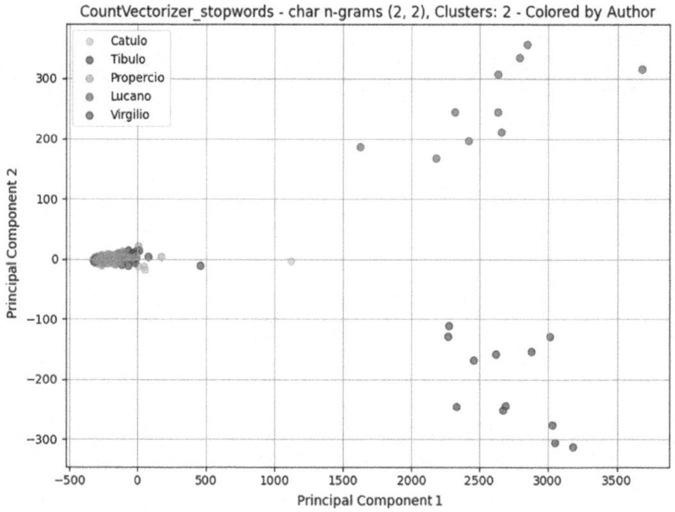

Fig. 2. Scatter plot of clustering by K Means using a frequency matrix of 2 character n-grams indicating the authors with different colors. Source: author's own work.

Applying the same technique but at the level of word n-grams, produced 3 clusters separating the elegiac poets on one side and Virgil and Lucan into two other clearly differentiated clusters (Figs. 3 and 4).

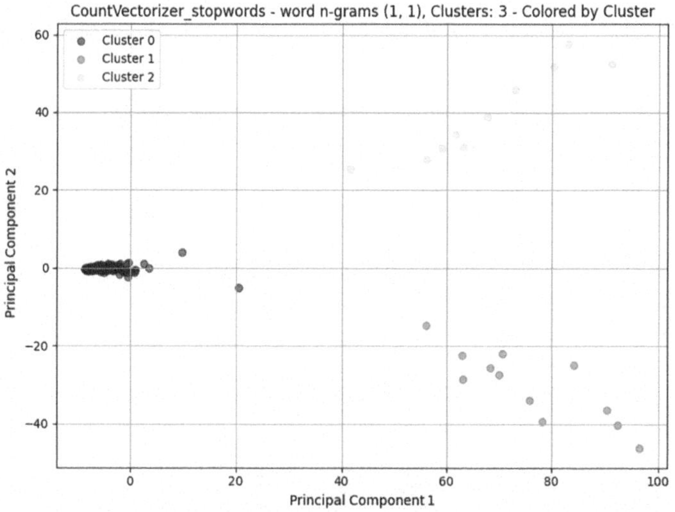

Fig. 3. Scatter plot of clustering by K Means using a frequency matrix of 1 word n-gram indicating the clusters with different colors. Source: author's own work.

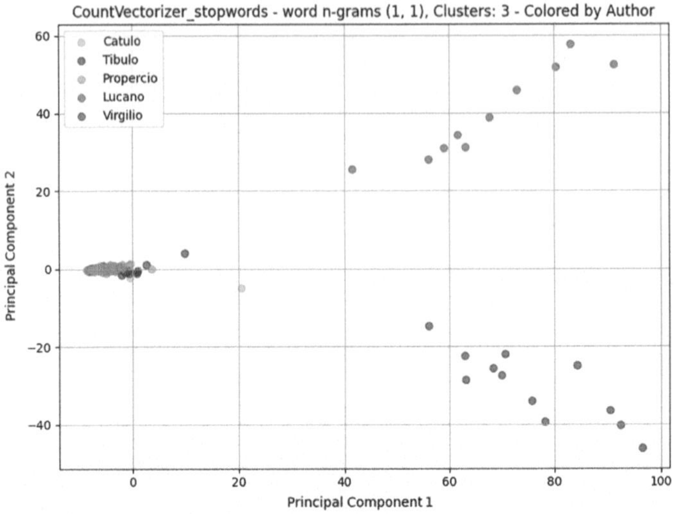

Fig. 4. Scatter plot of clustering by K Means using a frequency matrix of 1 word n-gram indicating the authors with different colors. Source: author's own work.

The use of a TF-IDF matrix both at the character and word levels produced scatter plots where the points (documents) were more dispersed across the plane. Specifically, at the level of 2 character n-grams, the poems of the epic authors are near those of Tibullus and Propertius, but occupy a distinct sector within the cluster. Conversely, the majority of Catullus's poetry is separated into a much less cohesive cluster (Figs. 5 and 6). At the level of word n-grams, the poetry of the epic authors coalesced into one cluster, and that

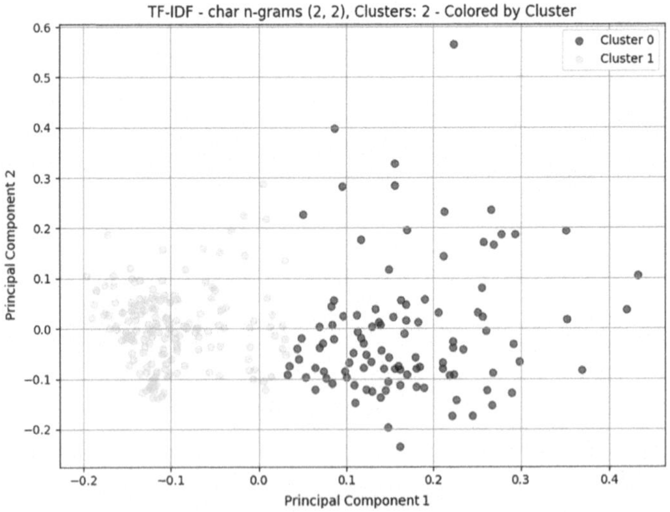

Fig. 5. Scatter plot of clustering by K Means using a TF-IDF matrix of 2 character n-grams indicating the clusters with different colors. Source: author's own work.

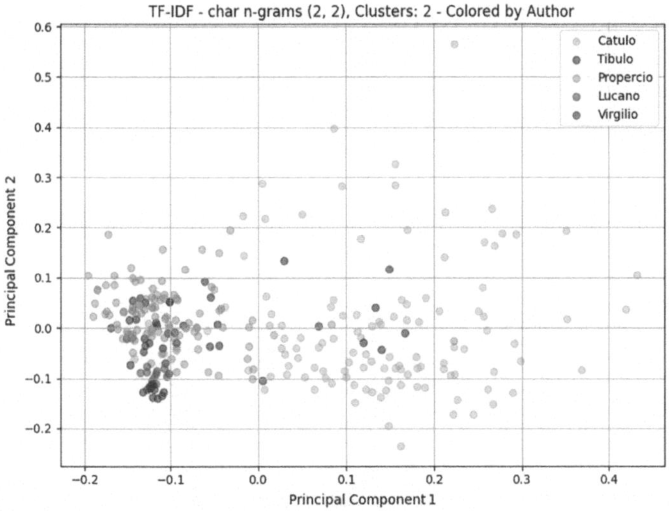

Fig. 6. Scatter plot of clustering by K Means using a TF-IDF matrix of 2 character n-grams indicating the authors with different colors. Source: author's own work.

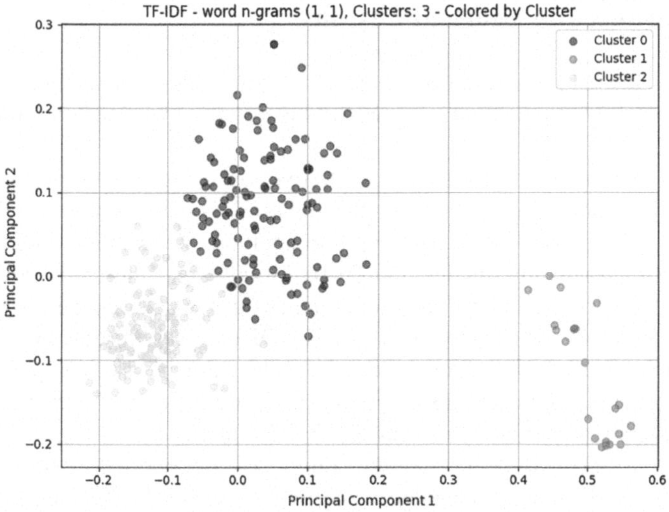

Fig. 7. Scatter plot of clustering by K Means using a TF-IDF matrix of 1 word n-gram indicating the clusters with different colors. Source: author's own work.

of Tibullus and Propertius formed another, albeit in close proximity to a third cluster encompassing nearly all of Catullus's poetry along with some texts from Tibullus. An interesting avenue for future investigation would be to explore why, using this technique, these documents from Tibullus appear to bear such a degree of similarity to those of Catullus (Figs. 7 and 8).

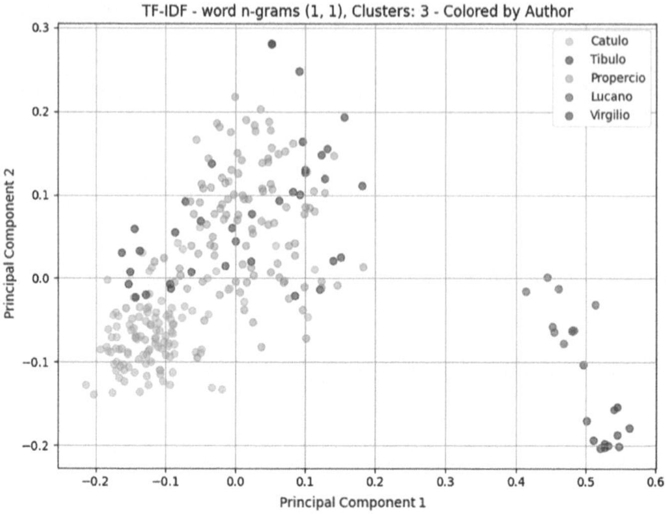

Fig. 8. Scatter plot of clustering by K Means using a TF-IDF matrix of 1 word n-gram indicating the authors with different colors. Source: author's own work.

7 Conclusions and Learned Lessons

Tests were conducted using two different types of stopwords, with negligible disparities observed for the K Means method using the Silhouette index to define the optimal number of clusters.

Different representations for the corpus were tested using various ranges of characters and word n-grams. The clusters with the highest Silhouette values were those using 2-character n-grams and 1-word n-gram, both applying the traditional Bag of Words method with stopwords filtering and the TF-IDF weighting. Contrary to the Silhouette results, which were close to 1 for the traditional frequency counting and stopwords filtering method and close to zero for the use of TF-IDF matrices, the outcomes from decision tree training presented conflicting data. The calculation of feature importance using Entropy, Information Gain, and Information Gain Ratio showed a better distribution of importance among the different features for TF-IDF matrices.

However, irrespective of the technique employed, the optimal number of clusters recommended by Silhouette remained consistent at the level of 2-character n-grams (two clusters) and 1-word n-gram (three clusters). The scatter plots obtained from the different representations show a match with the stylistic distribution reported by Forstall et. al. [8] who used a Support Vector Machine (SVM) approach to test the influence of Catullus on the poetry of Paul the Deacon[2].

Since this is a preliminary exploratory analysis, there is still a need to apply some other techniques such as variable ranges of character and word n-grams (only fixed ranges were used in this study), other similarity measures such as Jaccard, Cosine, or Soft Cosine, or other clustering methods like Gaussian Mixture Models, Density-based

[2] For a colored version of the scatter plot, see Coffe et al. [7].

spatial clustering of applications with noise (DBSCAN), or even hierarchical clustering methods. As for the representation of the documents, there is also a need to explore representation techniques with Embeddings like those recently developed by Burns et al., Bamman et al., and Johnson et al. [1, 3, 4, 11].

References

1. Bamman, D., Burns, P.J.: Latin BERT: a contextual language model for classical philology (2020). http://arxiv.org/abs/2009.10053, https://doi.org/10.48550/arXiv.2009.10053
2. Bracco, G., et al.: Data mining tools and GRID infrastructure for Assyriology text analysis (an Old-Babylonian situation studied through text analysis and data mining tools). In: RAI-Rencontre Assyriologique Internationale- Private and State in the Ancient Near East, Belgium (2013)
3. Burns, P.J.: Building a text analysis pipeline for classical languages. In: Berti, M. (ed.) Digital Classical Philology. Ancient Greek and Latin in the Digital Revolution, pp. 159–176 Walter de Gruyter GmbH, Berlin - Boston (2019)
4. Burns, P.J.: LatinCy: synthetic trained pipelines for Latin NLP (2023). http://arxiv.org/abs/2305.04365, https://doi.org/10.48550/arXiv.2305.04365
5. Cantaluppi, G., Passarotti, M.: Clustering the corpus of seneca: a lexical-based approach. In: Carpita, M., et al. (eds.) Advances in Latent Variables: Methods, Models and Applications, pp. 13–25. Springer, Cham (2015). https://doi.org/10.1007/10104_2014_6
6. Cerrato, L.M., Chavez, R.F.: Perseus classics collection: an overview. https://www.perseus.tufts.edu/hopper/text?doc=Perseus:text:1999.04.0053. Accessed 24 Mar 2023
7. Coffee, N., et al.: Modelling the interpretation of literary allusion with machine learning techniques. J. Digit. Humanit. 478–479 (2013)
8. Forstall, C.W., et al.: Evidence of intertextuality: investigating Paul the Deacon's Angustae Vitae. Lit. Linguist. Comput. **26**(3), 285–296 (2011). https://doi.org/10.1093/llc/fqr029
9. Forstall, C.W., Scheirer, W.: A statistical stylistic study of Latin elegiac couplets. Presented at the (2010)
10. Greenough, J.B.: The Bucolics, AEneid, and Georgics of Virgil. Ginn, Boston (1900)
11. Johnson, K.P., et al.: The classical language toolkit: an NLP framework for pre-modern languages. In: Ji, H., et al. (eds.) Proceedings of the 59th Annual Meeting of the Association for Computational Linguistics and the 11th International Joint Conference on Natural Language Processing: System Demonstrations, pp. 20–29 Association for Computational Linguistics, Online (2021). https://doi.org/10.18653/v1/2021.acl-demo.3
12. Lewis, C.S.: La alegoría del amor: un estudio sobre tradición medieval. Encuentro, Madrid (1936)
13. Lloyd, S.: Least squares quantization in PCM. IEEE Trans. Inf. Theory **28**(2), 129–137 (1982). https://doi.org/10.1109/TIT.1982.1056489
14. Martins, A., et al.: Historia augusta authorship: an approach based on measurements of complex networks. Appl. Netw. Sci. **6**(1), 1–23 (2021). https://doi.org/10.1007/s41109-021-00390-7
15. Merrill, E.T.: Catullus; edited by Elmer Truesdell Merrill. Boston Ginn (1893)
16. Moretti, F.: Distant Reading. Verso (2013)
17. Müller, L.: Sex. Propertii Elegiae. Teubner, Leipzig (1898)
18. Nagy, B.: Rhyme in classical Latin poetry: stylistic or stochastic? Digit. Scholarsh. Humanit. **37**(4), 1097–1118 (2022). https://doi.org/10.1093/llc/fqab105
19. Nusch, C.J.: Las Edades del Amor: una propuesta para el proyecto Aetates Amoris destinado a la poesía amorosa. Universidad Nacional de Educación a Distancia (UNED) (2021). https://doi.org/10.35537/10915/125629

20. Nusch, C.J.: Una breve exploración de la terminología amorosa en los corpora catullianum, tibullianum y propertianum con métodos y herramientas computacionales: etiquetado gramatical, lemas, bigramas y co-apariciones. Rev. Humanidades Digit. **9** (2024). https://doi.org/10.5944/rhd.vol.9.2024.38680
21. Postgate, J.P.: Tibulli aliorumque carminum libri tres. Scriptorum classicorum bibliotheca Oxoniensis, Oxford (1915)
22. Quinlan, J.R.: Induction of decision trees. Mach. Learn. **1**(1), 81–106 (1986). https://doi.org/10.1007/BF00116251
23. Ramsay, S.: Reading Machines: Toward an Algorithmic Criticism. University of Illinois Press (2011)
24. Rousseeuw, P.J.: Silhouettes: a graphical aid to the interpretation and validation of cluster analysis. J. Comput. Appl. Math. **20**, 53–65 (1987). https://doi.org/10.1016/0377-0427(87)90125-7
25. Salton, G., McGill, M.J.: Introduction to Modern Information Retrieval. McGraw-Hill Inc, New York (1986)
26. Shannon, C.E.: A mathematical theory of communication. Bell Syst. Tech. J. **27**(3), 379–423 (1948). https://doi.org/10.1002/j.1538-7305.1948.tb01338.x
27. Spärck Jones, K.: A statistical interpretation of term specificity and its application in retrieval. J. Doc. **28**(1), 11–21 (1972). https://doi.org/10.1108/eb026526
28. Weise, C.H.: Pharsaliae Libri X. M. Annaeus Lucanus. G. Bassus, Leipzig (1935)
29. Perseus Digital Library Homepage. https://www.perseus.tufts.edu/hopper/
30. Perseus Digital Library Stopwords. https://www.perseus.tufts.edu/hopper/stopwords
31. Stopwords ISO. https://github.com/stopwords-iso/stopwords-iso/blob/master/README.md

Management Model in Web Viewers that Incorporate Open Data - Case Study Geovisor SIG-SIR

Carlos A. Meneses E.(✉), Julio C. Chavarro P., and Cesar A. Jaramillo A.

Universidad Tecnológica de Pereira, Pereira, Colombia
{cmeneses,jchavar,swokosky}@utp.edu.co

Abstract. To display geographic data, Geoviewers are used that allow user interaction with cartographic data. Some viewing platforms are open source and others proprietary, but in general they do not meet the needs raised in the Law of Transparency and the Right of Access to National Public Information in Colombia, by which public entities have the obligation to disclose those primary data, which are in the public domain and are in standard and interoperable formats to facilitate access and reuse. The SIG-SIR platform is an open source web platform for the visualization of geographic information in the Eje Cafetero region used by autonomous corporations. This aforementioned law entails extending the functionalities and structuring of geographic data to guarantee the validity, efficiency and security of the information, facilitating the usability and interoperability of those spatial data disclosed. The model presented extends the functionalities and allows the visualization of geographic data within the framework of the Law that establishes the obligation to publish data that are public in nature to allow timely access to users. With this work, it is possible to determine the implications on the quality attributes of spatial information through a conceptual model, instantiated through the extension to the GIS-SIR viewer so that it has the capacity to publish open geographic data by adding new functionalities that allow giving compliance with the guidelines of the open data law.

Keywords: Geographic viewer · Open data · Geographic Information Systems

1 Introduction

In Colombia, access to public information is a right enshrined in the 1991 Constitution; In 2014, to reinforce compliance with this right and based on the Digital Government Policy, the Law of Transparency and the Right of Access to National Public Information [1], emerged, which requires public entities to disclose those primary or raw data, which are in standard and interoperable formats that facilitate access and reuse. These data fulfill public functions and are made available to any citizen freely and without restrictions, so that third parties can reuse them and create services derived from them.

A geographic information system (GIS) is "a computer tool capable of managing and analyzing information, with a view to solving territorial and environmental-based

V. Agredo-Delgado et al. (Eds.): DECISIONING 2024, CCIS 2369, pp. 135–146, 2025.
https://doi.org/10.1007/978-3-031-91690-8_11

problems" [2]. GIS are multipurpose tools that are used to solve spatial problems for cadastral management, risk prevention and market analysis. GIS allows any type of data to be related to a geographic location, in this way any distribution of resources can be located geographically. The basic functions of a GIS are the storage, visualization, query and analysis of spatial data.

There are various open source applications in which you can store and manage data, produce maps and create 2D and 3D data visualizations, perform raster and vector spatial analysis, geostatistical analysis, 3D analysis, satellite image analysis, automate tasks, capture data in the field, develop desktop applications, create web services or create web applications. [3].

The Regional Information System (SIR) of the Universidad Tecnológica de Pereira (UTP) contains a repository of spatial data that has been collected for more than a decade.

In the SIR, a Geographic Information System (GIS) has been developed that allows the use of atmospheric and geographic information, as a basis for analytical projects and visualization of useful data for the Autonomous Corporations of the Eje Cafetero Region.

With the Law of Transparency and the Right of Access to National Public Information, a new need has been created for autonomous corporations and that is, how to comply with this regulation to disclose primary spatial data, which are in standard and interoperable formats for facilitate their access and reuse.

Satisfying these regulations for the dissemination of open spatial data implies carrying out new developments as extensions of GIS. These extensions entail additional licensing and development costs unless open source technological tools are incorporated.

The research process was supported by the literature review and content analysis of documents with public policies on open data associated with geographic visualization systems. This study was carried out with an exploratory qualitative approach [4], based on the research question: What are the functionalities that extend a geographic data visualization system to incorporate the open data policy that allows autonomous corporations to comply with the spatial data disclosure regulations?

To incorporate open data into the geoviewer, a structured process was followed that ensures the quality and usefulness of the geospatial information. This methodology includes several stages in which there is a bibliographic review for the use of open data in geoviewers, the determination of the functionalities regarding the incorporation, publication and visualization of open data, implementation of the policy in the technological platform and validation to verify compliance with the functional requirements of the extension (Fig. 1).

With this work, it is possible to determine the implications on the quality attributes of spatial information through a conceptual model, instantiated through the extension to the GIS-SIR viewer so that it has the capacity to publish open geographic data by adding new functionalities that allow giving compliance with the guidelines of the aforementioned law.

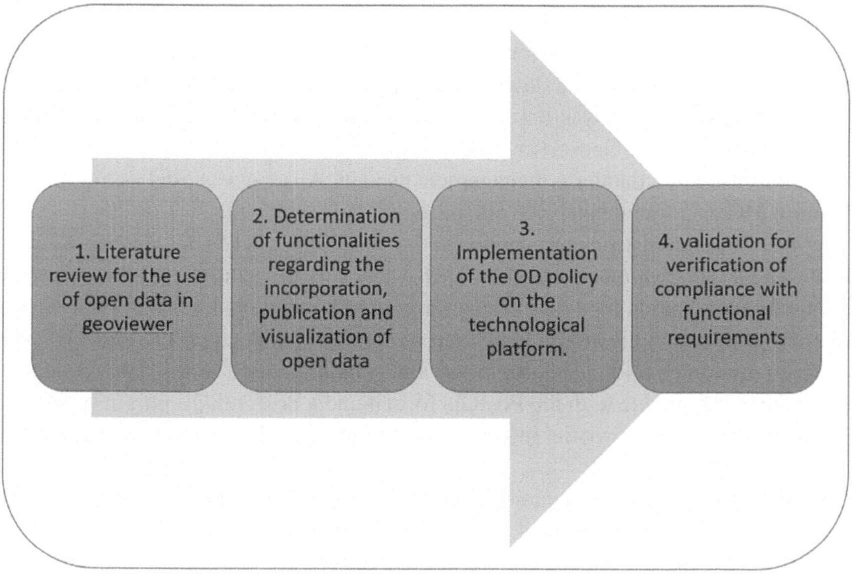

Fig. 1. Methodology for Construction process of the GIS-SIR Model (own authorship).

2 Literature Review

Some works have been aimed at the implementation of Geoviewers using open source tools, as is the case of the project "*Implementación de un Geovisor web para la información geográfica del MIES utilizando bases de datos espaciales y plataformas OpenGIS*" [5], in which carried out the implementation of a technological tool by the MIES (Ministry of Economic and Social Inclusion of Ecuador) that allows the integration, management and administration of geodata, through a database and web services that facilitate access to information of the entity by the users. In the implementation, ArcGis and open source technologies were used, for data management the PostgreSQL database engine was used together with the PostGis extension with geographic information objects and PHP was used for the backend and HTML with the Google Maps library for the frontend.

NASA has created a geographic information system, called *NASA World Wind*, that provides graphical access to terabytes of images and elevation models of planets and other celestial objects for mission operations, including satellite data. World Wind is also a customizable system that can be integrated as part of other applications. The international community has made significant open source contributions to make World Wind what it is today [6]. These projects are developed independently and externally to NASA taking advantage of its public open source version.

The research "*Desarrollo de un visor geográfico web para la gestión de información geodésica nacional*" from the Francisco José de Caldas District University in Colombia develops a geographic web viewer called RGN VIEWER. The viewer integrates geodetic data from different processes into a single source of information, allowing the visualization, consultation and download of data in a consistent and organized manner.

The visor consolidates data from different processes into a single source of information with its own functionalities for navigation on the map; In addition, it serves as a tool for viewing, consulting and downloading information in a consistent and organized manner. The development was based on the incremental model with analysis, design and development stages, Geoserver was used as a spatial data server, PostgreSQL with PostGIS was used as a database management system, Apache was used as a web server and Heron MC as a framework or workspace. [7].

Another implementation corresponds to the "*Visor Geográfico del Sistema Nacional de Información utilizando software libre*" [8], a new version of the Geographic Viewer of the National Information System of Ecuador with new functionalities that improve user interaction with the application. Open source tools such as PostgreSQL and PHP were used in the implementation. The migration and standardization of the data was carried out to make it compatible with the PostGis format and a PostgreSQL plugin specialized in the management of geospatial information, and the OpenLayers library was used for the frontend.

The Bogotá DC Environmental Geographic Viewer, [9] is the tool enabled by the District Environment Secretariat of Bogotá, to make environmental information that is of missionality available to academia, citizens and productive sectors. of the entity, on the environmental state of the city. The environmental geographic viewer based on the concept of policies, standards and interoperability of the Spatial Data Infrastructure for the Capital District (IDECA), and developed with free and open source software tools. The citizen is a participant in the generation and contribution of the entity's geographic data, supported by online tools on the Web platform and mobile devices.

In Mexico, government agencies are regulated by the General Law of Transparency and Access to Public Information. In the State of Colima, the Cadastre Directorate has a system to provide access to cadastral information, however, this system has been exceeded in the services it provides and in its availability, due to being implemented with registration software. Discharge. For this reason, the project Implementation of a Cadastral Geoportal for the Visualization of Cartography and Integration of Geospatial Services has been developed using open source technologies (Leaflet, CodeIgniter, GeoServer, PostGIS, among others) [10]. In the software engineering process, the Unified Agile Process (PUA) development methodology was used. The Geoportal includes a cartographic viewer for rendering and querying layers, an administration module for managing layers, geospatial services and users, and a geospatial services module with the Map Web Service standard so that the information can be interoperable.

There are many Geovisors that have been developed using open source to respond to specific needs of users and with a focus oriented to some productive sectors, as well as those for general use, but that do not respond to the specific needs that incorporate free access functionalities. to information based on georeferenced spatial data.

Geovision: "*una infraestructura abierta de datos espaciales*". This research from the State Distance University of Costa Rica presents the development of an open Spatial Data Infrastructure (SDI) called Geovision. This is an open IDE that allows the initial formation of a network of geoinformation suppliers and users, up to the enabling and publication of online geoinformation services; In addition, it facilitates the publication and exchange of geospatial information in accessible formats both for users without technical experience, as well as for specialized users. [11].

DERGeo is a cloud-based virtual interaction environment that allows access and interaction with free data and information related to produced road or thematic maps, as well as vector data, applications developed in the municipality and other information pertinent to the Highway System of the Federal District (SRDF), allows the management of the history of publications of road maps, SRDF legislation, downloads of public and open data both produced by the Department of Highways of the Federal District (DER/DF) and by other entities. Also, it is possible to access other functionalities in applications developed for specific topics, such as the Analytical Panel of Road Accidents of the Federal District (PARE/DF) and the creation and printing of personalized maps, in addition to consulting a series of spatial topics relevant to the SRDF [12].

3 Determination of the Functionalities that Incorporate Open Data in SIG-SIR

The Law on Transparency and Access to National Public Information establishes the obligation for public entities to publish open data taking into account the exceptions to access to information, associated with classified and reserved information established by third parties. Furthermore, the publication of open data must occur on websites free of charge, so that they are accessible to the general public, and arranged in formats that allow their use and reuse under an open license [13].

The issuance of the standard required an analysis of the existing functionalities in the SIG-SIR platform, concluding non-conformity with the new regulatory framework. Likewise, the lack of platforms available to manage geospatial data for CorpoCaldas that allow compliance with open data guidelines and that have also been carried out with open source technologies was established.

The activities developed in the methodological process included the identification of the minimum and mandatory requirements in order to comply with the open data policy, the identification of the deficiencies of the GIS-SIR platform with respect to the open data policy, the categorization of the data that is published on the platform, the specification of the data model for the platform, and finally, the implementation of the adjustments to the platform. The Fig. 2 shows the process by which the construction of the GIS-SIR model is carried out, corresponding to the objective of this work.

To identify the minimum and mandatory requirements in order to comply with the open data policy as a basis for carrying out the process model, an analysis of the National Open Data Policy was carried out, expressed in different standards enshrined in Article 74 of the Political Constitution of Colombia [14] that defines the concept of open data; Law 1712 of 2014 [1], with the principles by which the developments that comply with this law must be governed, such as the principle of free, effectiveness and quality of information, the availability of information through the website and the restrictions for the publication of data are defined; Decree 1078 of 2015 [15] determines the principles and foundations of the Online Government strategy in relation to the opening and reuse of public data to promote participation and control by citizens; the Guide for the Use and Exploitation of Open Data Colombia [16] and the ISO 19115 standard – "Geographic

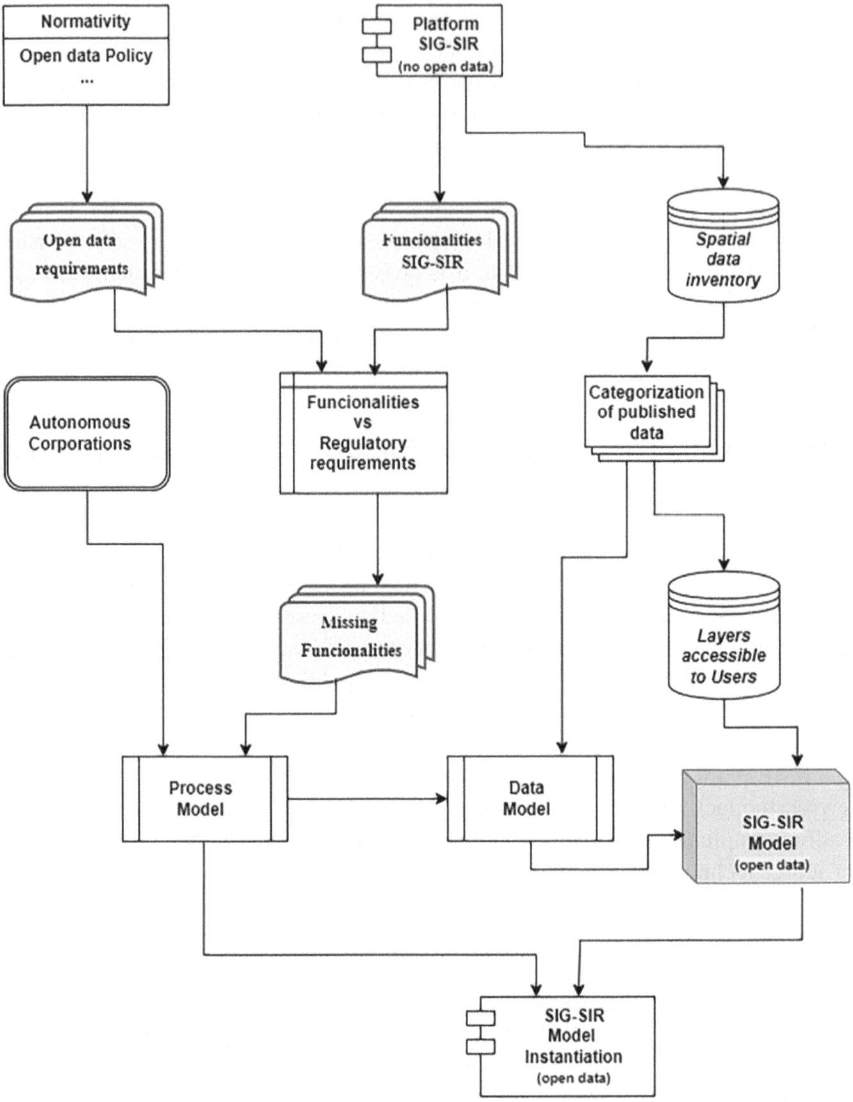

Fig. 2. Construction process of the GIS-SIR Model (own authorship).

information – Metadata" [17] regarding the metadata that is associated with each layer, and the monitoring of the quality of the data. Data uploaded to the platform.

To identify the shortcomings of the SIG-SIR platform with respect to the open data policy, a list was made of the functionalities that the SIG-SIR platform had and the functionalities that were associated with the requirements for compliance with the open-data law. data. A matrix of functionalities was created against regulatory requirements and subsequently with this information a cross-reference was made to obtain the missing functionalities, categorizing the functional and non-functional requirements to be implemented, with which the Process Model for the publication of Data Open could be established.

Among the missing functionalities that were determined are access to the information that the Corporation includes in open data, the management and visualization of the information layers and availability of the application.

4 Extension to the Geographic Information System SIG-SIR

The proposed model that includes the extension of the GIS-SIR Geoviewer was structured in two System Components: the Viewer Module, in which users will be able to observe and make the request to download layers, and the Layer Management and Visualization Module. Download log for Administrator management. In the Viewer Module, the information on the workspaces with their associated layers was arranged in a tree structure to facilitate searches. Additionally, existing functionalities were migrated to the new version of Geovisor. Figure 3 shows the GIS-SIR Model structured by components and the functionalities that determine the extension of the GIS-SIR Geovisor, which satisfies the legal provisions for the use and access of open spatial data.

The following Fig. 4 presents the Model Visualization Section and the Missing Functionalities regarding the download of open data information and the visualization of information repositories within the framework of the open data law.

In the Data Model for the platform (Entity Relationship Diagram, see Fig. 5) the entities were determined with their attributes and relationships that allow modeling the data categorized according to the layers stored for management and visualization. The resulting tables in the Relational Model correspond to the Users (with their roles and credentials), the work spaces that exist in the Corporation and that are the containers of the layers, the information of the layers, both their access level and the url that the service consumes to bring the layer, and the download requests of the existing layers on the platform, among others.

To instantiate the model, the Geovisor SIG-SIR platform was implemented using open source technologies, applying a classic approach to software engineering during the product life cycle, including the maintenance stage in aspects such as updating, support and adequacy; in addition to the testing, validation and verification process of the versioned product obtained.

5 Validation of the Geographic Information System SIG-SIR

The platform has different views that range from the table where the different layers that can be viewed are located, as well as the viewer where the graphic information can be observed. The viewer starts by loading the Open Street Map Topographic basemap by default and downloads services and other basemaps, as well as the layer that has been chosen for loading. Includes the search bar and the zoom tool in the interface; as well as access to the basemap change tool and the tool to control the layers. From this, you can find the geographic information download tool.

The Fig. 6, shows an example of visualization by layers, corresponding to the output of the functionality that allows viewing layers or in the filtered layers report. You

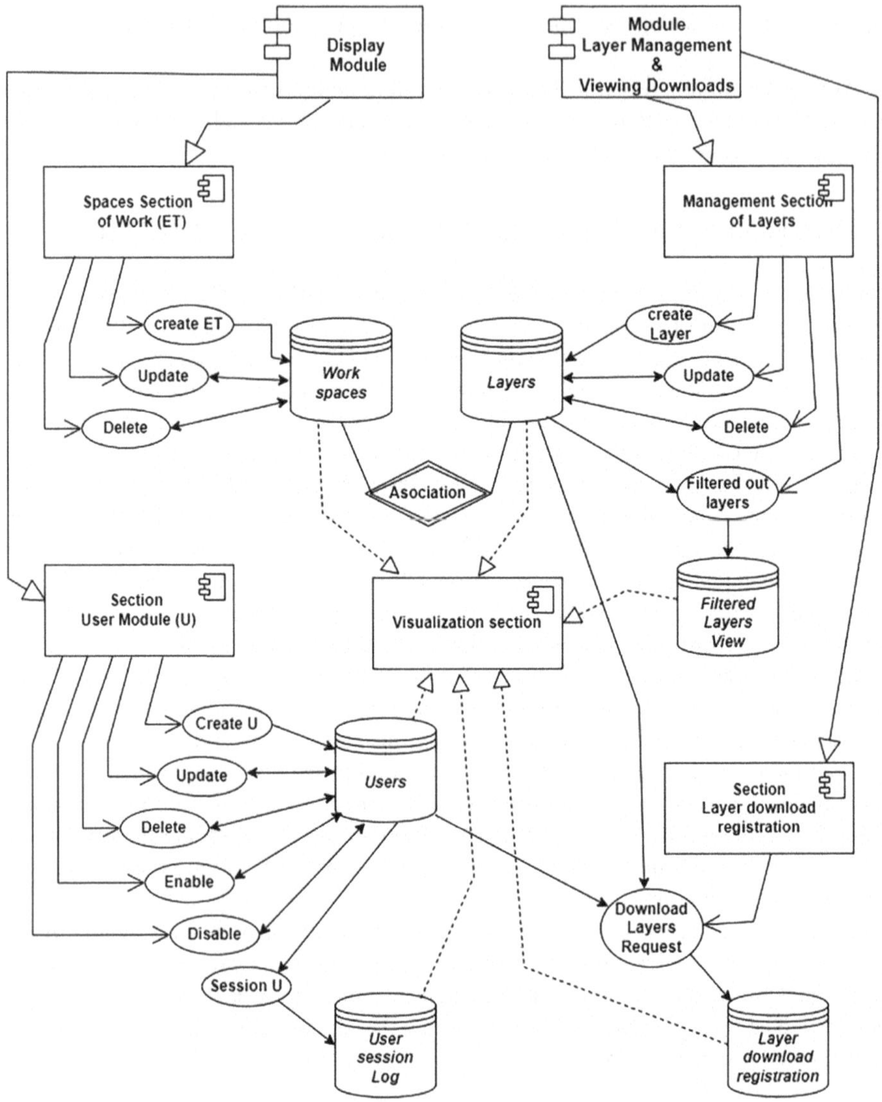

Fig. 3. GIS-SIR model by components and functionalities (own authorship).

can search from cities, municipalities, departments or addresses. It has an excellent geographic search engine.

To validate and categorize the data that is published on the SIG-SIR platform, an inventory was made and classified according to two criteria: the origin of the data (public or private, and verifying the validity of those that are property of third parties) and the sensitivity of the data, to determine what data is visible in each layer and the authorization levels to view layers that require it. The result of this process was the information on the

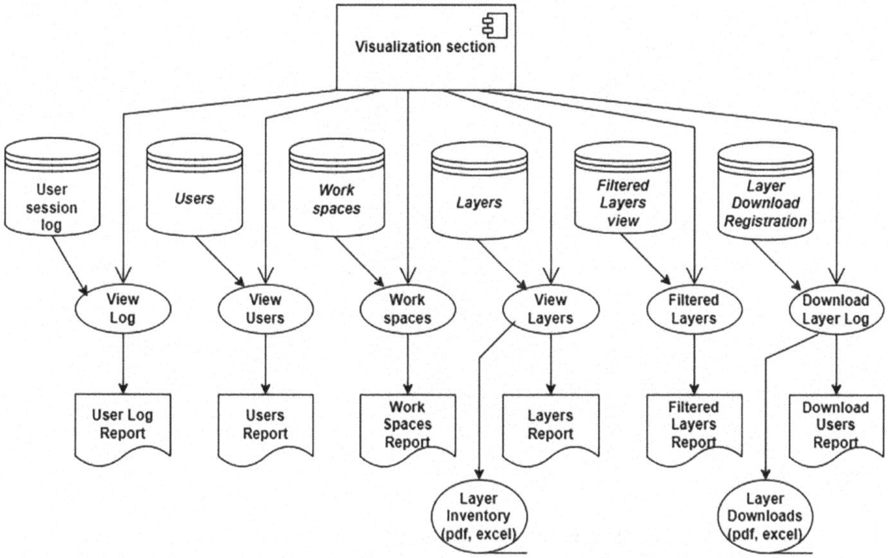

Fig. 4. Visualization of information in the SIG-SIR Model (own authorship).

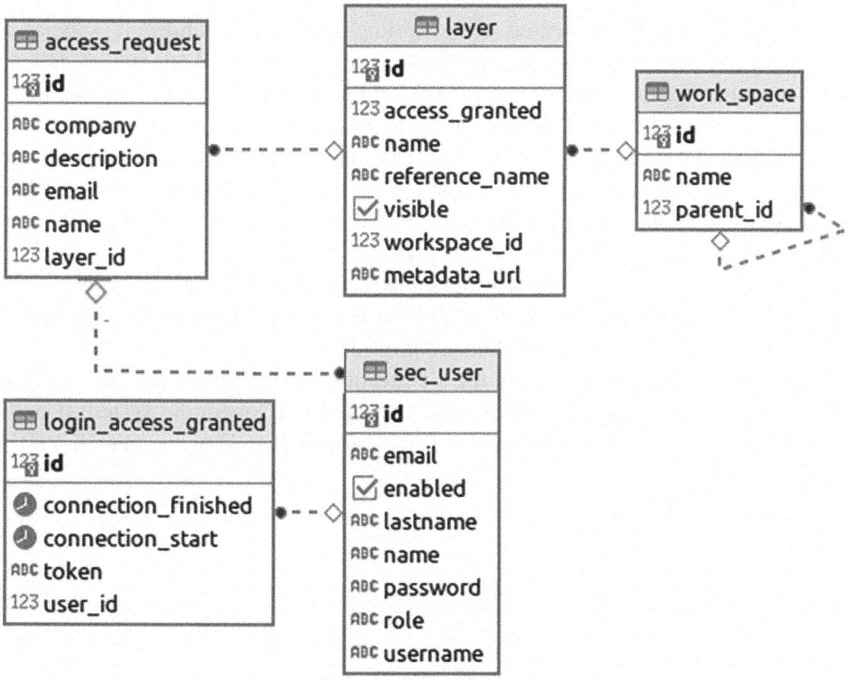

Fig. 5. Data model [4]

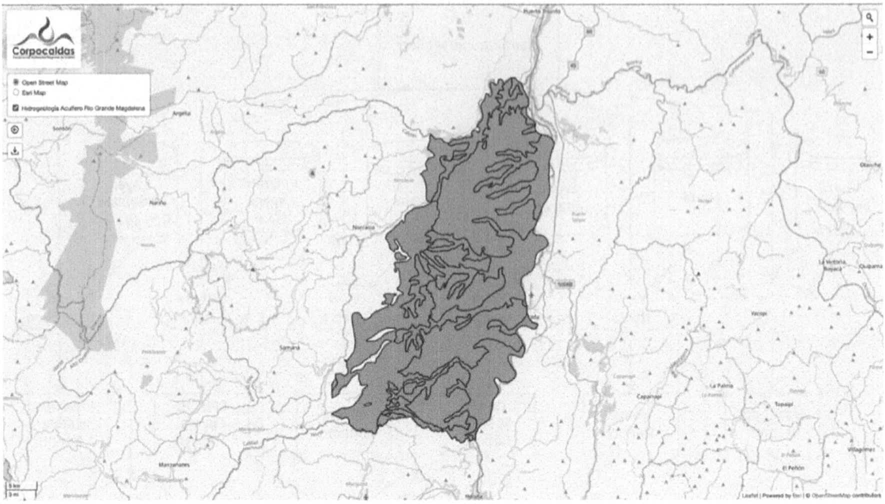

Fig. 6. Layer visualization view [4].

stored layers (classified according to the previous criteria) with their access permissions by the users.

The Backend was implemented using Spring Boot (Java Framework specialized in creating micro web services) and GeoServer (Server used to share spatial data and perform layer management and storage). The Frontend (see Fig. 7) was developed using Angular 8 (JavaScript Framework for creating dynamic views) and Leaflet JS (JavaScript Framework for creating and displaying interactive maps, and for loading layers with their metadata). In addition, the user interface was redesigned, in which an alert was added notifying that this application complies with open-data laws. In the management of open data, the PostgreSQL database engine was used.

It is possible to view the different downloads that have been made in the system, from which the records can be exported in both Excel and PDF formats. Each of the fields has a filter to search for more detailed information.

The desired working environment for the execution of the SIG-SIR Geovisor corresponds to the GeoServer server, which works on the Linux operating system (CentOS 8, Debian) or Windows 10, with Apache Tomcat 9 and Java Development Kit (JDK) version 8.

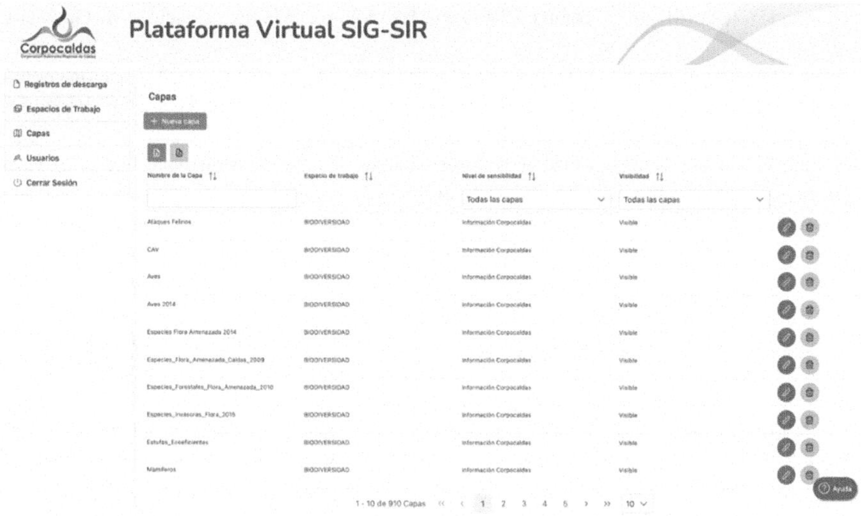

Fig. 7. Layer management section [13].

6 Conclusions

The extension to the GIS-SIR system is now available and is used by users of the Corporación Autónoma Regional de Caldas (CorpoCaldas), who benefit from being able to view and download the information they need from official sources, guaranteeing the validity of the data and reinforcing availability. of information at any time.

It was possible to implement one of the principles of the Open Data Law, improving governance and citizen participation through the opening of spatial data.

The adaptation carried out with the incorporation of the extension to the SIG-SIR platform was completed successfully, managing to migrate all the functionalities, improving the user experience visually and being more intuitive interactively; In addition, open-data standards were complied with so that access to public data is carried out efficiently and truthfully.

Open source technologies were used, with which an improvement in the performance and efficiency of executed processes could be achieved.

With the instantiation of the SIG_SIR Geovisor Extension Model, transparency in the use of data is favored, and allows the use of a useful tool in economic development, material well-being, and the strengthening of equity and social control.

References

1. Función Pública. Ley 712 de 2014. Ley de Transparencia y del Derecho de Acceso a la Información Pública Nacional. Congreso de la República (2014). https://www.funcionpublica.gov.co/eva/gestornormativo/norma.php?i=56882. Accessed 20 Feb 2024
2. Santos Preciado, J.M.: Sistemas de información geográfica, ed. UNED, p. 462 (2020)
3. Mapping GIS. https://mappinggis.com/2022/07/aplicaciones-gis-open-source/. Accessed 11 Apr 2024

4. Hernández, R., Collado, C., Baptista, M.D.P.: Metodología de la Investigación. Mc Graw Hill. (2014)
5. Baez Muñoz, M.F., Resl, R.: Implementación de un geovisor web para la información geográfica del MIES utilizando bases de datos espaciales y plataformas OpenGIS. Universidad San Francisco de Quito, Ed., Quito (2013)
6. Bell, D.G., et al.: NASA world wind: opensource GIS for mission operations. In: IEEE Aerospace Conference, Big Sky, MT, USA (2007)
7. Yepez, D.G., Ruiz, V.M.: Desarrollo de un visor geográfico web para la gestión de información geodésica nacional. Repositorio Universidad Francisco José de Caldas, Bogotá (2019)
8. Tulcanaza Revelo, J.P.: Visor Geográfico del Sistema Nacional de Información utilizando software libre. Universidad Central del Ecuador, Ed. (2016)
9. Secretaría Distrital de Ambiente. Datos Abiertos Bogotá (2020). https://datosabiertos.bogota.gov.co/dataset/a955f8f0-6119-416c-819a-51a0e3e29df1?_external=True. Accessed 08 Apr 2024
10. Gaytán Lugo, M., Farías Mendoza, N., Chávez Valdez, R., Cervantes Zambrano, F.: Implementación de un Geoportal Catastral para Visualización de Cartografía e Integración de Servicios Geoespaciales. Rev. Int. Invest. Innov. Tecnol. **8**(45) (2020)
11. Campos-Vargas, C., Mora-Zamora, R., Segura-Castillo, A.: Geovisión: una infraestructura abierta de datos espaciales. Tecnol. Marcha **28**(3), 15–24 (2015)
12. Santos, J.P., Guimarães, P.H., Alves Lorena da Silva, B., Rosa Campani, A., Vieira de Oliveira, J.M.: DERGeo: geovisualizador de informações geográficas para gestão do sistema rodoviário do distrito federal. Rev. Brasileira Transp. **3**(1), 62–85 (2023)
13. Castrillón, J.A.: Retos derivados de la Política Nacional de Datos Abiertos en Corporaciones Autónomas Regionales para el acceso de información geográfica a través de tecnologías open source. Universidad Tecnológica de Pereira, Pereira (2022)
14. República de Colombia. Constitución Política de Colombia art 74 (1991). https://www.mincit.gov.co/ministerio/normograma-sig/procesos-estrategicos/gestion-de-informacion-y-comunicacion/constitucion-politica/derechos/articulo-74.aspx#:~:text=Todas%20las%20personas%20tienen%20derecho,El%20secreto%20profesional%20es%20inviolable. Accessed 09 Apr 2024
15. SUIN – Juriscol. Ley 1078 (2015). https://www.suin-juriscol.gov.co/viewDocument.asp?id=30019521. Accessed 09 Apr 2024
16. Datos Abiertos Colombia. Guia para el Aprovechamiento de Datos Abiertos de Colombia. https://herramientas.datos.gov.co/sites/default/files/Guia%20de%20Datos%20Abiertos%20de%20Colombia.pdf. Accessed 09 Apr 2024
17. ISO. ISO 19115 Geographic Information – Metadata (2019). https://www.iso.org/standard/53798.html. Accessed 09 Apr 2024

Modeling Blockchain, Artificial Intelligence, and New Public Management Through a Semantic Ontology

Jhon Wilder Sánchez-Obando[1(✉)], Luis Fernando Castillo Ossa[2,3], and Néstor Darío Duque-Méndez[4]

[1] Departamento de Ingeniería Industrial, Corporación universitaria Minuto de Dios, Pereira, Risaralda, Colombia
jwsanchezo@unal.edu.co

[2] Grupo de Investigación en Inteligencia Artificial, Universidad de Caldas, Caldas, Manizales, Caldas, Colombia
lfcastilloos@unal.edu.co, luis.castillo@ucaldas.edu.co

[3] Departamento de Ingeniería Industrial, Universidad Nacional de Colombia sede Manizales, Manizales, Colombia

[4] Facultad de Administración, Grupo de Ambientes inteligentes y Adaptativos GAIA, Universidad Nacional de Colombia, Bogotá, Colombia
ndduqueme@unal.edu.co

Abstract. The integration of blockchain and artificial intelligence in new public management is an area of growing interest within academic communities worldwide. This article initiates a discussion on the theories, methods, tools, and practices of modeling and reasoning with blockchain, artificial intelligence, and new public management through a semantic ontology. This paper sets itself apart from related research by developing a semantic ontology that extends beyond a mere taxonomy of blockchain and artificial intelligence technology usage in the field of new public management. It also suggests the adoption of a cooperative procedure for future research to build the proposed ontological model. Based on the requirements for using blockchain and artificial intelligence technologies in new public management, an ontological model is constructed. Then, employing the reasoning rules of the ontological model, the model is processed through the HERMIT inference engine, which identifies the logical relationships among classes, subclasses, and individuals to create fields for querying the generated knowledge. In this way, the classification and generation of knowledge related to the operation of blockchain and artificial intelligence technologies in new public management are achieved.

Keywords: Artificial intelligence · Blockchain · New Public Management · Ontology

V. Agredo-Delgado et al. (Eds.): DECISIONING 2024, CCIS 2369, pp. 147–162, 2025.
https://doi.org/10.1007/978-3-031-91690-8_12

1 Introduction

According to H. R. Hassan and K. Sakah [1], it is stated that the market for blockchain and artificial intelligence technologies is projected to reach 13 trillion dollars by 2030. In addition, a taxonomy of blockchain for artificial intelligence is proposed, which defines applications of artificial intelligence in decentralized mechanisms based on: automatic computation, optimization, planning, knowledge management, reasoning, prediction, learning, and search.

Other studies have identified governance as a key challenge for the implementation of blockchains in the public sector [2, 3] and [4], other some propose exploring the implications of blockchains for public governance [5, 6]. However, blockchain governance is a challenge for public sector organizations, and instruments and models are needed to address the design, implementation, and monitoring of blockchain systems in public management [6]. According to J. Angelis and E. R. Da Silva [7], there are four levels of blockchain maturity:

- Blockchain 1.0 focused on transactions and was used for the development of cryptocurrencies in cash- related applications.
- Blockchain 2.0 adds privacy, smart contracts, and non-native tokens, among other features.
- Blockchain 3.0 incorporates decentralized applications (DApps), backend code that runs on a decentralized peer-to-peer network, expanding the uses of blockchain to different markets such as healthcare, supply chain, government, education, etc.
- Blockchain 4.0 introduces artificial intelligence (AI), which supports decentralized decision making based on reliable blockchain data without the need for direct human intervention.

On the other hand, there are a number of challenges facing blockchain based architecture for the development future research, including the consensus mechanism through the Proof of Work algorithm that consumes high levels of energy, which implies low performance in terms of transactions per second, making the application in public administration service cases difficult [8].

Based on the previous difficulty R. Beck, et al. [9], they propose a classification of blockchain and artificial intelligence assisted governance into 3 levels: micro level, meso level and macro level. The macro level is oriented to control and decision making by the public administration, assisted by blockchain architecture and artificial intelligence. According to M. Stephan, G. Marshall and M. McGinnis [10], they indicate that in a decentralized governance structure, it is a macro level governance model, because it guarantees the transparent, decentralized and participatory participation of the actors and whose decisions in the blockchain must be assisted by artificial intelligence architectures to improve the efficiency in decision making and the computational demand in the provision of services in the new public management.

On the other hand P. Dunleavy et al. [11] describe the new public management as the combination of three factors: disaggregation, competition, and incentives. M. Berzalay [12] indicates that the new public management can be understood as a field of professional discussion about how to structure, manage, and supervise government offices and the public sector as a whole, under an idea of cooperation and that discussions should focus on the implementation of efficient ways to meet the needs of citizens by an organized and diligent government, in such a way that public action should be governed by the principles of economy, efficiency, and effectiveness [13].

According to I. Jones and M. Pollit [14], eight characteristic factors of the NGP are characterized by: change in the management system approach: Identifies public administration management as the articulation of inputs (human talent), processes (basic education), outputs (people with basic knowledge measurable in knowledge tests) and results (literacy levels of the community). In G. Shen et al. [15] summarizes the above as the need to emphasize production controls.

In this paper, the architecture of the use of blockchain and artificial intelligence in the new public management is modeled from the dimension of semantic ontology. Based on the modeling and reasoning technology of semantic ontology, the identification, monitoring, and control related to the knowledge of blockchain and artificial intelligence in the new public management are achieved. This research is divided into the following sections: Section describes related work. Section indicates materials and method. Section describes results and discussion. The last section describes conclusions and future work.

1.1 Ontology

In 2000, Tim Berners-Lee, father of the World Wide Web, proposed the concept and hierarchy of the Semantic Web [16]. Based on URI (Uniform Resource Identifier) [17] and XML (Extensible Markup Language) [18], the W3C was officially launched in 2004, considered as the first basic ontology modeling language RDF (Resource Description Framework) [19]. RDF defines properties (the connection relationship between ontology resources) and resources in the form of individuals. The above provided the basis for the development of the semantic web and the way of representing relationships between knowledge entities. However, RDF has limitations in expressing concepts, classes, and attributes of entities. It can only be considered as the original ontology language.

Given the above, it is necessary to delve into the evolution of ontology modeling. To this end, it is considered that based on the inheritance of RDF grammar, the W3C was able to develop OWL (Web Ontology Language) [20], which is an ontology language oriented to the Semantic Web. OWL deepens the modeling capability by describing simple classes, individuals, simple properties, and property characteristics and Property Restrictions by defining description rules for classes and individuals, which allows ontology modeling to derive new classes or attributes in the form of equivalence based on existing classes and attributes. The introduction of ontology based on RDF enriches the expressive capability of modeling various ontologies.

Despite the strides made in ontology based on RDF, certain limitations persist. For instance, even with the existence of basic classes such as Person and data properties like Age, it is currently impossible to adequately express the concept of a PigSign Person a person whose age modulo 12 equals zero—as suggested by some 2019 research findings.

To enhance the modeling and expressive capabilities of OWL, the World Wide Web Consortium (W3C) introduced SWRL (Semantic Web Rule Language) [20], which builds upon RuleML [21]. SWRL significantly broadens the expressive scope of OWL by incorporating axioms into the ontology model. A SWRL rule is bifurcated into two segments: the antecedent and the consequent, each comprising multiple axioms. This structure facilitates the concurrent creation of numerous SWRL rules within the ontology modeling framework.

The axioms in SWRL are categorized as follows: class expression axioms, property expression axioms, data range restriction axioms, and SWRL core built-in axioms. SWRL further specifies a variety of core functionalities embedded within the swrlb description file. These functionalities are employed in the SWRL built-in axioms, enhancing the expressive power of SWRL's reasoning rules across mathematical calculations, string manipulations, and temporal processes.

1.2 Resource of Protégé

In this section, we examine the blockchain and artificial intelligence ontology model [1] as a practical example to illustrate the methodology for ontology modeling. The comprehensive ontology model is depicted in Fig. 1, although part of the content is condensed due to spatial limitations.

Initially, as a first procedure, the characteristics of the object property used in the ontology construction process are established, adhering to the grammatical rules of the OWL language, as shown in Fig. 1. Following this, the type of relationship between these object properties is delineated. Secondly, the process involves the creation of different classes within the ontological model. This includes defining the construction interactions between classes and the integration of subclasses, as well as outlining the relationships between subclasses and between classes, in accordance with the methodologies prescribed by the OWL language.

Based on Fig. 1, an observation of the syntax used in the development of the ontology highlights the relationships between classes and subclasses, as well as the characteristics of the object properties that constitute these classes and subclasses.

1.3 Tools for Ontology Modeling

Some academic communities have raised concerns regarding access to open-source tools for constructing ontology models, notable among which are Apollo [22], OILEd [23], Onto Editor [24], Protégé [25], WebODE [26], among others. Considering the open-source nature, the availability of complementary extension packages, and the extensive use of the tool, this article has chosen the Protégé tool for the ontological modeling of blockchain, artificial intelligence, and new public management.

One key feature of ontological models is the reasoning capability performed by the software unit known as a reasoner, which validates the rules of relationships among individuals, classes, etc. Protégé, developed by the Center for Biomedical Informatics at the Stanford University School of Medicine and based on the Java language, is the most widely used software for ontology editing and modeling. It serves as the primary development tool for ontology modeling in the Semantic Web. The latest release is version 5.6.1. A detailed introduction to the Protégé menu functions and their application is available in reference [27].

Utilizing Protégé for ontology modeling means that modelers are no longer burdened by the intricate grammatical rules of the description language typically used in

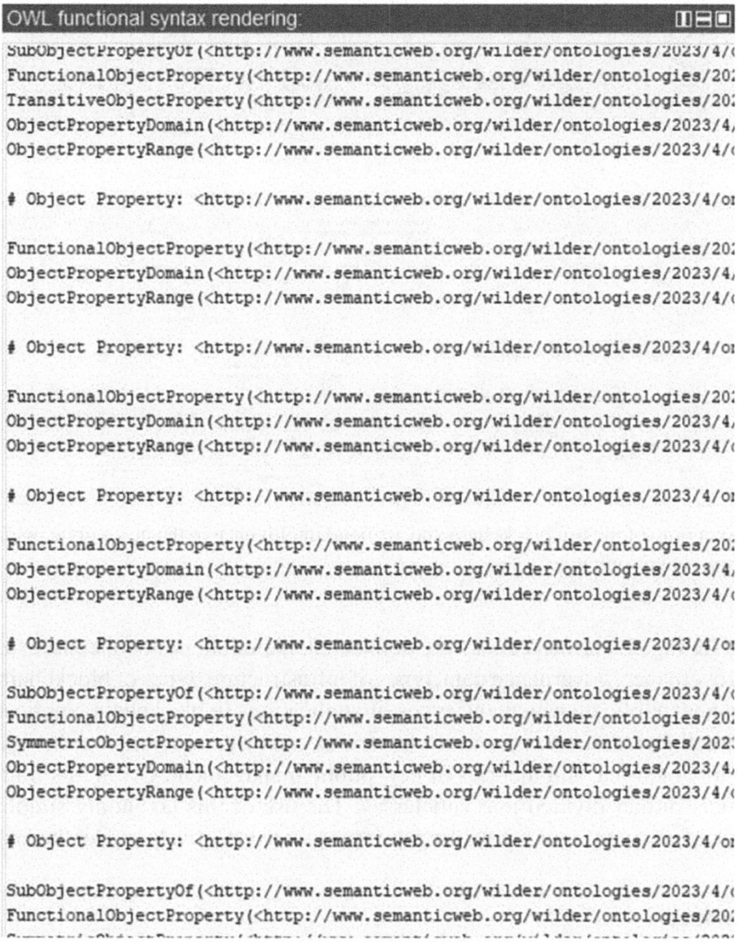

Fig. 1. Ontology modeling for classes, subclasses and individuals. (Own source)

ontologies. Instead, they need only grasp the attributes and restrictions described by the grammatical rules at a conceptual level, which facilitates the completion of domain ontology modeling or the field of study of interest, significantly enhancing the efficiency and effectiveness of the ontology reasoner. Given that RDF/XML-based ontology models and Protégé-based visual ontology models are fundamentally identical, all subsequent analysis is presented using the visual ontology model in Protégé.

It is important to note that while HERMIT outlines the reasoning rules within the ontology, it encounters difficulties with the reasoning of these rules. For the reasoner to function properly, it is necessary to establish relationships among classes, subclasses, and individuals, referred to as the taxonomy of the domain or field of knowledge being analyzed. For this purpose, Fig. 2 illustrates the taxonomy proposed in this research on the application of blockchain and artificial intelligence in new public management.

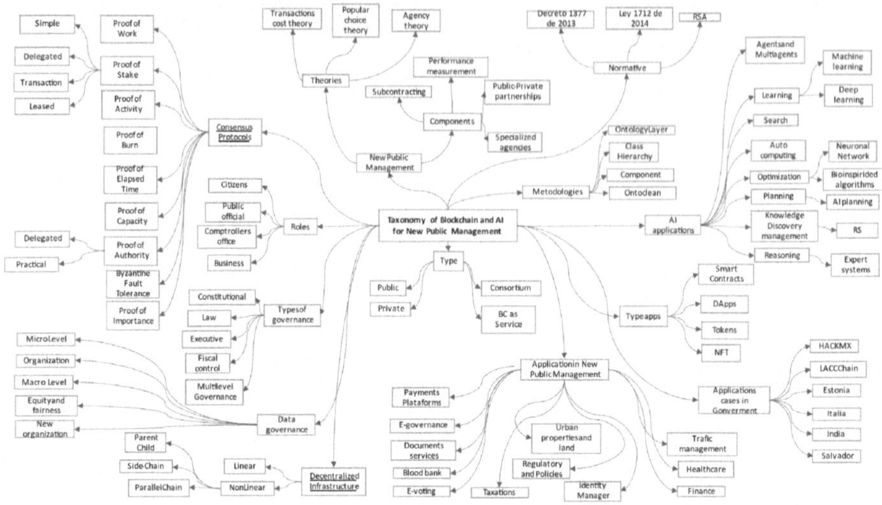

Fig. 2. Taxonomy of the use blockchain and artificial intelligence in the new public management in Colombia. (Own source)

Based on Fig. 2, various classes are delineated, including protocol consensus, roles, types of governance, governance data, types of infrastructure, types of blockchain, applications in new public management, types of applications in blockchain, applications of artificial intelligence, success stories from various countries, methodologies, regulations pertinent to Colombia, and theories of new public management. Given this framework, each class is further divided into subclasses. The use of this taxonomy simplifies the application of restriction rules, enabling the reasoner to effectively model the taxonomy.

1.4 Reasoner

Common inference reasoners for ontology models include Jess [28], Racer [29], Fact++ [29], Hermit [30], Jena [31], and Pellet [29], among others. The Hermit reasoner is pre-installed in Protégé 5.6.1, and additional reasoners like Pellet can be added via the Check for Plugin option in the "File" menu. In this research, as depicted in Fig. 3, the Hermit reasoner is utilized. The process involves selecting the inference engine or Hermit reasoner from the reasoner menu and then clicking on "start reasoner." On the right side of Fig. 3, the ontological model in Protégé for this article is displayed.

Based on Fig. 3, the chosen reasoner is Hermit, version 1.4.3.456. This inference engine is notable for its integration into the desktop version of Protégé and its convenience as it comes preloaded, unlike other inference engines that require a separate installation process. After the plugin download is complete, these typically function only in the web version of the tool. Conversely, the ontological model depicted illustrates the relationships and the types of relationships between the classes, centering around a main class called taxonomy where both symmetric and asymmetric relationships are demonstrated, which are not depicted in the taxonomy structure of Fig. 2. Each reasoner is

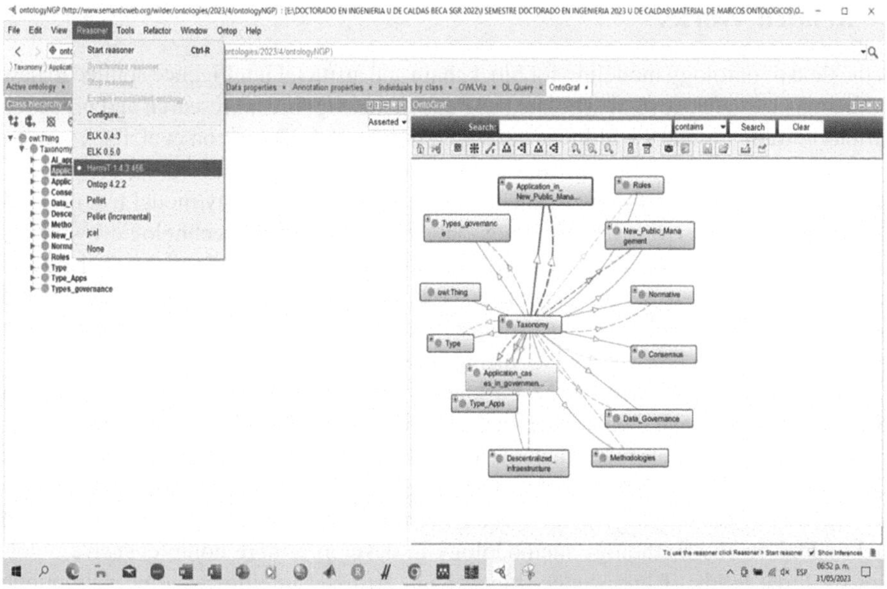

Fig. 3. Hermit reasoner and ontological model. (Own source)

delineated based on its operational properties, adherence to OWL rules of ontology, and the classes, properties, and data range restrictions as illustrated in Table 1.

Table 1. Support for the operation of the reasoner. (Own source)

Inference motor reasoner	Ontology rules OWL	Class and Properties	Data range and restrictions
Jess	Without support	With support	Without support
Racer	With support	Without support	Without support
Fact + +	With support	Without support	Without support
Jenna	With support	Without support	Without support
Hermit	With support	With support	With support
Pellet	With support	With support	With support

Based on the information presented in Table 1, it is noted that the primary performance characteristics of the reasoning engines are evaluated based on their support capabilities within the desktop or web versions of Protégé. The optimal reasoner is identified as one that supports all four properties listed in Table 1. Both the Hermit and Pellet reasoners fulfill this criterion. However, as previously mentioned, the Hermit reasoner is distinctively advantageous as it comes preloaded in the desktop version of Protégé, whereas the Pellet reasoner requires downloading from the plugins and is only available in the web version.

2 Related Works

In the field of ontology modeling for blockchain and artificial intelligence applied to new public management, several scholars have conducted significant research and proposed various ontology models within the academic sphere. In L. Besancon et al. [32], semantic ontology technology was utilized for decentralized applications on the blockchain, presenting a framework for automatically constructing an ontology model from textual information sources However, this study only selects one of the technologies, which is blockchain, and does not provide a comprehensive understanding of both blockchain and artificial intelligence in the context of new public administration. However, this study did not address the integration of blockchain technology with artificial intelligence within specific contexts such as new public management.

Conversely, in H. M. Kim and M. Laskowski [33], the modeling aspects of blockchain in supply chain management are detailed, proposing a framework for storing and invoking the ontology model. Nevertheless, it lacks a clear explanation on constructing an ontology model for blockchain and artificial intelligence and its application based on the construction of the ontology model. The current research enhances the work proposed by building on the methology methodology to develop a more comprehensive ontology for three fields of knowledge: blockchain, artificial intelligence, and new public administration.

Concerning the reasoning of the ontology of blockchain and artificial intelligence applied to new public management, P. S. Giannaris and N. E. Mastorakis [34] focuses on semantic collaboration for an ontology model based on prior taxonomies constructed on blockchain technology, analyzing key articles in taxonomy and ontology classification for the blockchain knowledge field. However, it lacks methods and examples for modeling ontology for blockchain, artificial intelligence, and new public management.

In W. Nohsen, M. Aref, and K. Elbahnasy [35], the development of a worldwide ontology ledger (WOL) platform was proposed for collaborative development of functional ontological architectures and models and the evolutionary development of artifacts designed for blockchain technology. However, a limitation of this research is the absence of evidence on the use of ontological models and a robust platform for collaborative development of artifacts, and its methodology remains unclear.

3 Methodology

The ontology modeling approach presented in this paper employs the semantic ontology approach of the class hierarchy model type, as utilized by the Protégé program [25]. However, the methodology for constructing the ontology model in this study is oriented towards capturing tacit knowledge, as depicted in Fig. 4.

Section 3.1 outlines the basic structure of the ontological model for blockchain and artificial intelligence within new public management. Meanwhile, Sect. 3.2 details the operational rules for the reasoner.

3.1 Steps for the Build of the Ontology

This paper draws on certain modeling concepts from SSN [36] and [37], such as environment, resources, and behavior, which are fundamental to the ontology of blockchain, artificial intelligence, and new public management. However, it does not directly utilize the conceptual classes or properties found within the SSN ontology. To meet the needs of the simulation experiment and to introduce the ontology-based modeling method for the architecture, a simplified basic ontology model of blockchain, artificial intelligence, and new public management has been developed, as illustrated in Fig. 4. This model encompasses only the essential concepts and attributes necessary for the integrated application of blockchain and artificial intelligence technologies in new public management.

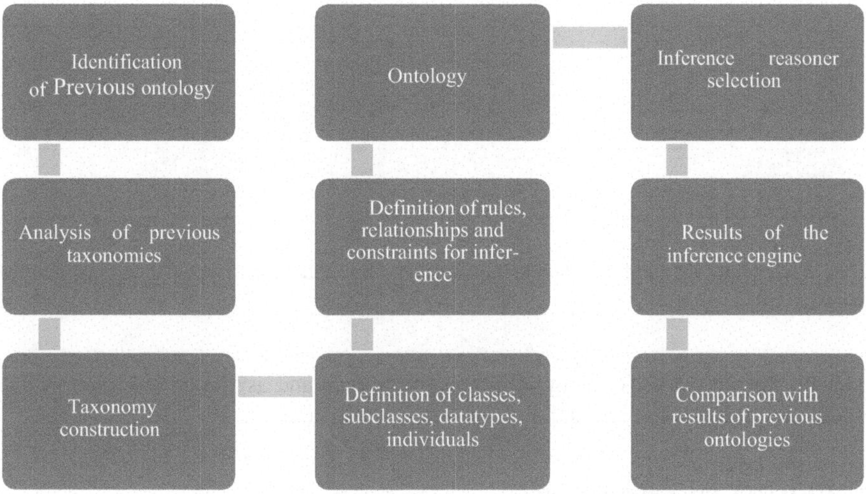

Fig. 4. Procedure for tacit knowledge in an ontology. Source: based on [38]

Based on Fig. 4, the diagram illustrates a cooperative procedure for constructing ontology models. This process begins with the identification of existing ontologies and taxonomies relevant to the domain of interest—blockchain and artificial intelligence within new public management for this study. This foundational step facilitates the development of a new ontology model. Utilizing a specified inference engine embedded within a tool that employs a semantic ontology approach of the hierarchical modeling type [39], this method generates results. These outcomes are then compared with prior ontologies, allowing for the identification of both limitations and contributions that the new knowledge brings to the study domain in the Fig. 5.

Based on Fig. 5, it is evident that the left side of the ontological model includes a total of 15 classes, 92 subclasses, 13 main relationships, 74 sub-relationships, 5 types of data, 9 operating rules, and 7 individuals representing interactions with various components such as citizens, public officials, and regulatory bodies. These interactions within the model facilitate the evaluation of the functioning of the inference rules tailored for the HERMIT reasoner.

On the right side of Fig. 5, an organized structure for the ontological model and its relationships is proposed. Given the complexity of the model and its inability to fit entirely within the image, the clustering option was utilized to represent each of

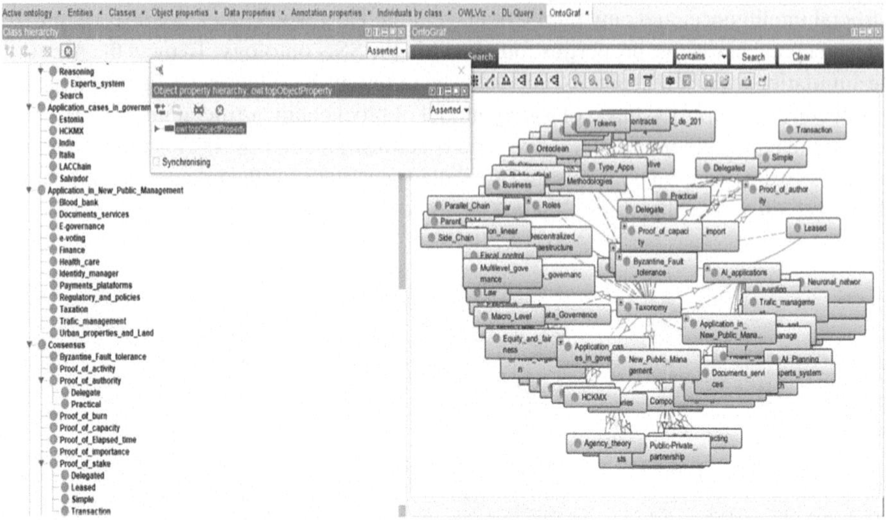

Fig. 5. Basic Ontology model for blockchain, artificial intelligence and new public management. (Own source)

the subclasses and classes, along with the symmetrical and asymmetrical relationships developed in the ontology model as proposed in the article.

3.2 HERMIT Inference Engine

From the established ontological model concerning blockchain, artificial intelligence, and their application in new public management, it is feasible to further develop the SWRL reasoning rules of the ontological model proposed in this article, as detailed in Table 2. These reasoning rules are designed to enhance the attributes of classes, subclasses, relations, and individuals within the ontological model of blockchain, artificial intelligence, and new public management.

The reasoning rules outlined above were formulated in accordance with the types of rules typically employed in constructing hierarchical ontology models, as well as the principles of semantic ontology, which encompass restrictions related to quantification, cardinality, and specific values. Quantification restrictions, also known as existential restrictions, are applied to the relationships between classes and individuals. In the context of this article, these are exemplified by the rules governing behavior. The "has value" restrictions denote a specific value for an individual or a class, implying the existence of semantics for classes, subclasses, and individuals; in this article, this type of restriction is depicted by the classification rule.

The cardinality constraint indicates the context in which classes or individuals are linked with other classes or subclasses, representing a particular scenario within the knowledge domain. Table 2 illustrates each of these constraints as rules, where the general rules of the proposed ontological model are displayed in the format used by the JavaScript extension in the Protégé 5.6.1 tool.

Table 2. General rules for the HERMI. (Own source)

Rule Type	Expressions	Relations/results
Rule of conduct 1	Taxonomy: Behavior ^ taxonomy: targetURI(? r) ^ taxonomy: identyURI (?r, ?r URL) ^ hermit: resolveURI (?burl, ?rurl, "http") → taxonomy: targetResource(?b, ?r) ^ taxonomy: takeBehavior(?r, ?b)	Is Groups of New Public Management
Rule of conduct 2	Taxonomy: Behavior ^ taxonomy: targetURI(?r) ^ taxonomy: identyURI (?r, ?r URL) ^ hermit: resolveURI (?burl, ?rurl, "http") →	Has Applications of artificial intelligence
Rule of conduct 3	Taxonomy:Environment(?e) ^ taxonomy: belongSystem(?e, ?s) → taxonomy: currentTime(?b,?r)^ taxonomy: execBehavior(?e, ?t)	Is Network type of blockchain
Classification rule 1	Casg: noBehavior(? r, "All", "All") taxonomy: Resource(?r) taxonomy: UnknowResource (?r)	Has methodologies
System composition 1	Taxonomy: Service(?s) taxonomy: FaultResource (?s) taxonomy: belongSystem(?s, ?sys) taxonomy: hasFaultService(?sys, ?s)	Has Type applications

4 Results and Discussion

Building on the outlined stages and procedures for constructing the ontology model discussed in this article, a comprehensive and real-time foundational fact model is derived. This model encapsulates various aspects crucial to new public management, including governance, data governance, and the types of blockchain networks. It also covers the hybrid operation of artificial intelligence and blockchain, detailing case studies where these integrations have been successfully implemented. Moreover, the model addresses the types of applications, the various representations of knowledge produced by artificial intelligence, and the necessary technological infrastructure required for the effective deployment of blockchain and artificial intelligence technologies within the realm of new public management.

4.1 Ontological Model

As illustrated in Table 2, the rules Behavior Rule 1 and Classification Rule 1 are instrumental in linking behavior with classes, subclasses, and relationships within the ontology model proposed in this paper. Specifically, these rules facilitate the interaction within the blockchain, artificial intelligence, and new governance ontology model. The URI of the source is retrievable via the property from URI, while the URI of the class and/or subclass receiving the behavior can be accessed through the property target URI. By comparing these URIs, the association between the behaviors take Behavior and "exec Behavior" is established. Additionally, Fig. 6 displays the configuration in Protégé of the constraints for the inference engine, highlighting how these relationships are systematically managed within the tool.

Fig. 6. Reasoner results for the ontological model of blockchain, artificial intelligence and new public management. (Own source)

Based on Fig. 6, we observe the functioning of the ontological model for blockchain, artificial intelligence, and new public management. This illustration reveals a specific outcome from the reasoner, wherein it associates the individual named types of cases with the class named application cases in government. This association is facilitated through the relationship named something types of cases, which includes a data property for both the class and the individual named has application governance. This data property functions as a value restriction, signifying a decremented value in the relationship constructed by the inference engine.

Based on the system composition rule found in Table 2, the cardinality and value restrictions subject to the proper functioning of the inference engine for the construction of the three types of restrictions socialized in restriction 4.1 can be accurately perceived. Since the correct functioning of the reasoner allows real-time consultation of the relationships between the different types of individuals in the proposed ontological model and the different classes and subclasses in the ontological model.

Cardinality constraint control allows individuals: cases, types, governance, and citizens to interact with all classes and subclasses through each of the queries that are performed through the tab called data query in Protégé 5.6.1 for the simulation of the feasibility of implementing blockchain and artificial intelligence technologies in the new public management.

Despite the implementation of three key constraints, gaps remain in the automatic control of the ontological model that integrates blockchain, artificial intelligence and new public governance. These gaps include the lack of compilation and deployment rules for simulating the ontological model, as well as rules defining the relationship between specific AI and blockchain techniques in governance applications. Addressing these challenges requires significant effort, as such rules must be manually introduced into Protégé, rather than being integrated in real-time. Addressing these issues is largely dependent on the availability of data sets that comply with the CRISP-DM methodology. In addition, exploring the Pellet inference engine, identified in Table 1 as the second reasoner supporting inference, or integrating the HERMIT inference engine into a framework that facilitates the registration of governance behaviours through real-time data mining, could enhance inference capabilities. Based on the system composition rule in Table 2, the cardinality and value restrictions essential for optimal performance of the inference engine are clearly defined, enabling real-time querying of relationships between individuals, classes and subclasses within the ontological model. The hermit reasoner, based on descriptive logic, operates in two scenarios: classification inference related to the taxonomy in Fig. 2, and inference related to the role of blockchain and AI in the new public management.

5 Conclusions

The ontological model of blockchain, artificial intelligence, and new public management serves as a graphical and formal representation of the composition and operational principles of these technologies, exploring their implementation feasibility in various perspectives and contexts of new public management. This model was developed through the lens of semantic ontology, blending theoretical insights and practical applications from new public management. This document delves into the theory and modeling methodology of the semantic ontology dimension pertaining to blockchain, artificial intelligence, and new public management.

This paper proposes a framework that utilizes taxonomy and collaborative procedures to construct a real-time semantic ontology model of blockchain, artificial intelligence, and new public management. Leveraging semantic reasoning technology, this framework facilitates the high-level knowledge modeling, classifying classes, subclasses, and individuals based on the control of restrictions formulated as rules within the proposed ontological model.

To ensure the efficient querying of behavior in the ontological realms of blockchain, artificial intelligence, and new public management, it becomes essential to explore data storage technologies for ontology instances and assess their implementation feasibility. Moreover, the real-time perception and fault diagnosis of the developed ontological model depend on the updated behavior of the inference engine or reasoner.

The challenge of cleaning and updating some outdated behaviors in the ontological model also warrants further investigation.

To fully harness the potential of the semantic ontology dimension in the ontological model of blockchain, artificial intelligence, and new public management, future research, as discussed in Sect. 4.2, could also focus on advancing semantic reasoning technologies and developing knowledge graphs. Establishing a reasoner or inference engine within a framework would enable real-time awareness of resource states, anomaly monitoring of failures, and a richer semantic and intelligent automatic control of the ontology model.

References

1. Hasan, H.R., Salah, K.: Combating deepfake videos using blockchain and smart contracts. IEEE Access **7**, 41596–41606 (2019). https://doi.org/10.1109/ACCESS.2019.2905689
2. Babu, S.D., Pamula, R.: An effective block-chain based authentication technique for cloud based IoT. In: Singh, M., Gupta, P., Tyagi, V., Flusser, J., Ören, T., Valentino, G. (eds.) ICACDS 2020. CCIS, vol. 1244, pp. 305–319. Springer, Cham (2020). https://doi.org/10.1007/978-981-15-6634-9_28
3. Ølnes, S., Ubacht, J., Janssen, M.: Blockchain in government: benefits and implications of distributed ledger technology for information sharing. Govern. Inf. Q. **34**(3), 355–364 (2017)
4. Atzori, L., Iera, A., Morabito, G.: Understanding the Internet of Things: definition, potentials, and societal role of a fast evolving paradigm. Ad Hoc Netw. **56**, 122–140 (2017)
5. Werbach, K.: The Blockchain and the New Architecture of Trust. Mit Press (2018)
6. Janssen, M., Weerakkody, V., Ismagilova, E., Sivarajah, U., Irani, Z.: A framework for analysing blockchain technology adoption: integrating institutional, market and technical factors. Int. J. Inf. Manage. **50**, 302–309 (2020). https://doi.org/10.1016/j.ijinfomgt.2019.08.012
7. Angelis, J., Da Silva, E.R.: Blockchain adoption: a value driver perspective. Bus. Horiz. **62**(3), 307–314 (2019)
8. Palumbo, R., Manesh, M.F., Pellegrini, M.M., Caputo, A., Flamini, G.: Organizing a sustainable smart urban ecosystem: perspectives and insights from a bibliometric analysis and literature review. J. Clean. Prod. **297** (2021). https://doi.org/10.1016/j.jclepro.2021.126622
9. Beck, R., Müller-Bloch, C., King, J.: Governance in the blockchain economy: a framework and research agenda. J. Assoc. Inf. Syst. **19**(10) (2018). https://aisel.aisnet.org/jais/vol19/iss10/1. Accessed 05 Nov 2021
10. Stephan, M., Marshall, G., McGinnis, M.: An introduction to polycentricity and governance. Gov. Complex. Anal. Appl. Polycentricity 21–44 (2019)
11. Dunleavy, P., Margetts, H., Bastow, S., Tinkler, J.: New public management is dead—long live digital-era governance. J. Public Adm. Res. Theory **16**(3), 467–494 (2006)
12. Barzelay, M.: Learning from second-hand experience: methodology for extrapolation-oriented case research. Governance **20**(3), 521–543 (2007)
13. Ramon Gil-Garcia, J., Chengalur-Smith, I., Duchessi, P.: Collaborative e-government: impediments and benefits of information-sharing projects in the public sector. Eur. J. Inf. Syst. **16**(2), 121–133 (2007)
14. Jones, I., Pollitt, M.: Understanding how issues in corporate governance develop: cadbury report to Higgs review. Corp. Govern. Int. Rev. **12**(2), 162–171 (2004)
15. Hood, C.: A public management for all seasons? Public Adm. **69**(1), 3–19 (1991)
16. Chen, G., Jiang, T., Wang, M., Tang, X., Ji, W.: Modeling and reasoning of IoT architecture in semantic ontology dimension. Comput. Commun. **153**, 580–594 (2020)
17. Li, Y., Chu, X., Mou, X., Dong, C., Chen, H.: Practical study of deterministic regular expressions from large-scale XML and schema data. In: Proceedings of the 22nd International Database Engineering & Applications Symposium, pp. 45–53 (2018)
18. Masinter, L., Berners-Lee, T., Fielding, R.T.: Uniform resource identifier (URI): generic syntax. Network Working Group, Fremont, CA, USA (2005)

19. Le, D.X.T., Heon, M., Volmer, N.: Towards semantic applications: from knowledge management to data publishing on the web (2017)
20. Sosa, J.D.T.G., Domínguez, V.H.M., Bolaños, M.E.C., Montalvo, J.R.G.: Use of an ontological model to assess the relevance of scientific production. IEEE Lat. Am. Trans. **17**(09), 1424–1431 (2019)
21. Bassiliades, N.: SWRL2SPIN: a tool for transforming SWRL rule bases in OWL ontologies to object-oriented SPIN rules. arXiv Preprint arXiv:1801.09061 (2018)
22. Shen, W., Wang, J., Luo, P., Wang, M.: Apollo: a general framework for populating ontology with named entities via random walks on graphs. In: Proceedings of the 21st International Conference on World Wide Web, pp. 595–596 (2012)
23. Bechhofer, S., Horrocks, I., Goble, C., Stevens, R.: OilEd: a reason-able ontology editor for the semantic web. In: KI 2001: Advances in Artificial Intelligence: Joint German/Austrian Conference on AI Vienna, Austria, 19–21 September 2001, Proceedings 24, pp. 396–408 (2001)
24. Sure, Y., Erdmann, M., Angele, J., Staab, S., Studer, R., Wenke, D.: OntoEdit: collaborative ontology development for the semantic web. In: The Semantic Web—ISWC 2002: First International Semantic Web Conference Sardinia, Italy, 9–12 June 2002, Proceedings 1, pp. 221–235 (2002)
25. Noy, N.F., Sintek, M., Decker, S., Crubézy, M., Fergerson, R.W., Musen, M.A.: Creating semantic web contents with protege-2000. IEEE Intell. Syst. **16**(2), 60–71 (2001)
26. Corcho, O., Fernández-López, M., Gómez-Pérez, A., López-Cima, A.: Building legal ontologies with METHONTOLOGY and WebODE. In: Law and the Semantic Web: Legal Ontologies, Methodologies, Legal Information Retrieval, and Applications, pp. 142–157 (2005)
27. Horridge, M., Jupp, S., Moulton, G., Rector, A., Stevens, R., Wroe, C.: A practical guide to building owl ontologies using protégé 4 and co-ode tools edition1. 2. University of Manchester, vol. 107 (2009)
28. Eriksson, H.: Using jesstab to integrate protégé and jess. IEEE Intell. Syst. **18**(2), 43–50 (2003)
29. Huang, T., Li, W., Yang, C.: Comparison of ontology reasoners: racer, pellet, Fact++. In: AGU Fall Meeting Abstracts, vol. 2008, pp. IN13A-1068 (2008)
30. Glimm, B., Horrocks, I., Motik, B., Stoilos, G., Wang, Z.: HermiT: an OWL 2 reasoner. J. Autom. Reason. **53**, 245–269 (2014)
31. Alves, M.B., Damásio, C.V., Correia, N.: SPARQL commands in Jena rules. In: Knowledge Engineering and Semantic Web: 6th International Conference, KESW 2015, Moscow, Russia, 30 September–2 October 2015, Proceedings 6, pp. 253–262 (2015)
32. Besançon, L., Da Silva, C.F., Ghodous, P., Gelas, J.-P.: A blockchain ontology for DApps development. IEEE Access **10**, 49905–49933 (2022)
33. Kim, H.M., Laskowski, M.: Toward an ontology-driven blockchain design for supply-chain provenance. Intell. Syst. Account. Financ. Manag. **25**(1), 18–27 (2018)
34. Giannaris, P.S., Mastorakis, N.E.: Overview of taxonomy and ontology approaches for the classification of blockchain components. WSEAS Trans. Comput. Res. **11**, 33–56 (2023)
35. Mohsen, W., Aref, M., ElBahnasy, K.: Blockchain as a platform for collaborative ontology evolution. In: Proceedings of the 6th International Conference on Frontiers of Educational Technologies, pp. 183–190 (2020)
36. Compton, M., et al.: The SSN ontology of the W3C semantic sensor network incubator group. J. Web Semant. **17**, 25–32 (2012)
37. Feng, J., Song, S., Kong, L.: Research on semantic association and decision method of internet of things. Acta Autom. Sin. **42**(11), 1691–1701 (2016)

38. Sinha, D., Roy Chowdhury, S.: Blockchain-based smart contract for international business – a framework. J. Glob. Oper. Strateg. Sourc. **14**(1), 224–260 (2021). https://doi.org/10.1108/JGOSS-06-2020-0031
39. Hwang, S.-H., Kim, H.-G., Yang, H.-S.: A FCA-based ontology construction for the design of class hierarchy. In: Proceedings of the Computational Science and Its Applications–ICCSA 2005: International Conference, Part III 5, Singapore, 9–12 May 2005, pp. 827–835 (2005)

Police Report Linking Algorithm Based on Named Entity Recognition

Mauro Daniel Alvarez[1](✉) and Leandro Antonelli[2,3]

[1] Facultad de Informática, UNLP, La Plata, Buenos Aires, Argentina
mauro.alvarez@info.unlp.edu.ar

[2] LIFIA, Facultad de Informática, UNLP, La Plata, Argentina
leandro.antonelli@lifia.info.unlp.edu.ar

[3] CAETI, Facultad de Tecnología Informática, Universidad Abierta Interamericana, Santa Fe, Argentina

Abstract. When a crime is committed, authorities such as police officers, employees of the prosecutor's office, etc. create a report with the details of the crime usually narrated by the victim. These reports include a complaint made by the victim of a crime. This complaint is a story that describes the facts from the victim's point of view. Most of the time, crimes are perpetrated by unknown authors. This causes cases to be shelved until new evidence arrives. The use of natural language processing allows us to take advantage of non-structured text in victim's complaints by generating links that could lead to the reopening of an archived investigation. Through the use of NER (Named Entity Recognition), it is possible to extract entities of interest from a report of a complaint that arrives and link it with other reports of existing complaints, allowing the generation of a maps of links in order to detect similarities between cases. This idea will increase the possibility that cases in archived status being opened.

Keywords: NLP · NER · police reports · criminal justice · graphs · similarity

1 Introduction

Victim's complaints are composed of non-structured text. Some of them contain information that can be categorized such as names, places, timetables, etc.

With a knowledge base of complaints, it is possible to compare similarities between a report of an entry complaint and the existing ones.

Initially, it is necessary to reduce the number of reports in the existing complaint database, i.e., to allow only those reports of complaints that have some degree of similarity to the incoming complaint.

The aim of this paper is to propose a NER-based strategy for the identification of similar complaints. This strategy is made up of two phases.

The first phase consists of reducing the number of reports in the existing complaint database, i.e., reducing and preserving only those reports of complaints the have some degree of similarity to the incoming complaint.

V. Agredo-Delgado et al. (Eds.): DECISIONING 2024, CCIS 2369, pp. 163–172, 2025.
https://doi.org/10.1007/978-3-031-91690-8_13

The second phase consists of the recognition of named entities or NERs. From this moment on, the aim is to compare those reports of complaints that have some relationship in categories such as names, people, locations, timetables, etc.

From the result of this comparison, the most similar entities are selected in terms of named entities and an appropriate visualization is generated for the user.

The following section describes the theoretical framework that was used for the development of the algorithm.

The contribution section details the two-phase algorithm and finally gives a brief conclusion about the algorithm.

2 Theoretical Framework

Natural language processing (NLP) enables machines to understand and generate written text that can be interpreted by humans.

All natural language processing requires standardization [1], that is, the removal of words and symbols that do not add meaning to the text, such as punctuation symbols, white spaces and also the conversion of lowercase letters from the text, since, for machines, the capitalization of words is indistinct.

The process also encompasses the extraction of lemmas [2]. An interesting case is made up of verbs. With lemma extraction, we avoid having to deal with conjugated forms of verbs. The goal is to unify as much as possible the language in order to apply Jaccard similarity index more efficiently.

The unification of vocabulary is necessary due to the fact that this method does not perform any kind of semantic comparison, only syntactic, so that conjugated verbs and their root base or lemma do not belong to the intersection, they are simply considered two words that have no relationship at all.

Jaccard method is defined as the intersection divided by the union of the sets [3].

For example, with sets A and B, the Jaccard similarity index indicates that they are the numbers of common elements that A and B have, divided by the number of elements that the union of those sets have.

On the other hand, there is the recognition of named entities [4], which allow the extraction, as their name indicates, of entities.

The entities are classified in different categories, in order to allow grouping unstructured texts where these entities participate. For example, the texts could be grouped where certain proper nouns appear, or even use the geographical location to determine how many articles refer to that area. The above idea es reinforced by the crime pattern theory [5].

The aforementioned grouping would make it possible to detect patterns in order to identify people who commit crimes based on data such as type of crimes, locations, schedules, among others.

3 Contribution

In this case, the concept of corpus will be used to describe a set of stories of complaints which are composed of unstructured text.

Figure 1 shows an example of a real complaint structure; however, the real data has been modified because this information may contain sensible data.

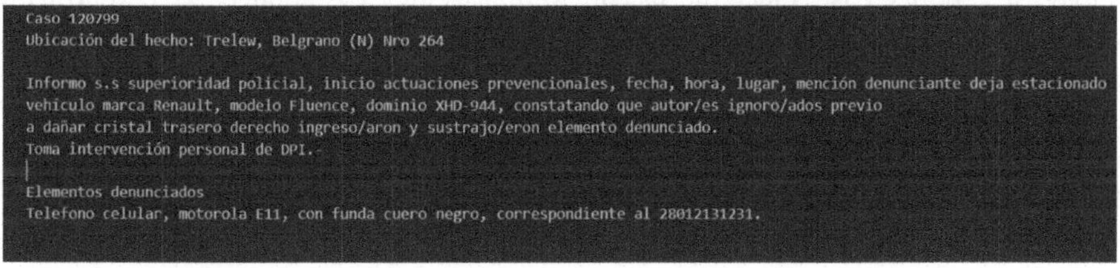
Caso 120799
Ubicación del hecho: Trelew, Belgrano (N) Nro 264

Informo s.s superioridad policial, inicio actuaciones prevencionales, fecha, hora, lugar, mención denunciante deja estacionado vehiculo marca Renault, modelo Fluence, dominio XHD-944, constatando que autor/es ignoro/ados previo a dañar cristal trasero derecho ingreso/aron y sustrajo/eron elemento denunciado.
Toma intervención personal de DPI.-

Elementos denunciados
Telefono celular, motorola E11, con funda cuero negro, correspondiente al 28012131231.

Fig. 1. Complaint from case 120799. Source: Own Elaboration

Each complaint is basically unstructured text, so it needs to be standardized first, otherwise the text may contain information that is not useful and can interfere by adding unwanted noise. For the non-Spanish speaker, the complaint is about an unknown criminal that broke into a car and steal the belongings from the owner.

An example of noise or unwanted information in this complaint are verbs such as ingreso/aron, sustrajo/eron. As this is an unknown author case, the description is not clear whether the burglar is singular or plural which means the existence of multiple burglars, so authorities employ these phrases with slashes to note that situation. This is a specific case for Spanish language, and it may not represent an issue in other languages.

Another problem that usually happens is the irregular patterns that appear in complaints as this is an activity that is performed under stressful situations and the victim may not be in their best emotional state to provide a precise description. So, complaints for similar crimes can be similar as the situation is alike, but the structure could differ in various degrees depending the victim. Also, the complaint is not necessary described by the victim, it could be described by a witness that was present at the moment of the crime.

3.1 Overview of the Algorithm

The overall strategy is shown in Fig. 2.

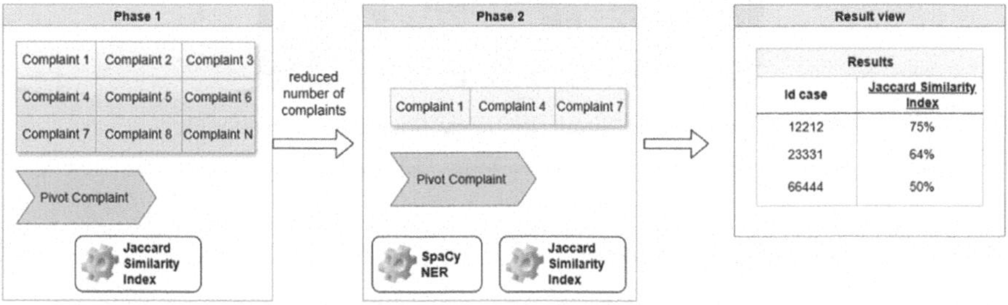

Fig. 2. Overview of the algorithm. Source: Own Elaboration.

As mentioned before, the algorithm consists in two phases. It is a pipeline, where the output of a phase is fed into the next one.

In the beginning we start with a considerable amount of complaints. Each complaint belongs to a police case. Once the Jaccard similarity index is applied, we end up with a subset of complaints. These complaints are the most similar syntactically to the pivot complaint.

The subset of complaints is fed to the next phase, which then proceeds to detect named entities in the complaints, finally Jaccard Similarity index is applied again but this time with named entities. In the following sections, each phase is described in more detail.

3.2 First Phase of the Strategy

When a new complaint arrives, it could be determined how similar it is with respect to the knowledge available in the model, that is, what degree of similarity corresponds to the reports available in the knowledge base. To determine this similarity, the Jaccard similarity index is used in order to yield those complaints that are most similar to the new document.

In order to reduce the number of documents, complaints with higher similarity index are selected and named entities are extracted from the new document and the similar ones, ending phase one of the algorithm. The selection criteria for documents is based on Jaccard similarity higher or equal to twenty five percent (25%), those below that value are consider negligible.

Be it the following complaints and a recently arrived complaint called a pivot, in Fig. 3. It can be seen the comparison made of the pivot against nine (documents. In this case it can be noted that the complaints differ greatly syntactically, with the first three complaints being selected.

Caso	Indice de similitud
Caso 120928	0.42857142857142855
Caso 120927	0.4166666666666667
Caso 122633	0.3333333333333333
Caso 122531	0.2222222222222222
Caso 122521	0.20689655172413793
Caso 122693	0.2
Caso 120924	0.19642857142857142
Caso 122709	0.16666666666666666
Caso 122355	0.09375

Fig. 3. Table - Jaccard Similarity Index. Source: Own Elaboration.

3.3 Second Phase of the Strategy

For the extraction of named entities, the SpaCy [6] library is used, which already has support for this task. This library generates automatic tagging of named entities, for instance, it can differentiate between ORG, LOC, PERSON, TIME, etc.

The idea is as follows, a model will be trained for the NER module of SpaCy. For that matter, the NER Annotator [7] tool will be used.

The NER module is part of the SpaCy pipeline. This module can be extracted to perform adjustments to the model. In this case, the model will be trained in the criminal justice domain, such as crimes, related legal articles and some other more general sections like street names and their belonging to a neighborhood.

This training gives the model the ability to link words like robbery with the penal code article that corresponds to that crime, or to recognize the neighborhood that belongs to a certain street.

Tentative training sets for the NER module are detailed below (Tables 1, 2 and 3).

Table 1. Crimes training template[1]. Source: Own Elaboration.

Word	NER	Additional information
Robbery	Article 140 of penal code	Common theft
Burglary	Article 140 of penal code	Common theft
Vandalism	Article 201 of penal code	Damage of property
Car theft	Article 163 of penal code	Car theft
…	…	…
Word N	Article N of penal code	Description N

Table 2. Neighborhood training template. Source: Own Elaboration.

Street	Number	NER
San Martín	0	Centro neighborhood
Muzio	10	Padre Juan neighborhood
Urquiza	20	Padre Juan neighborhood
Marconi and. San Martín	S/D	Centro neighborhood
…	…	…
Street N	Number N	Neighborhood N

Once the new named entities have been obtained, the Jaccard method is re-executed with recognized entities, i.e., with the categories, in order to obtain a successive refinement and thus determine which ones are most similar to the story of the new complaint.

This process will yield the most similar cases just like the representation shown in Fig. 1. This information will then be processed by the visualization tool [8] to generate a

[1] They do not correspond to actual articles numbers, they are for example purposes only. Besides each country has it own penal code.

Table 3. Suspects template. Source: Own Elaboration.

Full Name	Alias	NER
John Doe	Doey	John Doe + Doey SUSPECT
Ron J	Joey	Ron J + Joey SUSPECT
...	...	...
N	N	N SUSPECT

graphed map composed of the crime, the neighborhood where the event occurred, those involved if they exist, otherwise they are categorized as unknown authors.

Figure 4 depicts the resulting schema with graphs.

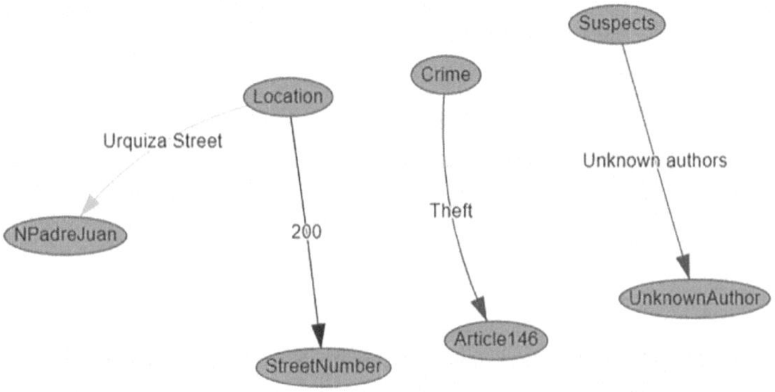

Fig. 4. Representation of a complaint story with the Vis tool. Source: Own Elaboration.

This idea could be extended to the N most similar cases to the pivot, in order to obtain a visualization of a set of N cases that can provide the investigator with clues, such as detection of crime patterns on the cases.

This would make it possible to expand the possibility of reopening cases currently shelved for further investigation.

3.4 Initial Implementation

This algorithm is currently under development. We proceeded to with a proof of concept[2]. The idea is to determine feasibility through a minimum implementation and then proceed to a definitive implementation.

The PoC of phase one of the algorithm is available, it was tested with a sample of nine complaints and the pivot. The application of the PoC of phase one reduced the complaints of interest to three as can be seen in Fig. 3.

[2] Proof of Concept or PoC.

The next step is the development of the phase two PoC. It consists of the training of a NER model. In this case, a simplified model of named entities related to justice system language will be defined.

Taking the results from the PoC of phase one, it will be fed into the PoC of phase two to perform the extraction of named entities from both the complaints and the pivot complaint.

The output of this process consists of a JSON-formatted object. It will contain the links and details of the cases as well as the named entities. This information in this state does not represent an adequate form, and it is necessary to send this object with links to the Visjs library, in order to obtain a graphical representation of the object and its relations.

4 Algorithm Validation

The algorithm contains two phases and the validation of both is independent, because phase one consists of the implementation of the Jaccard similarity index. It will be composed of unit tests with the unitest library [9] of Python.

As for the NER model, being a machine learning model, validation is carried out by making changes to the hyperparameters and controlling the loss rate.

It is important to define which complaints will be in the training set, which ones in the test set and finally which will be in the validation set. Omitting this separation of sets will result in overfitting the model, and it would not perform properly to information the model has not previously seen.

The above validations are of a technical nature, and it is also necessary to validate manually. In this case, it is proposed to assemble a corpus with complaints of cases in solved state. The idea is to determine the output generated graphically in order to verify if it is consistent with what happened in the case history and if the related cases are linked appropriately.

To determine the degree of accuracy, it is necessary to involve domain stakeholders such as prosecutors, who can verify whether the maps generated would be useful in an investigation.

5 Evaluation

This section describes an increment of the initial implementation described in Sect. 3.3. It is an evaluation performed in the algorithm. As this is a preliminary test, the amount of data is rather small and only intends to show the viability of the algorithm.

For this test, 10 complaints have been used as a base of knowledge. We also employed the complaint that we need to solve, this complaint is known as the pivot.

The pivot complaint could be seen as the complaint that belongs to the case we are interested in resolving.

The previous description involves phase one of the algorithm only. Regarding phase two, a NER model has been trained. This also contains a limited amount of data. For this model, 70 examples have been used. The data employed consists in a mixture between articles from the penal code [10], streets that belong to a particular neighborhood as well license plates and car models.

This dataset has been divided in two sets. One for training and the other for validation. Usually the dataset is divided in a 80–20 proportion. This means that the training set will contain 80% of the data whereas the validation set will contain 20%. [11]. The training set contains 56 examples and the validation the remaining, in other words 14 examples.

Figure 5 shows the output of the result of the algorithm first phase. A threshold of 25% similarity has been established in order to discard most of the non-similar complaints but it also allows some freedom, otherwise the threshold will be too tight and it is likely to discard most of complaints. As stated in Sect. 3.1 this phase performs a syntactic comparison between complaints.

The most similar complaints which are over or equal the threshold are kept for the second phase. In this case we select the first three complaints.

Phase two performs the comparison between entities that have been extracted from each complaint against the pivot complaint. This allows a more precise comparison and it is only performed in named entities.

Figure 6 shows the Jaccard similarity index between pivot and the three complaints.

Case	Jaccard Similarity index - pivot
Caso 120928	0.7352941176470589
Caso 120927	0.3068181818181818
Caso 122633	0.2894736842105263
Caso 122709	0.2116788321167883
Caso 122693	0.2033898305084746
Caso 122531	0.20161290322580644
Caso 120924	0.19811320754716982
Caso 122521	0.15126050420168066
Caso 122355	0.1504424778761062

Fig. 5. Jaccard Similarity Index preliminary evaluation – Phase 1. Source: Own Elaboration.

Case number	Jaccard Similarity Index - pivot
120928	60.0
120927	66.7
122633	50.0

Fig. 6. Jaccard Similarity Index preliminary evaluation – Phase 2. Source: Own Elaboration.

The table above shown in Fig. 6, indicates the cases that contains similar named entities in both the pivot and the case.

6 Related Work

There are different articles that aim to provide investigators, police officers and other actors with tools to solve cases that are currently waiting for new clues. The article A distance Measure for Determining Similarity between Criminal Investigations [12] takes advantage of the volume of data to determine what crimes may have been committed by a set of individuals. It is a system composed of several modules, such as a text miner, transformers, etc., and after going through this pipeline, a visual report is generated for police officers.

Regarding phase two of the algorithm, we can reference plenty of interesting works such as Chau et al. [13]. This paper describes an extractor of named entities to deal with textual police reports. Cargnaz et al. [14] and Schraagen et al. [15] describes named entity recognition in different languages such as Portuguese and Dutch and also describes the standardization of the models used in those languages.

Hafedh et al. [16] and Sedik et al. [17] perform entity extraction from different resources from internet such as newspapers, news agencies, blogs, forums, and so on.

One of the articles considered the starting point of the current work is [18]. This article applies the Jaccard similarity index in software engineering scenarios.

Other articles that can be considered are [19]. This focus on named entity extraction from medical reports and [20], this paper proposes a chatbot that uses named entity recognition for improving their answers. Finally, the article entitled Deep Analysis and Advancements in Named Entity Recognition [21] offers detailed information regarding named entity recognition and the latest advancements on the subject.

7 Future Work

The PoC presented as such is not suitable for use in real environment, therefore, it is proposed to evolve the PoC into a final product.

In this case, a large part of work will consist of collecting data about cases, and their classification for the subsequent training of the NER model. In the author's work environment, there are large amounts of information about cases and bibliography on legal concepts and also the advice of professionals in the area such as prosecutors.

8 Conclusion

The algorithm described constitutes a starting point that provides support for the investigation of criminal offences. The inclusion of a graphical interface will complement this algorithm, making it intuitive for operators in the organization to use.

Considering the possibilities offered by natural language processing, the failure to automate the available information, in this case the reports of complaints, represent a waste of data that could open new paths in stagnant investigations.

As a note of interest, the implementation of this tool in the future will represent a milestone in the organization in which the main author of this paper currently works, since there is no tool based on artificial intelligence.

This work presents a general overview of the algorithm and two implementations. The first implementation was intended to develop the general strategy whereas the second implementation attempts to complete the strategy and show the viability of it.

References

1. Aliero, A., Bashir, S., Aliyu, H., Tafida, A., Kangiwa, B., Dankolo, N.: Systematic review on text normalization techniques and its approach to non-standard words. Int. J. Comput. Appl. **185**, 975–8887 (2023)
2. Khyani, D., Siddhartha, B.S.: An interpretation of lemmatization and stemming in natural language processing. Shanghai Ligong Daxue Xuebao/J. Univ. Shanghai Sci. Technol. **22**, 350–357 (2021)
3. vor der Brück, T., Pouly, M.: Text similarity estimation based on word embeddings and matrix norms for targeted marketing. In: Proceedings of the 2019 Conference of the North American Chapter of the Association for Computational Linguistics: Human Language Technologies, vol. 1, pp. 1827–1836 (2019). https://doi.org/10.18653/v1/N19-1181
4. Salman, N., et al.: Named Entity Recognition (NER) in NLP Techniques, Tools Accuracy and Performance (2022)
5. Brantingham, P., Brantingham, P.: Crime pattern theory. In: Environmental Criminology and Crime Analysis, pp. 78–93 (2013). https://doi.org/10.4324/9780203118214
6. SpaCy. https://spacy.io/. Accessed 10 Apr 2024
7. NER Annotator. https://tecoholic.github.io/ner-annotator/. Accessed 8 Apr 2024
8. Vis JS. https://visjs.org/. Accessed 7 Apr 2024
9. Unittest. https://docs.python.org/3/library/unittest.html. Accessed 18 Apr 2024
10. Código Penal Argentino. https://servicios.infoleg.gob.ar/infolegInternet/anexos/15000-19999/16546/texact.htm. Accessed 22 July 2024
11. Collet, F.: Deep Learning with Python Second Edition, pp. 133–138. Manning Publications (2021). ISBN 9781617296864
12. Cocx, T., Kosters, W.: A Distance Measure for Determining Similarity Between Criminal Investigations, pp. 511–525 (2006). https://doi.org/10.1007/11790853_40
13. Chau, M., Xu, J., Chen, H.: Extracting Meaningful Entities from Police Narrative Reports (2002)
14. Carnaz, G., Nogueira, V., Antunes, M., Ferreira, N.: Named-Entity Recognition for Portuguese Police Reports (2019)
15. Schraagen, M., Bex, F., Brinkhuis, M.: Evaluation of named entity recognition in Dutch online criminal complaints. Comput. Linguist. Netherlands J. **7** (2017)
16. Hafedh, S., Nazlia, O., Khamael, R.: Named Entity Recognition in Crime Using Machine Learning Approach, pp. 280–288 (2014). https://doi.org/10.1007/978-3-319-12844-3_24
17. Sedik, R., Romadhony, A.: Information Extraction from Indonesian Crime News with Named Entity Recognition, pp. 1–5 (2023). https://doi.org/10.1109/KST57286.2023.10086789
18. Delle Ville, J., Torres, D., Fernández, A., Antonelli, L.: An Approach to Cluster Scenarios According to their Similarity using Natural Language Processing. Lifia, Fac. de Informática, UNLP, La Plata, Bs As, Argentina (2020). https://doi.org/10.13140/RG.2.2.15098.26564
19. Wen, C., Chen, T., Jia, X., Zhu, J.: Medical named entity recognition from un-labelled medical records based on pre-trained language models and domain dictionary. Data Intell. **3**, 1–13 (2021). https://doi.org/10.1162/dint_a_00105
20. Ali, N.: Chatbot: A Conversational Agent employed with Named Entity Recognition Model using Artificial Neural Network (2020). https://doi.org/10.48550/arXiv.2007.04248
21. Madhu, N., Suraparaju, V., Mallaiah, S.: Deep analysis and advancements in named entity recognition-NER. **45**, 171 (2024)

Prospective User Interfaces for Decision-Making Processes in Multidimensional Agriculture

Erika Andrea Valencia Arango[1(✉)], Alejandro Fernandez[2], and Cesar Collazos[1]

[1] Universidad del Cauca, Popayán-Cauca, Colombia
vaerika@unicauca.edu.co, casco@lifia.info.unlp.edu.ar
[2] Universidad de La Plata, La Plata, Argentina
ccollazo@unicauca.edu.co

Abstract. Prospective user interfaces play a crucial role in supporting decision-making processes within the multifaceted landscape of agriculture. This study aims to develop a software tool that integrates prospective user interfaces with the Analytic Hierarchy Process (AHP) model to assist in selecting agrochemicals based on criteria such as price, environmental impact, and toxicity. By leveraging dynamic visual tools and interactive interfaces, the proposed system empowers farmers and stakeholders to anticipate and evaluate future scenarios effectively in the context of diverse agricultural dimensions. The integration of prospective user interfaces with the AHP model enhances decision-making by providing a structured framework to prioritize criteria and alternatives. This facilitates informed and sustainable agricultural practices while addressing complex challenges related to environmental impact and economic viability. The software tool will enable users to input their preferences, weigh different criteria according to their importance, and generate recommendations based on the AHP analysis. This study highlights the importance of technological innovation in advancing decision-making capabilities within multidimensional agriculture, ultimately contributing to more efficient and responsible agricultural practices.

Keywords: Analytic hierarchy process · decision-making · multifunctional agriculture · human-computer interaction · prospective user interface

1 Introduction

Agriculture plays a crucial role in modern society, providing food, employment, and contributing significantly to the global economy. However, the current growth model of agricultural production presents challenges that raise concerns about environmental and social sustainability. This study aims to develop a comprehensive decision-making model for agriculture. It considers economic factors, environmental impact, and consumer safety. By addressing these dimensions, the goal is to improve economic profitability while promoting sustainable and safer agricultural practices.

V. Agredo-Delgado et al. (Eds.): DECISIONING 2024, CCIS 2369, pp. 173–184, 2025.
https://doi.org/10.1007/978-3-031-91690-8_14

1.1 The Problem Statement

The current trajectory of agricultural production growth is unsustainable due to its negative impacts on natural resources and the environment. Up to 40% of the planet's land is degraded, affecting half of humanity, as prices rise in the context of rapid climate change, increasing scarcity, and the rapid degradation of natural resources and other factors affecting the planet. A crisis approach is needed to conserve, restore, and use land sustainably [1]. Given the various issues in the agricultural sector and the growing need for a new perspective and growth in the development of technologies in this field, and since this is an area where research and development of functional prototypes are quite necessary, given that many developed models are redundant as noted in the development of the state of the art, the development of new technologies and techniques is necessary to meet the needs of the new agricultural model, which no longer relies on indicators such as performance or profit but instead ventures into the new multidimensional model that is based on or incorporates the three dimensions of sustainability: environmental, social, and economic, with objectives including environmental conservation, rural development, human nutrition and health, and farmer productivity and profitability [2]. Furthermore, given the continuous change in how user interfaces are developed and modeled, with a focus on making them increasingly user-friendly, innovative, and effective, improving communication between devices and users, and focusing on design, usability, and user experience [3].

A prospective interface refers to a tool or approach used to explore, understand, and/or evaluate potential future scenarios and facilitate informed decision-making. These provide a framework for user visualization and interaction with information, allowing them to anticipate changes and identify future opportunities and challenges in a given context. Prospective interfaces in agriculture provide farmers and planners with the ability to foresee and prepare for impending changes, helping them to identify and adopt more sustainable and resilient agricultural practices. They provide valuable information for evidence-based decision-making, and the use of prospective tools in agriculture helps farmers better understand risks and opportunities, enabling them to make more informed and strategic decisions. According to a report from the Food and Agriculture Organization (FAO) [4], prospective planning is crucial for addressing the challenges of climate change, resource scarcity, and increasing food demand. With the development of the following thesis work, we seek to develop a system to support decision-making, using an efficient method for multicriteria decision-making and implementing the concept of prospective interfaces. This system should meet the requirements of the new agriculture, known as multidimensional or multifunctional agriculture, allowing improvements in this sector, and supporting research and technology implementation in this area, while also considering the concept of responsible innovation.

1.2 Objectives

General Objective: Design prospective user interfaces for decision-making in the agricultural field that support concepts such as sustainable agriculture and multidimensional agricultural systems, based on the pillars of the three dimensions of sustainability: environmental, social, and economic.

Specific objectives

- Analyze the data of decision-makers in the multidimensional agriculture sector and characterize them through user profiles.
- Develop a prototype (software) based on prospective user interfaces corresponding to user profiles, enabling the evaluation of decision-making in multidimensional agricultural systems.
- Validate the proposed system to analyze and confirm the correct implementation of interfaces for user profiles and effective decision-making in a multidimensional agricultural context.

2 Methodology

This study aims to implement technology that supports decision-making in the field of multidimensional agriculture, utilizing the Analytic Hierarchy Process (AHP) decision-making method. This field encompasses various dimensions and criteria, making it extensive and complex, requiring consideration of multiple aspects to ensure effective decision-making. It is crucial in this context to address the diverse perspectives and criteria involved in agricultural decision-making, avoiding conflicts between farmers' prioritized objectives and those inherent in multidimensional agriculture. Additionally, the goal is to characterize each user involved in this process to understand their needs and preferences better. To achieve this, a tool will be implemented using AHP to select the appropriate agrochemical based on the user's preferred criteria model(s). Prospective interfaces will be utilized to enhance the user's understanding of the selection model(s), facilitating more effective decision-making in multidimensional agriculture.

2.1 Multidimensional Agriculture

Agricultural research must move beyond measuring farm "performance" through single indicators like yield and profit and adopt a multidimensional approach that incorporates the three dimensions of sustainability: environmental, social, and economic [2]. This concept of multidimensional agriculture goes beyond food production and considers interconnected dimensions, balancing agricultural production with sustainability and human well-being.

Key dimensions of multidimensional agriculture [2]:

- **Social Dimension:** This dimension addresses human interactions, rural communities, and agriculture's societal impact. It connects economic, environmental, and political factors, involving public and private entities like municipal authorities, NGOs, cooperatives, and producer-consumer associations. Social organizations and solidarity economies play a significant role in improving the quality of life for those involved in food production and consumption.
- **Economic Dimension:** Agriculture plays a crucial role in national economic development, particularly in developing countries, where it provides vital income and contributes significantly to the GDP. It supports other economic sectors and helps reduce poverty while serving as an internal market and a source of foreign exchange through agro-exports.

- **Environmental Dimension:** Population growth and increasing consumption place unprecedented demands on agriculture and natural resources, leading to global environmental degradation. Addressing future food security while reducing agriculture's environmental impact is essential for sustainability. Critical issues include global warming, biodiversity loss, deforestation, and land degradation.

Multidimensional agriculture strives for environmentally sound, socially acceptable, and economically viable food production, ensuring sustainability and equity across all sectors.

2.2 Analytic Hierarchy Process

Since its inception, the Analytic Hierarchy Process (AHP) has been a valuable tool for decision-makers and researchers, establishing itself as one of the most widely used tools for decision-making involving multiple criteria. Over the years, numerous prominent works based on AHP have been published, addressing a wide variety of applications in various fields. These applications range from planning and selecting the best alternative to resource allocation, conflict resolution, optimization, and many other areas. Additionally, extensions and numerical enhancements of AHP have been developed, further enriching its utility and versatility in the decision-making domain [5].

The Analytic Hierarchy Process (AHP) is based on the following steps for decision-making:

1. The objective to be achieved is determined.
2. The criteria and sub-criteria to be considered are defined, structuring them in a hierarchy.
3. Each criterion is compared with its sibling criteria (same parent) using pairwise comparisons to determine the importance of each criterion in the hierarchy.
4. For each criterion C, pairwise comparisons between alternatives must be made to obtain the priorities of each alternative with respect to C. This step should only be carried out for those criteria that do not contain sub-criteria.
5. All priority vectors obtained in the previous step are combined, resulting in a new vector representing the final ranking of the alternatives.

The comparisons are made considering the Saaty scale (Fig. 1):

With the above, we present the Analytic Hierarchy Process (AHP) Tree Diagram for Decision Making that will encompass our solution. This AHP (Analytic Hierarchy Process) diagram will be essential for analyzing and prioritizing evaluation criteria such as price, toxicity, and environmental impact, helping us make informed and effective decisions. Through this process, we will establish a clear and objective hierarchy of relevant factors, facilitating the selection of the best option within our solution (Fig. 2).

2.3 Prospective User Interface

The field of Human-Computer Interaction (HCI) is paramount in the design of interactive systems. HCI focuses on understanding how humans interact with technology

Intensity of importance	Definition
1	Equal importance
3	Somewhat more important
5	Much more important
7	Very much more important
9	Absolutely more important
2, 4, 6, 8	Intermediate values

Fig. 1. The fundamental scale of AHP. Source: Application of fuzzy Delphi AHP method for the estimation and classification of Ghomrud tunnel from groundwater flow hazard - Scientific Figure on ResearchGate. Available from: https://www.researchgate.net/figure/The-fundamental-scale-of-AHP-Saaty-1980_tbl1_251224190

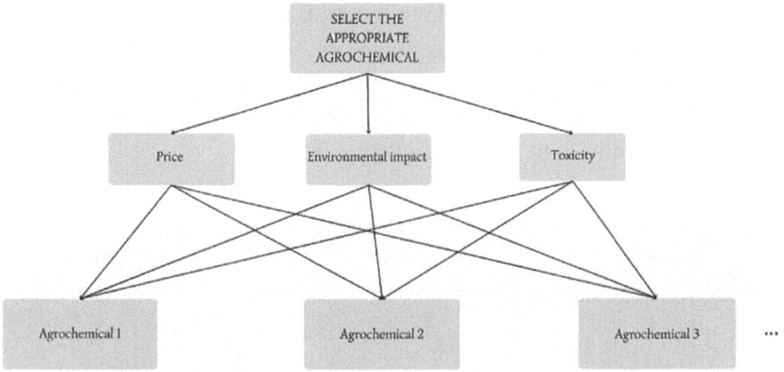

Fig. 2. Analytic hierarchy process (AHP) tree diagram for decision making. Source: Created by the author

and aims to improve this interaction to optimize usability, accessibility, and user satisfaction. Strategies are discussed for designing more effective and appealing interfaces, along with ethical considerations in the design of interactive systems. In summary, HCI underscores the importance of creating technology systems that are more user-friendly, accessible, and impactful, ultimately enhancing the relationship between humans and technology.[6].

The focus of Human-Computer Interaction (HCI) is to create interfaces where users have greater control and understanding of their decisions. This is where the concept of prospective user interfaces comes into play. These interfaces serve as tools or approaches to explore, understand, and evaluate potential future scenarios. They facilitate informed decision-making by providing users with a framework to visualize and interact with information. This enables users to anticipate changes, identify future opportunities, and recognize challenges within a specific context. Lastly, our software will implement these prospective interfaces when users rank criteria using sliders and visualize this model through matrices and pie charts. This will allow them to interact more effectively with the information, enabling exploration of future scenarios and informed decision-making.

3 Results

Presented below are the latest advancements in our solution, which enable users to dynamically rank various criteria using interactive selection and slider controls. This approach enhances usability by providing a more intuitive and flexible way for users to engage with the ranking process. By allowing dynamic selection and adjustments through sliders, users can efficiently assess and prioritize criteria according to their preferences and needs. Users will have the ability to log in to the tool, ensuring that their data is securely stored within it. Our solution leverages modern technologies such as React for frontend development and MongoDB for data storage, ensuring efficiency and scalability.

- Home Page: When the user accesses the web application, they will encounter a simple start interface. The screen will display the solution's logo and three options on the right side. One option leads to the application's main home page, another offers a summary of what AgroAHP is, and the third allows the user to log in. In the main area of the screen, the user will see a slogan alongside a button that provides access to a tutorial video on how to use the tool (Fig. 3).

Fig. 3. Home page. Source: Created by the author

- Login Interface: The login interface is designed to be simple and functional. On this screen, users can enter their email and password to access the application. If they don't have an account, a clearly visible link provides the option to register. This design aims to offer a smooth and straightforward experience, ensuring that the login process is quick and accessible for both new and registered users (Fig. 4).
- Main Menu Interface: The main menu interface of the AgroAHP solution, designed to assist users in agricultural decision-making, features a large button labeled "WELCOME." Below it, four available options are presented:

  - Create New Decision Model: Allows users to establish a new decision model by evaluating different existing criteria, such as price, environmental impact, and toxicity.
  - Make a New Decision: Enables users to carry out a new evaluation and selection of phytosanitary or agrochemical products using an existing decision model.

Fig. 4. Login interface. Source: Created by the author

- Edit Decision Model: Provides users with the ability to modify a previously created decision model.
- Decision History: Displays a record of all decisions made by the user.

In the top right corner of the interface, two additional buttons are located: "My Profile" and "Log Out." The "My Profile" button gives access to the user's personal information and settings, while the "Log Out" button allows the user to exit the application.

- The evaluation and criteria model creation interface in AgroAHP has been designed to be intuitive and easy to understand. Users can visualize their evaluations and make comparisons using sliders, enabling simple and precise interaction. Additionally, the Saaty scale is clearly described, ensuring quick and effective comprehension of the relative importance of each criterion. The interface and its functionalities are described below:

  - Step 1: Assign a name to the criteria model: The user assigns a name to their model, corresponding to the specific decision or set of criteria they are creating. Example: "Economic Model."
  - Step 2: Compare criteria: The user performs pairwise comparisons of the criteria for their decision. To do this, the user must: Visualize the criteria being compared and select which one is more important. These comparisons are made in pairs. Example: choosing whether price or environmental impact is more important. Evaluate how important one criterion is relative to another using a scale from 1 to 9, based on the values of the Saaty scale. This scale is described below the table and in Chapter 2 of the user manual. Ratings are made using sliders, allowing for intuitive and precise value selection.
  - Step 3: Analyze results: The user can visualize their decision and weighting by clicking the 'Calculate AHP Matrix' button. This action displays the calculated matrix and a pie chart with the calculated percentages for each criterion. These values can be modified and recalculated, providing the user with visual support for the criteria model they are creating and reflecting their preferences (Fig. 5).

Once the user has confirmed their selections and criteria rankings, our tool will automatically generate the AHP matrix specific to their evaluation model. This AHP matrix

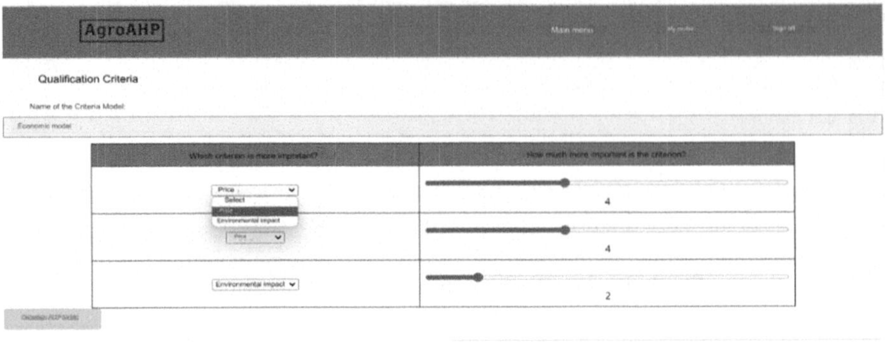

Fig. 5. Ranking criteria: user interface for evaluating economic, environmental, and toxicity. Source: Created by the author

will provide a structured representation of preference relationships between criteria, enabling a more accurate and objective assessment. In addition to the AHP matrix, we will present a pie chart that visually illustrates the percentage of importance assigned to each criterion by the user. This graphical representation will facilitate result interpretation by highlighting the most relevant criteria within the decision-making context (Fig. 6).

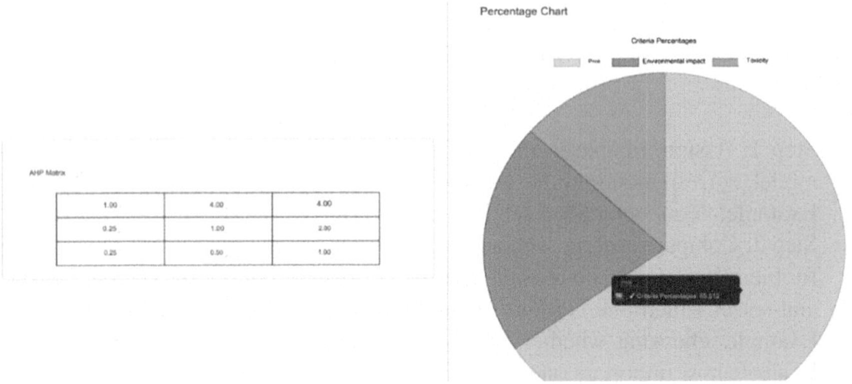

Fig. 6. Visualizing criteria evaluation: matrix and pie chart. Source: Created by the author

- The user interface for the selection of phytosanitary products or agrochemicals has been designed to be intuitive and easy to use, allowing the user to consider different criteria for evaluating alternatives and to properly weigh each pairwise comparison (Fig. 7).

The interface initially includes the following fields:

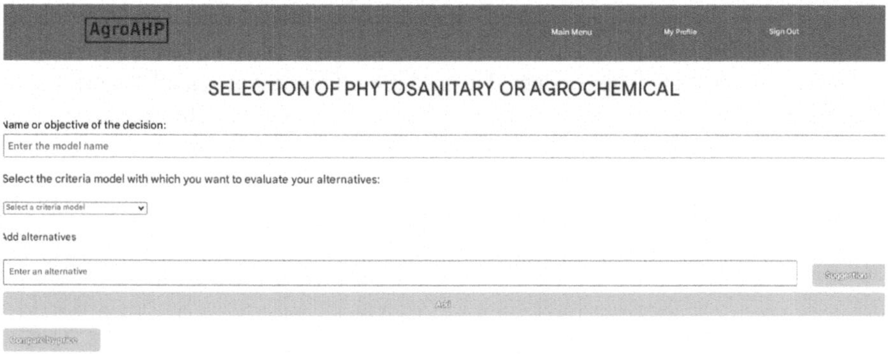

Fig. 7. Selection of phytosanitary. Source: Created by the author

- **Decision name or objective:** The user is asked to enter the name or objective of the decision to be made. Example: "Selection of a phytosanitary product for whitefly control."
- **Select the criteria model:** The user is prompted to select a previously defined criteria model to evaluate the alternatives of phytosanitary products or agrochemicals. These models are available in a drop-down list.
- **Enter an alternative:** A text field to enter the name of a new alternative.

The interface also includes the following buttons:

- **Suggestions:** A button that displays a list of suggested or recommended alternatives.
- **Add:** A button to add the entered alternative to the list of options.
- **Compare by price:** An option to compare alternatives based on their price.

The process starts by adding a decision name and selecting a previously created criteria model. For this example, two alternatives with optional names will be added to demonstrate the interface's functionality. Once the alternatives are entered, the user can proceed to compare them based on the selected criteria and finally visualize the results. These steps enable a complete and accurate evaluation, facilitating well-informed and effective decision-making (Fig. 8).

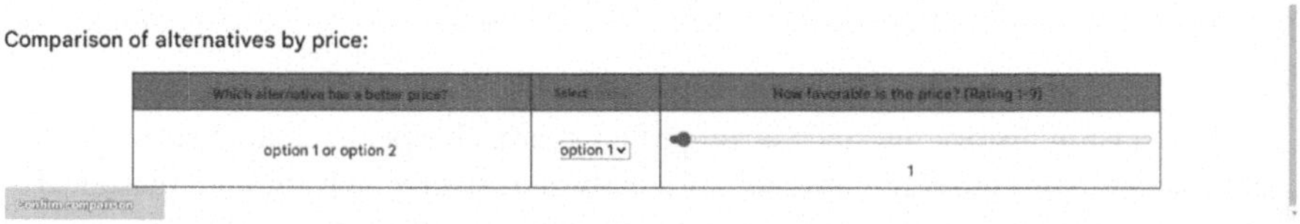

Fig. 8. Comparison of alternatives by price. Source: Created by the author

After the user adds the alternatives, they can proceed with the first comparison, which focuses on the price of the available alternatives. Once this comparison is confirmed, the button to proceed to the next stage will be enabled, where the environmental impact of the alternatives will be evaluated. Finally, the comparison based on the toxicity of each alternative will take place.

These evaluations will be conducted using a drop-down menu that allows the user to select the best alternative for each criterion. Additionally, a slider will be used to rate each criterion, following Saaty's fundamental scale, making it easier to carry out a precise and structured evaluation of all available options. Once the user is confident in their ratings, they can confirm their comparisons and view their evaluations and decisions.

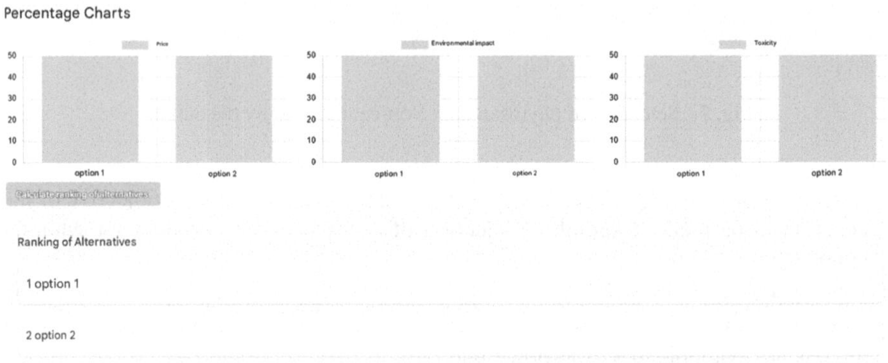

Fig. 9. Percentage charts. Source: Created by the author

Finally, as shown in Fig. 9, once the user has completed all the necessary comparisons and evaluations, they will be able to calculate the ranking of the alternatives. This process will display a detailed list that includes the position and name of each alternative, allowing the user to clearly see which options are best ranked according to the evaluated criteria. This final step provides a structured and objective conclusion based on the data collected and the decisions made during the evaluation process.

This visualization is important because it provides the user with a clear and detailed graphical representation, using bar charts, of how each alternative performs in relation to the different evaluated criteria (price, environmental impact, toxicity). It allows for a quick understanding of the differences between alternatives and facilitates the validation of the assessments made. Additionally, it helps the user make informed decisions by providing a visual image that supports their choices based on objective and comparative data.

- In the decision history interface, a simplified approach has been adopted to enhance ease of use. In this interface, the user can clearly and directly view the name assigned to each decision and the final ranking of the corresponding alternatives. This presentation allows the user to quickly access the most relevant information for each decision made, without complications or unnecessary elements (Fig. 10).

The interfaces designed in this project provide an intuitive and efficient platform for decision-making in the field of multidimensional agriculture. Using the Analytic Hierarchy Process (AHP), users can evaluate key criteria such as price, environmental impact,

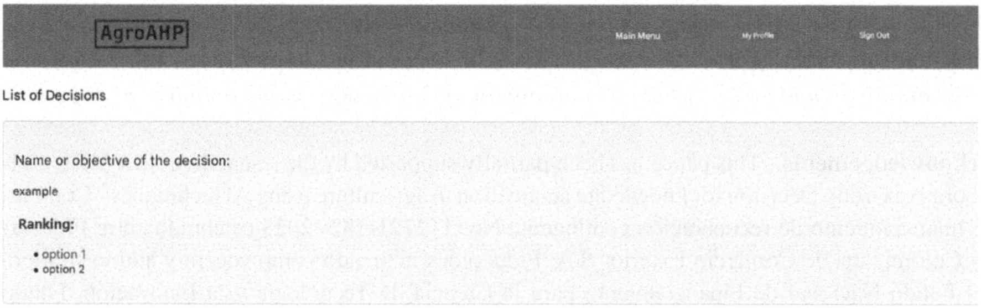

Fig. 10. List of decisions made. Source: Created by the author

and toxicity to select suitable phytosanitary products and agrochemicals. The implementation of the Saaty scale allows for a precise quantitative comparison of these criteria. Users can use sliders and selectors to assess and adjust the criteria and alternatives, enabling optimal customization.

These interfaces have been developed following user-centered design (HCI) principles, ensuring they are accessible and easy to use. Strategic meetings were held with agricultural experts and end users, enabling iterative modifications to the initial interfaces, adapting them to real needs and expectations. The result is a solution that not only meets technical requirements but also provides an enhanced user experience, aiming to encourage greater user participation in the decision-making process.

4 Conclusions

The Analytic Hierarchy Process (AHP) is an effective tool for supporting complex decision-making. It facilitates the process by breaking down the problem into a hierarchy of criteria and alternatives, allowing for clearer and more structured evaluations. By integrating both quantitative and qualitative data, AHP helps assign weights to criteria based on their relative importance, reducing subjectivity, and improving decision quality. Its transparency and methodological rigor also enhance communication and consensus among decision-makers. In summary, AHP is a valuable tool that enhances and justifies complex decisions.

The developed solution enables users to anticipate the economic, human health, and environmental impact of their decisions, promoting sustainable agricultural practices. This is crucial for fostering agriculture that minimizes ecosystem degradation and ensures overall health and well-being.

Visualizing the percentage of importance assigned to each criterion, users will gain a clearer understanding of their preferences and be able to identify the most important criteria and their relative impact on decision-making. If the initial results are not satisfactory, users can adjust the weights to see how they impact decisions. This flexibility supports continuous improvement, allowing for better decision-making over time as priorities and insights evolve. Visual representations like diagrams or matrices make these changes visible to users, enhancing their understanding of the decision-making process.

Additionally, AHP opens avenues for further research and development. Its versatility and applicability across various domains encourage exploration into additional methodologies and tools that can complement and enhance decision-making processes.

Acknowledgements. This papee has been partially supported by the research project 6131: Collaborative Group Decision for knowledge acquisition in agriculture using AI techniques - Contrato de financiamiento de recuperación contingente No. 112721-182- 2023 celebrado entre Fiduciaria Colombiana de Comercio Exterior S.A. Fiducoldex actuando como vocera y administradora del Fondo Nacional de Financiamiento para la Ciencia, la Tecnología y la Innovación, Fondo Francisco José de Caldas y la Universidad del Cauca.

References

1. United Nations: Global Land Outlook, 2nd edn. United Nations (2022)
2. Drinkwater, L.E., Friedman, D., Buck, L.: Systems Research for Agriculture. SARE Outreach (2016)
3. ¿Qué es el diseño centrado en el usuario? DCU. https://platzi.com/blog/diseno-centrado-en-el-usuario-y-su-importancia/. Accessed 08 Apr 2024
4. OECD and Food and Agriculture Organization of the United Nations: OCDE-FAO Pespectivas Agrícolas 2017–2026, OECD Publishing (2017)
5. Vaidya, O.S., Kumar, S.: Analytic hierarchy process: an overview of applications. Eur. J. Oper. Res. **169**, 1–29 (2006)
6. Ali, H.: Human-computer interaction: enhancing user experience in interactive systems. Kufa J. Eng. **14**, 23–41 (2023)

RDF Graph GPT - Building Knowledge Graphs with Chat GPT

Juana Borrelli Zara[1(✉)], Alejandro Fernández[1], and Diego Torres[1,2]

[1] LIFIA, CICPBA-Facultad de Informática, Universidad Nacional de La Plata, 50 y 120, La Plata, Buenos Aires, Argentina
{jbzara,casco,dtorres}@lifia.info.unlp.edu.ar

[2] Depto CyT, Universidad Nacional de Quilmes, Roque Saenz Peña 352, Bernal, Buenos Aires, Argentina

Abstract. This paper introduces RDF Graph GPT app as a tool to automatically translate natural language texts into RDF format knowledge graphs using Artificial Intelligence. Throughout its reading we will dissect and elaborate the various aspects of the functionality mentioned above, as well as some more that this app provides such as graph visualization of any RDF format text with the possibility to choose between two graph types. It also presents an overview of the connection with the AI, more precisely Chat GPT, and the prompts structure that leads to the desired results. The app was tested using different types of natural language texts and different prompts in order to make a richer analysis of the results. This evaluation process was made by experts who gave us some conclusions about the scope and limitations of the tool. It has promising results that show us how interesting this task is along with the potential that the resultant app has. This app, then, puts the focus on the IA as a resource on the matter of developing powerful tools for translating natural language texts into structured formats such as RDF. A very desired task to do automatically due to its implications and applications in the matter of adding semantics to the data.

Keywords: Resource Description Framework (RDF) · Large Language Models (LLMs) · Artificial Intelligence · Chat GPT · Knowledge Graph

1 Introduction

The Semantic Web is a visualization of the Web in which the data is structured and presented in a certain way to make it more machine-readable [1]. This is of great significance when it comes to automatic tasks and intelligent web searches. Machines are good in automatic and repetitive tasks where humans tend to make mistakes; humans, on the other hand, have the ability to understand the semantics of language, as long as computers only see it as symbol concatenation. As a result, the realization of the Semantic Web vision is led by a collection of standards and techniques to make data structured [2].

One of the most powerful techniques to make data machine-readable is the natural language text translation into knowledge graphs, whose nodes represent the text entities

V. Agredo-Delgado et al. (Eds.): DECISIONING 2024, CCIS 2369, pp. 185–199, 2025.
https://doi.org/10.1007/978-3-031-91690-8_15

and whose edges represent the relationships between them [3].There are various graph models, such as Directed Edge-labelled Graphs in which we find nodes and binary relations between them, where we can recognize the subject, from which the arrow will start, and the object, where the arrow will aim, and finally, the predicate will be the arrow's label. A standard data model based on this kind of graph is the Resource Description Framework (RDF) used for globally identifying entities and relations on the Web [4].

That is, then, the motivation of this article, given an unstructured text in natural language, to obtain a correct knowledge graph in RDF format. We can visualize this motivation in the translation from Listing 1 to Listing 2. There are important characteristics of natural language texts that need to be analyzed and processed to be translated properly. Furthermore, in natural language, ambiguities are usual, where the same word has different meanings depending on the context. It commonly has lexical substitutions also, where, in order not to repeat a word, we refer to it differently. To this, we shall add syntactic dependencies where some entities are bound to others. Lastly, humans can extract and recognize different entities that have a global meaning, like companies, countries, or languages, that should be properly identified in our graph.

Listing 1. Natural language text example. Source: Authors.

```
The La Plata National University (Spanish : Universidad
Nacional de La Plata , UNLP) is a national public re-
search university located in the city of La Plata , capi-
tal of Buenos Aires Province, Argentina.
```

Listing 2. RDF graph for text in Listing 1. Source: Authors.

```
@prefix ex: http://lifia.ar/ontology/ .
@prefix rdf: http://www.w3.org/1999/02/22-rdf-syntax-ns .
ex: LaPlataNationalUniversity  rdf: type ex: University;
  ex: hasName ''La Plata National University''@en ;
  ex: hasName ''Universidad Nacional de La Plata''@es ;
  ex: isLocatedIn ex: LaPlataCity ;
  ex: isLocatedIn ex: BuenosAiresProvince ;
  ex: isLocatedIn ex: Argentina ;
  ex: isPublic ''true''^^ xsd: boolean ;
  ex: isResearchUniversity ''true''^^ xsd: boolean .
ex: LaPlataCity rdf: type ex: City ;
  ex: isCapitalOf ex: BuenosAiresProvince .
ex: BuenosAiresProvince rdf: type ex: Province ;
  ex: isLocatedIn ex: Argentina .
  ex: Argentina rdf: type ex: Country .
  ex: University rdf: type rdf: Class .
  ex: City rdf: type rdf: Class .
  ex: Province rdf: type rdf: Class .
  ex: Country rdf: type rdf: Class .
```

In this context, the translation from text to knowledge graph automatically is a desired goal. However, the mechanism used to do it must have the ability to process natural language texts as it must recognize the mentioned characteristics of these texts to express them in the correct RDF format. Several approaches are capable of doing that using regular NLP tools, using DBpedia tools as DBPedia Spotlights in the NER and NEL detection [5] or using the Web LOD cloud [6]. In this article, we analyze the use of a Large Language Model to analyze the natural language. Particularly, this article uses Chat GPT as it is innovative natural language processing. This, added to a detailed prompt to give context to the query, makes Chat GPT a very interesting tool for this task.

A previous open source project named Graph GPT interacts with Chat GPT through its API to build knowledge graphs based on unstructured natural language texts using a prompt. For the graph it maintains an array for entities or nodes and other for relationships or edges. The obtained graph can be extended by writing more information and once it is done it can be stored as a png image. The state of the graph is entirely maintained within the browser and it is not sent in the prompt as, how Graph GPT creator explains, it would make the prompt more expensive and bigger at each query.

This article presents an extension of Graph GPT with different approaches in the type of output and the interaction with the generated graph. With RDF Graph GPT we use Chat GPT to translate natural language text into an RDF turtle format. This makes the first difference with Graph GPT as the Chat GPT prompt won't ask for an extraction of entities and relationships but for a translation to a specific format that requires more processing and the recognition of many aspects in the text, taking advantage of Chat GPT capacities. This RDF is saved in a file, which gives us a lot of opportunities to work with it; we don't need to maintain any structure in order to generate or extend our graphs, the RDF file itself allows us to do these things only by writing or recovering it. Throughout this paper, we will present the RDF Graph GPT operation in detail.

The following sections are organized as follows. In Sect. 2 the related work is presented. In Sect. 3 we find the methodology, while in Sect. 4 the text to knowledge graph process is described. In Sect. 5 the approach is presented. Lastly, in Sect. 6 the evaluation is presented, in Sect. 7 we discuss the limitations of the tool; and Sect. 8 shares conclusions and future work.

2 Related Work

There is a long history of attempts to automatically generate knowledge graphs. The one that prompted this project was Graph GPT, which, built as a toy over a weekend, may not be very powerful, but it introduces the idea of using Chat GPT to generate knowledge graphs from unstructured natural language. It also makes good use of prompt structuring, with the idea of stateless prompts.

As we mentioned in Sect. 1, Graph GPT maintains a JSON object with the nodes and edges of the actual graph, ones that keeps updating any time that more data is added. One of the limitations of Graph GPT is that it runs entirely on the browser, preventing any kind of saving for the structured data we obtain. The only way to save the graph is as a png image, but that wouldn't allow us to keep extending it after. Other of its limitations is that it doesn't allow more than one relationship between two nodes and that sometimes when the same node is mentioned with a tiny difference, it would take it as a new node.

These issues are resolved with RDF Graph GPT by improving the detailing of the prompt and the way of maintaining the state of the graph. The identification of the nodes is also solved with RDF terms that not only make our graph more readable but also compatible with any other knowledge graph on the web. This means that the same resource will be labeled the same way in our graph and in any other graph.

There are other related works in the matter of knowledge graphs and information extraction with LLMs. A systematic analysis of the KB completion potential of GPT, where we focus on high precision [7]. We meticulously design an open-world evaluation set incorporated in INSTRUCTOPENWIKI to assess Open-world IE capabilities thoroughly, focusing on the generalization of unseen instructions and out-of-ontology entities [8]. Extensive experiments to evaluate the performance, time, and cost-effectiveness of 3 different GPT-3 based data annotation approaches for both sequence- and token-level NLP tasks [9]. This last one also introduces the idea of having a Prompt-Guided Unlabeled Data Annotation that we adopt for our prompts.

3 Methodology

The study introduced in this article carried out the Design Science Research methodology [10], which is based on the creation of meaningful artifacts in the resolution of particular problems [11].

The methodology proposes five steps: (1) Awareness of Problem; (2) Suggestion; (3) Development; (4) Evaluation; and (5) Conclusion. This article focuses on the problem of (1) generation of knowledge graphs from text using LLM. An analysis of Knowledge Graphs in RDF language and the activities needs of the mapping are described below, then RDF Graph GPT is the proposed artifact to solve the problem. Finally, RDF Graph GPT is evaluated with different types of text prompts, and experts analyze the results.

4 Text to Knowledge Graph

The translation of unstructured text to a knowledge graph is lead by a natural language processing (NLP) group of techniques, each corresponding to an aspect of natural language texts. These are, the entity recognition (NER), the entity linking (NEL), the relationship recognition (REN) and the relationship linking (REL), that we will discuss in Subsects. 4.1, 4.2, 4.3 and 4.4 respectively. The following are the steps needed in order to obtain good results in the translation, the ones that we desire our tool could do well. Once they are done, we will have a data structure with identified entities and relations, basically, a knowledge graph, where the nodes will be our entities and the edges will be our relationships.

4.1 Entity Recognition

One of the natural language texts characteristics is that, when we read them, we instantly recognize things that have significance for us without the need of having an explanation. This means that we can implicitly put them in context. Named entity recognition or NER is the process by which we can recognize and categorize entities in a text that have a global meaning. This entails the identification of the tokens that represent entities and their subsequent classification in known subgroups like country, organization, language, etc.

4.2 Entity Linking

Another thing to mention about natural language texts is the appearances of words that are written exactly the same but have different meanings depending on the context. To disambiguate this or any other possible confusion, we use named entity linking or NEL, that, as its name suggests, links all entities with a unique identifier from some knowledge base like DBpedia or Wikidata.

4.3 Relationship Recognition

In texts, we will find connectors between the different entities. There is the need to recognize these relationships too, as they will be the connectors of our graph nodes. To achieve this, we use relationship extraction or REN, not only to recognize them but also to categorize them, as they could be of different kinds like a class, a property, etc.

4.4 Relationship Linking

Lastly, we shall do with relationships like with entities; globally identify them in the context of the language. For that, we use relationship linking or REL.

5 Approach

5.1 RDF Graph GPT Functionalities

A visualization of RDF Graph GPT is provided by Fig. 1. We can split its functionalities in the subsequent parts:

Translation. Initially, this app translates natural language into RDF format. To do so, it is necessary to count on a translation tool that recognizes the entities in the text. Especially with RDF the tool should not only recognize them but also categorize these entities to use a proper term for them, as they are usually existent wikidata terms. The terms are the tool that RDF gives us to identify our resources globally. RDF describes the resources in a subject-predicate-object structure, these three elements, when they are put together, is what we call a triplet in RDF. So, in addition to the entities, we need a tool that recognizes the relations between them, as long as the objects of the sentence, in order to form all the triplets.

Once that is settled, there are other details that the tool needs to acknowledge. When it comes to the identification of a resource, the tool may use different kinds of terms depending on the resources semantic. If it is a unique resource it should use an IRI as its ID, so it's globally identified in one and only one way, but if it's a name, an address, or some kind of human readable information, it should use Literals to identify them, as we want these resources to maintain its string state. Lastly if there is need to represent a resource that is actually unknown, for example the author of a book, it should resort to a blank node. On the other hand, in natural language is common to find lists as the object of the sentence; in those cases, the tool should be aware of that, as there is a certain way to express the lists in RDF format [12]. The chosen tool for the translation is Chat GPT with which we interact through its API using a prompt.

Prompt Flexibility. Although RDF Graph GPT's user interface doesn't allow any interaction with the prompt, in the visualization of it as a framework it's a very easy task to do. We can add as many prompts as we want and use any of them to do the request to the API, thus to consult Chat GPT. This is a very interesting aspect as it could be helpful to try different kinds of prompts and see the obtained results depending on which we use. By changing the prompt, for example, we could change the instructions that we send to the model, or the example we use to present our desired output, as, how we were able to see, the improvement in any of the aspects of the prompt means a direct improvement on the generated graph. In order to do this, we need to create a.prompt file, then write on it the desire prompt, always adding a variable that we are going to replace with the text that we want to translate. Then, when doing the fetch to the API we have to take that prompt with the text injected and send it.

Graphic Flexibility. In RDF Graph GPT, our RDF graph will be visually graphed through nodes and edges. The platform offers a variety of possibilities to interact with the obtained graph. For example, in addition to graph an existent file if it is in RDF format or create one in a new file, one could extend an existent file by adding more information to it, which will be displayed in a new graph.

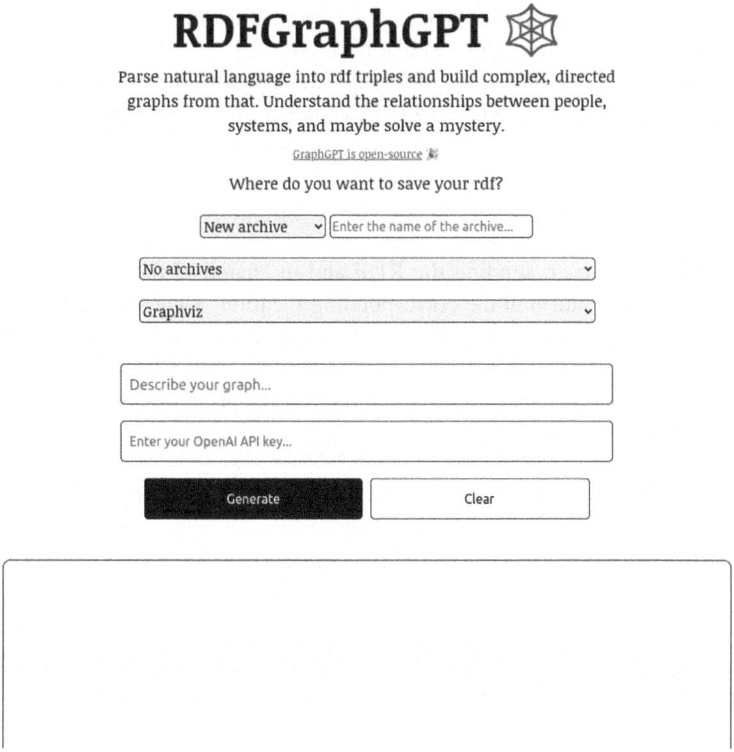

Fig. 1. Visualization of RDF Graph GPT. Source: Authors.

Furthermore, one can choose the graph framework between Graphviz and Cytoscape. While Graphviz draws a more visual and simple graph, the last one allows the user to customize the nodes and edges names, in a visual approach, as it will not change the file content.

RDF Improvement. Lastly, RDF Graph GPT allows the improvement of the result in two different ways. One is with the help of Chat GPT and the other is on hands of the user. The first one uses a prompt to request the API to swap some IRIs for the ones that the user enters. The second one lets the user change any part of the RDF resultant code, either change the IRIs or triplets or add new ones. This change, in contradistinction to the one Cytoscape offers, will change the involved file content; as long as the graph, as it will generate a new one.

5.2 RDF Graph GPT Architecture

An overview of the RDF Graph GPT architecture is provided by Fig. 2. The architec-tonic elements that conform this app are mainly the react app, the node server that continually interacts with the file system and finally the API that we consult and which represents our communication with Chat GPT.

The process begins when the user inserts a natural language text and an API key, and requests to generate the graph. On that point, the app takes the general prompt and inserts the input text in it, then the app fetches the API with the entire prompt and the API key. The response comes in an array in which we find some options, such as the reason of the response to end. Also, one of the options and the most important in this case, is the text field, as in it we find the RDF.

Once it has the response RDF the app checks the location where the user wants to save it. Could be, as we said before, a new or an existent file. With that information, the app reaches the server, sending the RDF and the name of the file. It is the server which saves the information in the corresponding location. Meanwhile, the app checks which of the two graph frameworks were chosen and depending on that, it translates the RDF into a DOT or JSON format and graph the entire RDF with it. To clarify, if the user is extending an existent file, the app will recover the previous RDF and add the new extension so all of it is graphed.

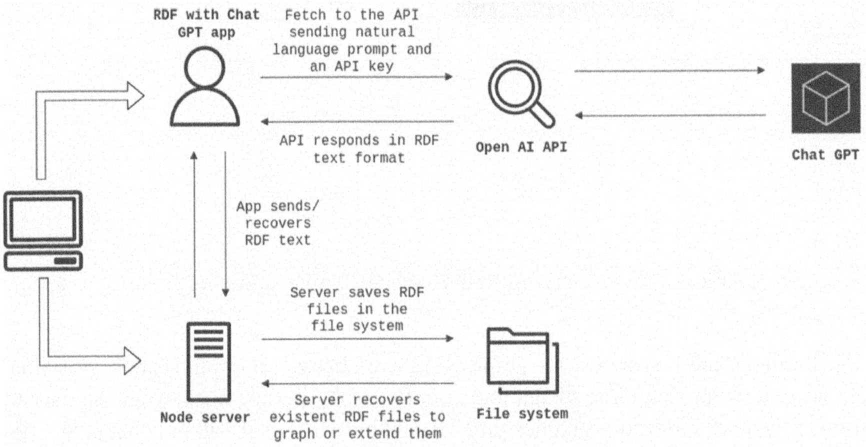

Fig. 2. Architecture of RDF Graph GPT. Source: Authors.

5.3 RDF Graph GPT Prompts

When it comes to interacting with an AI, one of the most important things are the prompts, as they are the way for us to ensure we reach an accurate and coherent answer.

Listing 3. Guided prompt with abbreviated example. Source: Authors.

```
Please represent the following natural language input as
an RDF turtle format. If necessary, clarify any ambiguous
entities or relationships. Avoid using incorrect wikidata
ids or dbpedia ids. Use several vocabularies such as wik-
idata, dbpedia, schema.org, yago, foaf and other type of
rdf vocabularies that appears on the web. Make the de-
scription complete and correct! For wikidata you can
search for IRIs in https://www.wikidata.org/?uselang=en
and for dbpedia from https://www.dbpedia.org. For ele-
ments without a DBpedia or wikidata URI use the follow-
ing: http://lifia.ar/ontology/. Please use all the tools
that the turtle format allows, as the collections and
classes. When the response ends, please put the string
''eof'', so i can know if i have all the information.
Example:
Input:
''The apartment block with address 146, 5th Avenue, New
York, US, has 24 floors and 120 apartments. It was con-
structed in the year 1976. The second floor of the apart-
ment block has 5 apartments: 201, 202, 203, 204 and 205.
. . . ''
Output:
@prefix ex: http://lifia.ar/ontology/ .
@prefix rdf: http://www.w3.org/1999/02/22-rdf-syntax-ns .
@prefix foaf: http://xmlns.com/foaf/0.1/
ex: ApartmentBlock rdf: type ex: ApartmentBlock ;
  ex: hasAddress ''146, 5th Avenue, New York, US'' ;
  ex: hasFloors ''24''^^xsd: integer ;
  ex: hasApartments ''120''^^xsd: integer ;
  ex: wasConstructedInYear ''1976''^^xsd: gYear .
  ex: hasFloor ex: SecondFloor .
ex: SecondFloor rdf: type ex: Floor ;
  ex: belongsTo ex: ApartmentBlock ;
  ex: hasApartments (ex: Apartment201, ex: Apartment202,
ex: Apartment203, ex: Apartment204, ex: Apartment205) .
ex: ApartmentBlock rdf: type rdf: Class .
ex: Floor rdf: type rdf: Class .
eof
Input: $prompt
Output:
```

In this app we use a non-chat completion model, which means that the endpoint is expecting a single string prompt instead of a list of messages [13]. An example of the prompt is shown by Listing 3.

The examples turned out to be a powerful tool for the prompts; the tests showed that without them the responses were very varied and not accurate. As a result, the app prompts are guided ones, which structure is made of a brief description of what we want to obtain from the model. After, we find an example of input followed by an example of the perfect output for the given input. Then a variable that will be replaced with the input of the user and lastly a hook that will be the trigger for the model response.

RDF Graph GPT uses two different prompts depending on the action we intend to do. One for creating a new RDF and the other for improving an existent one. Both of them follow the structure we already described. An important thing to consider is that when it comes to extending the RDF Graph, we use the first prompt as if we were creating a new RDF. We do this in order to make the prompt stateless, as we don't need to send the actual state of the RDF in order to ask Chat GPT to extend it, we can just create a new RDF with the new information and then save it in the original file; that way, we are automatically making the RDF bigger, taking advantage of RDF graphs union capacity. The stateless capacity of the prompt is very important given that if we send the actual state of our graph in each request, the request would be not only more expensive but also bigger each time we extend the graph, leading a point where the API will reject our petition because it will exceed the maximum token amount.

6 Evaluation

Given the context and the desired results in the matter of knowledge graphs, we are going to evaluate the resultant RDF graph correctness. As we mentioned in Sect. 4 there are some needed tasks that the translation tool must perform, whose outcomes are of our interest. So, in the resultant RDF graph, we are going to evaluate (1) Correct entities and literals, (2) Correct relationships, (3) Vocabulary reuse, and (4) Usage of a given IRI when there isn't reuse. The correctness of relations and entities has two important aspects, one is the existence of those entities and relations in the natural language text that we use in the prompt, basically, that the resultant graph makes sense; and the other involves the point (3), that is the correct linking, this means that both relations and entities are linked to existent vocabularies in RDF published on the Web. Lastly we will expect that when no reuse is possible, the tool use a given IRI that we will provide or generates a coherent IRI.

We will evaluate these aspects trying different prompts. As we mentioned, our prompt is a guided one, this means that it could be separated in two parts; the training data and the actual text that we want to convert into RDF. This evaluation will consider changing not only the training part but also the type of text that we give to the model.

When it comes to the configuration of the guide part, we will be trying three different prompts. The first is a training part with detailed instructions and a short example (inst-1); the second has also detailed instructions but no example (inst-2); and the third has simplified instructions and a large example (inst-3). We want to analyze how the model reacts to more details in the instructions and to the examples.

On the other hand, for the texts we choose two types of texts fragments. The first is a wikipedia fragment where we know that the entities come from wikidata (txt-1); and the second is a fragment of a book (txt-2), as we want to analyze how the model reacts to entities that may not have a wikidata IRI.

This evaluation will be done by experts that given a text and a type of prompt will analyze the sense of the resultant RDF graph and the correctness of the IRIs. This analysis will have a (1) quantitative and a (2) qualitative aspect. The first one refers to the amount of correctness, this is, given a graph, how many relations and entities are correct considering both meaning and linking and how many are incorrect; and the second are the possible improvements that would lead to better RDF graphs; lastly, having this information we will evaluate if the graphs can be improved by the existent editing functionality.

On the Table 1 we can see the different variations of instructions and text fragments with the resultant RDF for each. They are identified by an id that matches with other in the document which link we left below, where these three resources are written, as they would take a lot of lines in this paper.

Table 1. Table with results. Source: Authors.

Prompt	Chosen text	Generated RDF
Inst-1	Txt-1	Res-1
Inst-2	Txt-1	Res-3
Inst-3	Txt-1	Res-5
Inst-1	Txt-2	Res-2
Inst-2	Txt-2	Res-4
Inst-3	Txt-2	Res-6

On the other hand, Table 2 shows the different expected entities by both evaluators for each text fragment.

6.1 Evaluator 1 – Analysis

inst-1, txt-1 (res-1). The generated entities match with the expected ones except for two of them. Besides, the result shows some extra entities. When it comes to the correctness of these entities 20 of them are correct and 1 is incorrect, it generates clas-ses with semantic problems. The relations are correct; it generated 58 syntactic and semantic correct triplets. There was zero vocabulary reuse founded, every IRI was new except for rdf:type.

inst-2, txt-1 (res-3). 3 expected entities where detected but with bad IRIs, 11 of them weren't detected and 7 new entities were founded of which 6 were incorrect and 1 was correct. For the relationships 24 triplets with correct relations were founded in a total of 49 triplets. When it comes to vocabulary reuse, on the majority of the triplets the tool intended to use schema or wikidata IRIs but they are not correct; it generates properties that doesn't exist or uses wikidata IRIs that match with elements with no sense in the context. In this case we didn't find much sense on the results, the IRIs don't match with the text and the descriptions don't seem right.

Table 2. Table with expected entities. Source: Authors.

Text	Expected entities by evaluator 1	Expected entities by evaluator 2
Txt-1	La Plata National University; Universidad Nacional de La Plata; UNLP; University; La Plata; Buenos Aires Province; Argentina; 90000 Literal; 10000 literal; 17; 106; University reform; movement; National University of Cordoba; 1918 literal; Argentine university systems; free university education; autonomy; curricular flexibility; university extension; Latin America	Universitary reform; Q1570489 (UNC); Q784171 (UNLP); Q44059 (La Plata); Q44754 (Buenos Aires); Q414 (Argentina); "University reform in Argentina was a…. as well as many others in Latin America."; "1918"; "106"; "17"; "10000"; "over 90000"
Txt-2	Game mechanic; term; rule; set of rules; player action; cause-and-effect relationship; player/s; Action; game status; expected consequence; game; simulation; (novel) mechanics; repurpose; recombine; modify; example (of game mechanic); stealth game mechanic; ability to avoid been seen; penalty; educational games; situations; person's perspective	Stealth-game-mechanic Q1751513 (game mechanic class) "Giving the players the ability to avoid… another person's perspective."; "The term "game mechanic"… lots of games.";

inst-3, txt-1 (res-5). In this combination, 19 entities were correctly detected, 3 weren't detected and 5 new entities were generated, all of them correct. For relationships, 47 triplets make sense as they use the base URI as reference but there are some class definition triplets that are conceptually incorrect. There wasn't vocabulary reuse except for rdf:type and rdf:Class, all the rest triplets used the base IRI generating or inventing possible relations or classes.

inst-1, txt-2 (res-2). Only 5 of the expected entities where found, Game mechanics, game, simulation, stealth game mechanic and mechanic type. All of them are correct but there are a lot missing. When it comes to the relationships, 12 of the triplets were correct, 4 incorrect. The incorrect have the structure "Game rdf:type Game" which is incorrect because it says that an entity is of the type of itself. Except rdf:type and rdf:Class there isn't vocabulary reuse, the properties are created using the prefix ex:.

inst-2, txt-2 (res-4). 6 of the generated entities weren't expected but we can take them as correct because they are bounded to the expected ones. 33 triplets were generated but with questionable correctness as the class definition triplets don't use the prefix rdf but owl which is incorrect on the context; and when it comes to the comments that the tool adds to the class definition, they are invented, not extracted from the text. As to the vocabulary reuse, the analysis is similar from the ones above, it adds the rfds:label and rfds:comment. The RDF looks coherent but not correct as it incorporates elements that don't come from the text.

inst-3, txt-2 (res-6). 14 of the expected entities and 6 extra entities were generated, from the not expected ones, one is correct and in the text, one is correct but wasn't in the text and the other four were incorrect. As for the relationships, 41 correct triplets were generated. The model didn't reused almost any vocabulary, just the rdf:type label. When it comes to the coherence of the RDF this result is better than the one above but it is important to observe that the model takes comments from other sources outside the text.

ddd.

6.2 Evaluator 2 – Analysis

inst-1, txt-1 (res-1). All of the expected entities except three were generated; but not with the wikidata syntax as it was expected. Moreover the model generated 7 new entities that weren't expected. Some of these weren't directly on the text like "Cordoba" or the seek changes of the university reform, which have sense, but it's interesting that the model inferred them from the text. As for the relationships, all of them are considered correct. The model was coherent on the generation and usage of entities and relationships.

inst-2, txt-1 (res-3). The generated entities are questionable, the tool intended to use wikidata IRIs but they were all wrong; besides, to model that UNLP has 17 depart-ments it generated a collection with a different id for each one of them. On the other hand, it correctly used schema.org relations. Beyond that, the tool didn't reuse vocabulary; it redefines identifiers from the space-name of wikidata without considering that they already exist.

int-3, txt-1 (res-5). All of the generated entities were correct and expected, they make sense for the context. The relationships that the model defined were correct. However the model did not use vocabulary reuse.

int-1, txt2 (res-2). Just two of the generated entities were correct, another was questionable, and the two others were incorrect. The model initialized some classes as instances of themselves, which is incorrect. In summary, the model didn't use existent vocabulary but it was consistent with what it defined.

7 Limitations

Although Chat GPT is quite good at natural language processing, the model presents some limitations when it comes to our task. What we need is a translation, not between languages but between data formats. NLP plays a very important role in this translation but there are other things to take into account. In our case, these things are the specific RDF turtle syntax and the usage of existing IRIs. The fact that Chat GPT can't be pre-trained makes us unable to impose the context that we want to the model, so we usually find some syntax errors or invented IRIs on the resultant RDFs. The first limitation can be avoided by providing the model a prompt that includes an example in which the syntax is shown or using a fine-tuned model; but the second comprise a higher degree of difficulty as we can't neither show all the possible IRIs in an example or fine-tunning task, nor train the model to generate them. We think this problem might be solved with Chat GPT 4, which has access to the internet, and, therefore, to the different defined ontologies. On the other hand, another solution for this problem is to train an open-source LLM like LLaMA that we can shape for our specific task.

8 Conclusions and Future Work

Throughout this paper we have presented RDF Graph GPT as a tool to translate natu-ral language into knowledge graphs, particularly using RDF format. We have gone over the importance of knowledge graphs in order to provide semantics to the data, as long as the promising and ongoing tool that the IA represents for us in this context. This app, then, puts the focus on the IA as a tool on the matter of developing powerful tools for this translation, and demonstrates that tools like Chat GPT can bring us up-and-coming results that are in continuous improvement.

Based on the analysis made by experts, we have seen that this tool works quite good when it comes to processing natural language, especially when we provide it with a detailed guided prompt with an example; this was proved by the amount of correct entities and relationships that the tool could recognize using inst-1. However, the results where different on the matter of vocabulary reuse. Instead of finding an existent RDF IRI, it invents it using the correct structure or finds a real IRI that makes no sense for the entity. This and other details may be fixed with GPT-4 that has access to the web. In the meanwhile, it is a task that we are able to do with the improvement functionalities that RDF Graph GPT provides, although they require of our intervention and knowledge.

On the other hand, another conclusion that the evaluation gives us is that the results are significantly better when the text that we request to translate comes from the Wikipedia. We observed that with txt-1 the inst-1 prompt recognized almost every expected entity and all of the relationships were correct. On the contrary, using that same instructions with txt-2 a lot of entities were missing, although the ones that it indeed found were correct.

Beyond this analysis, we have to take into account that it was made looking at a particular LLM results. There are new models of GPT and other LLMs with powerful qualities that we consider will be of great importance on the matter of translating natural language texts into knowledge graphs.

As a future work we would like to make this same analysis but using other LLMs or Chat GPT-4 in order to find the most compatible model for our task.

References

1. Berners-Lee, T., Hendler, J., Lassila, O.: The semantic web. Sci. Am. **284**(5), 34–43 (2001)
2. Hogan, A.: Web of data. In: The Web of Data, pp. 15–57. Springer, Cham (2020). https://doi.org/10.1007/978-3-030-51580-5
3. Jain, N., et al.: Generating domain-specific knowledge graphs: challenges with open information extraction. In: Text2KG 2022: International Workshop on Knowledge Graph Generation from Text. CEUR Workshop Proceedings (2022). https://ceur-ws.org/Vol-3184/TEXT2KG_Paper_4.pdf

4. Hogan, A., et al.: Knowledge graphs. Synth. Lect. Data Semant. Knowl. **12**, 1–257 (2021). https://doi.org/10.2200/S01125ED1V01Y202109DSK022
5. Daiber, J., Jakob, M., Hokamp, C., Mendes, P.N.: Improving efficiency and accuracy in multilingual entity extraction. In: Proceedings of the 9th International Conference on Semantic Systems, pp. 121–124. Association for Computing Machinery, New York (2013). https://doi.org/10.1145/2506182.2506198
6. Rincon-Yanez, D., Senatore, S.: FAIR knowledge graph construction from text, an approach applied to fictional novels. In: TEXT2KG/MK@ ESWC, pp. 94–108 (2022)
7. Keming, L., Xiaoman, P., Kaiqiang, S., Hongming, Z., Dong, Y., Jianshu, C.: PIVOINE: instruction tuning for open-world information extraction. arXiv preprint. https://arxiv.org/pdf/2305.14898.pdf (2023)
8. Veseli, B., Razniewski, S., Kalo, J.C., Weikum, G.: Evaluating the knowledge base completion potential of GPT. arXiv preprint. https://arxiv.org/pdf/2310.14771.pdf (2023)
9. Bosheng, D., et al.: Is GPT-3 a good data annotator? arXiv preprint. https://arxiv.org/pdf/2212.10450.pdf (2022)
10. Vaishnavi, V.K., Kuechler, W.: Design Science Research Methods and Patterns: Innovating Information and Communication Technology, 2nd edn. CRC Press (2015)
11. Hevner, A.R., March, S.T., Park, J., Ram, S.: Design science in information systems research. Manag. Inf. Syst. Q. **28**(1), 75–105 (2004)
12. Hogan, A.: Resource description framework. In: The Web of Data, pp. 59–109. Springer, Cham (2020). https://doi.org/10.1007/978-3-030-51580-5_3
13. OpenAI: Overview - OpenAI API. https://platform.openai.com (2020). Accessed Mar 2024. Accessed 25 Oct 2023

Selection of a Machine Learning Model for Automated Massive Valuation in the Context of the Colombian Cadastre

Maritza Ospina Parra[1](✉), Carlos Orlando Lozada Riascos[2], and Julio Cesar Chavarro Porras[1]

[1] Universidad Tecnológica de Pereira, Pereira, Colombia
{marospina,jchavar}@utp.edu.co
[2] Instituto Geográfico Agustín Codazzi, Bogotá, Colombia
ingeocar@utp.edu.co

Abstract. Knowledge of land values is crucial for the development of economic and fiscal policies that enable the estimation of comprehensive property values in alignment with the dynamic nature of the real estate market. In Colombia, the cadastre has undergone a significant transformation, evolving from a purely fiscal model to a multipurpose cadastre aimed at addressing contemporary challenges such as outdated records, incomplete coverage, and the lack of systematic training. Consequently, continuous cadastral updating and professional training are essential to accurately reflect economic development, urban expansion, and administrative changes. However, despite advancements in technology, the available tools have not been sufficient to efficiently capture, process, and analyze the vast volume of information required for an accurate valuation system. This paper presents a theoretical approach to evaluating and selecting an artificial intelligence-based methodology to improve urban land valuation. The machine learning models analyzed include Random Forest (RF), Support Vector Machine (SVM), Artificial Neural Network (ANN), and Gradient Boosting Model (GB). Ultimately, the study highlights the effectiveness of Random Forest (RF), which, when integrated with the Kriging geostatistical model (KG) to incorporate spatial dependencies, achieves a superior predictive accuracy.

Keywords: Multipurpose Cadastre · Automated Massive Valuation · Random Forest · Kriging

1 Introduction

The cadastre, as an official and systematic register of real estate, is a fundamental piece of the economic value of a society. From the accurate valuation of property for tax collection to ease of access to credit and sustainable urban planning, the cadastre is the foundation on which multiple economic, political and social activities take place. By providing transparency, legal certainty and reliable data for decision-making, the cadastre encourages investment, promotes economic development and contributes to stability and equity in the region. The distribution of wealth, thus strengthening the foundations of a prosperous and just society.

V. Agredo-Delgado et al. (Eds.): DECISIONING 2024, CCIS 2369, pp. 200–211, 2025.
https://doi.org/10.1007/978-3-031-91690-8_16

The traditional cadastre or orthodox cadastre in Colombia has had a fiscal and tax approach (value, dimensions, location and tenure) physical, economic and legal data of a property. Where, the physical cadastre contains cartographic documents and alphanumeric data that characterize each plot and its buildings; The legal cadastre (also called legal cadastre) contains documents that demonstrate the relationship of ownership or tenure between people and the land, and the economic cadastre records data that allows the values of real estate to be determined [1]. This traditional cadastre model has some shortcomings that lie in its reduced coverage and incompleteness, and in the valuation inequity that is generated by treating similar properties as different [2, 3], leaving in the background the real ownership of the territory and its tenure, which leads to ignorance of the value of a particular territory. Likewise, this situation translates into a high lack of horizontal equity in the tax system [3].

The National Government in CONPES 3958 of 2019 [4] recognizes the described problems that the country is going through and proposes a multipurpose cadastre model with a new policy for the updating of properties that seeks to have accurate and updated information on the territory for the development of infrastructure and territorial planning. This is evident if we look at the information published by IGAC 2022 in CONPES 4071 [5], where there are 23,283,380 million hectares updated cadastrally, equivalent to 20.4% of the national area; Of the remaining area of the Colombian territory, 29.31% does not have cadastral formation and 50.91% is outdated.

The updating of the cadastral formation becomes an opportunity for the application of massive instruments that eliminate in the economic element the disparities caused by physical changes, variations in use or productivity, public works, or local conditions of the real estate market (art. 97 Resolution 70 of 2011 of the IGAC) [6]; Therefore, the cadastral authorities have the permanent obligation to update the cadastral and establish models for the updating that allow approximation to the reality of the value of the land.

The cadastral appraisal in Colombia is based on the determination of the independent value of the land or unit value that is carried out specifying the physiographic conditions of the property and the value of the constructions where the clear definition of public services, roads, is made.

For a better physical identification of the properties, it is recommended to consult the homogeneous physical and geoeconomic zones determined by the cadastral entity, which provide integrated information on the potential value, slope, climate, roads, availability of surface water, land use, in the rural area. The slope, use of land and buildings, domestic public services, roads and typology of constructions dedicated to housing in urban areas.

Direct methods are related to traditional methods of capturing land value, including:

1) Comparison or market method.
2) Method of capitalization of rents or incomes.
3) Replacement cost method.
4) Residual method.

Generated by the economy, government decisions, and the community at large. Indirect methods are also linked to government decisions and are of great value to understand the background of the generation and capture of the highest value of urban land given the analytical nature they have, indirect methods such as:

1) Remote sensing images.
2) Integration administrative records.
3) Statistical and econometric models.
4) Analysis with Intelligence Techniques Artificial and all those that are derived from the real estate observatories and can be added to the cadastral base.

Collaborative methods refer to approaches and tools that foster cooperation between different government entities, private organizations, and citizens to collect, maintain, and update cadastral information efficiently and accurately. These methods leverage the participation of diverse actors to improve the quality of cadastral data and pro-mote smart governance in its main aspects (open, transparent, accountable, equitable, responsive, participatory and collaborative) [7].

In the Colombian urban environment, the mass valuation of properties has focused on the determination of cadastral appraisals as the basis for the calculation of property tax, in order to reflect the commercial value of properties in an objective and equitable manner.

2 Methodology

This research corresponds to the initial phase of the project titled "Identification of Automated Mass Valuation Methods in the Context of the Multipurpose Cadastre in Colombia." The main objective of this phase is to systematically identify and analyze machine learning methods that have been applied in mass appraisal processes, with a particular focus on their integration into cadastral valuation frameworks. Given the increasing complexity of land valuation and the need for efficient, scalable, and precise methodologies, this study aims to establish a solid theoretical foundation for the selection of the most suitable artificial intelligence techniques.

2.1 Methodological Approach

A Systematic Mapping Study (SMS) was conducted to identify relevant machine learning methods that have been used in mass land valuation. The methodological process was structured as follows:

Definition of Research Questions: The central research question that guided this study was: Which machine learning methods have been applied in automated mass valuation processes?

To refine the scope, secondary questions were formulated: What are the most frequently used machine learning techniques in cadastral valuation?. What evaluation metrics are commonly employed to assess these models?. What are the main challenges and limitations identified in the literature regarding automated valuation?

Selection of Keywords and Search Strategy: Based on the research objectives, a set of keywords was established to ensure comprehensive coverage of relevant studies. The primary terms used included: Automated Mass Valuation, Cadastre, Massive Land Valuation, Land Value, Mass Appraisal and Computer-Assisted Mass Appraisal (CAMA).

Table 1. Comparison direct and indirect methods.

Criterion	Direct Valuation Methods	Indirect Valuation Methods
Definition	Methods that determine land value based on observable real estate market information, construction costs, and income generation	Methods that use analytical models, geospatial data, artificial intelligence, and statistical techniques to estimate land value
Main Techniques	Market Comparison Income Capitalization Replacement Cost Residual Method	Remote Sensing and Satellite Imagery Integration of Administrative Records Statistical and Econometric Models Artificial Intelligence (Random Forest, Artificial Neural Net-works, etc.)
Data Sources	Real estate market data, recent transactions, construction costs, and profitability rates	Large-scale cadastral data, satellite images, econometric models, and machine learning outputs
Accuracy	High in markets with abundant and transparent information	Higher in contexts where real estate markets lack transparency or data is fragmented
Information Requirements	Accurate data on transactions, costs, and land profitability	Large volumes of data, machine learning models, and advanced computational capabilities
Information Requirements	Accurate data on transactions, costs, and land profitability	Large volumes of data, machine learning models, and advanced computational capabilities
Limitations	Requires updated and accessible data Can be influenced by speculation and market fluctuations Difficult to apply in inactive or underdeveloped markets	Depends on the quality of input data Requires advanced analytical and modeling tools May be challenging to interpret without specialized technical knowledge
Application Areas	Urban and rural real estate markets Tax assessment and fiscal appraisals Infrastructure development and urban planning	Cadastral zoning and land-use planning Land value prediction in areas without transactional data Large-scale automated valuation processes

These keywords were adapted according to the syntax and indexing rules of the selected academic databases to maximize retrieval efficiency. Boolean operators and wildcard characters were employed to refine search queries and retrieve a broad yet relevant dataset of publications.

Selection of Academic Databases: To ensure high-quality and peer-reviewed literature, the following scientific databases were consulted: Springer, ScienceDirect, Web of Science (WOS), IEEE Xplore and Scopus.

These databases were selected due to their extensive repositories of high-impact research in machine learning, geospatial sciences, and cadastral valuation.

Inclusion and Exclusion Criteria: To refine the dataset, a set of inclusion and exclusion criteria was applied:

1. Inclusion criteria: Studies published in indexed journals or conference proceedings. Articles published within a five-year window (2018–2023) to ensure up-to-date findings. Studies explicitly addressing machine learning applications in mass appraisal or cadastral valuation.
2. Exclusion criteria: Studies focused solely on traditional valuation methods without AI integration. Research without empirical validation or case studies. Articles published in non-peer-reviewed sources.

Bibliometric and Content Analysis: To complement the SMS, a bibliometric review was incorporated to identify trends, research gaps, and key contributors in the field. Articles selected through the systematic review were analyzed and categorized based on the machine learning models employed. The classification included:

1. Supervised learning models: Random Forest (RF), Support Vector Machine (SVM), Artificial Neural Networks (ANN), Gradient Boosting (GB).
2. Hybrid models: Combinations of AI techniques with geostatistical approaches, such as Random Forest + Kriging interpolation.
3. Emerging techniques: The use of deep learning models or ensemble techniques beyond traditional machine learning.

2.2 Rationale for Methodological Choices

The choice of an SMS, combined with bibliometric analysis, ensures a structured and reproducible review process. Given that this research is intended to support the development of automated mass valuation methods for Colombia's multipurpose cadastre, it was essential to establish a comprehensive understanding of existing methodologies and their applicability to geospatial and economic valuation contexts.

Moreover, by incorporating a five-year evaluation window, this study captures the most recent advancements in AI-driven valuation while maintaining a focus on methods that have demonstrated empirical validity. The integration of Kriging geostatistical models alongside machine learning techniques is of particular interest, as this hybrid approach has shown promising results in enhancing spatial interpolation and predictive accuracy in cadastral valuation.

3 Methods Analyzed

Aspects of mass valuation are understood as a mechanism for large-scale estimation of values. It is not an individual appraisal that takes into account the particular characteristics of each property, but a valuation process whose objective is to set the most probable values of all the properties [8].

The accelerated evolution of the methods and techniques of valuation and market data capture reveals that economic cadasters can be transformed very quickly [1] therefore, according to de Oliveira [9], the need to innovate in the establishment of technical criteria for the preparation, measurement and execution of The market values are significant. In this context, automated valuation models (AVMs) that use state-of-the-art statistical models are presented as a concrete alternative to ensure the sustainability of a correct and up-to-date valuation of urban land that incorporates the rapid transformations that occur in the territory and the way in which these are reflected in the real estate markets.

To compare the different methods, we searched for relevant information on the most commonly used algorithms and their application to the cadastral context and the weighting of the articles identified to these algorithms.

Random Forest (RF). Breiman developed the concept of Random Forest (RF) in 2001 [10] as an extension of CART. RF is a set (or assembly) of decision trees, where each tree is trained on a random subset of data and uses a random selection of features in each node division. This randomness approach helps improve generalization and reduce overfitting in data that is particularly noisy. The idea of RF is to improve the reduction of Bagging variance by reducing the correlation between trees, without increasing the variance too much [11]. In addition, the correlation between trees is reduced, resulting in a decrease in overfitting [9]. RF is known for its ability to handle complex data and nonlinear relationships, which can be beneficial when modeling soil properties that can depend on multiple factors.

In the context of cadastre, RF can be used in application areas such as land value prediction, land use management, geographic change detection, and risk assessment. The Random Forest method has been applied in various cities around the world for cadastral valuation and other tasks related to urban and territorial management.

Recent research has focused on establishing model accuracy and performance by calculating errors, where RF presents the best results for predicting land prices [12, 13]. On the other hand, the algorithm has shown a better performance when spatial independence is incorporated through Kriging for the management of the waste generated in the unobserved variables [3, 14–17]. Some additional experiences with RF:

1. New York, USA: In New York, Random Forest has been used to improve estimates of real estate values in a context where property values can vary significantly within small geographic areas due to diversity of land uses and variability in property characteristics. The city's Finance Department uses advanced machine learning models, including Random Forest, to update and maintain its cadastral record.
2. Amsterdam, Netherlands: Amsterdam has applied machine learning techniques, including Random Forest, for automatic property appraisal. Models are used to estimate land and structure values based on cadastral data, property transaction information, and urban features.

3. Melbourne, Australia: In Melbourne, the use of Random Forest to assess and predict urban land prices has been investigated as part of efforts to improve the accuracy of cadastral data and support decision-making in urban planning and development.

Other significant work using RF on correlated topics such as House Price Prediction: in South Korea [18], Boston USA [19].

Support Vector Machine. (SVM) is a supervised learning algorithm that seeks to find the optimal hyperplane to separate data from different classes, maximizing the mar-gin between classes and minimizing classification errors. It can be constructed with different core functions (linear, radial-based, sigmoid, and polynomial) [13].

In the context of cadastre, SVMs can be used for tasks such as land classification, detection of changes in land cover, identification of relevant features in satellite imagery, prediction of land values, and data quality analysis.

According to [13], the application of the method in automated mass appraisal does not achieve a good performance. In other correlated fields, such as funding rate inference, SVM is used with acceptable results that are close to the actual projection [20].

Artificial Neural Network. (ANN) are machine learning models inspired by how the human brain works. These models are made up of layers of interconnected artificial neurons that work together. Input neurons represent predictive variables that connect to the hidden neuron layers and then link to the output.

In the context of cadastre, they can be used for image segmentation, land use classification, detection of changes in the landscape, correction of errors in cadastral data, prediction of real estate values, optimization of urban planning. NNAs can be applied in a variety of ways to improve the efficiency, accuracy and quality of cadastral information [12, 13, 16].

In other topics related to the cadastre, there are works that use neural networks: prediction of real estate values [22], extraction of characteristics of buildings in medium-resolution satellite images [23], calculating the cadastral appraisal of a rural property in Colombia [24]. These show the breadth of topics addressed by the ANNs.

Gradient Boosting Model. (GB) is a machine learning technique used to build robust predictive models, usually for regression and classification tasks. The core idea behind gradient boosting is to combine multiple simpler models, usually decision trees, to form a more powerful and accurate model. This model is built iteratively, with each new tree focusing on correcting the errors made by the existing set of trees. In the context of the land registry, the GB has several applications: prediction of real estate values [21], detection of anomalies in data, customer segmentation, optimization of resource allocation, and prediction of real estate trends.

The comparative analysis of machine learning techniques for automated mass valuation highlights the superior performance of Random Forest (RF) and Artificial Neural Networks (ANNs) in terms of accuracy, scalability, and the ability to handle nonlinear relationships in real estate data. RF demonstrates robustness in managing heterogeneous datasets while maintaining computational efficiency, whereas ANNs excel in capturing complex patterns within large-scale valuation models. However, both methods show limitations in spatial dependency integration, which can be mitigated through hybrid approaches such as RF-Kriging. The findings emphasize the necessity of incorporating

Table 2. Comparison of Machine Learning Techniques for Automated Mass Valuation.

Criterion	Random Forest (RF)	Support Vector Machine (SVM)	Artificial Neural Networks (ANNs)	Gradient Boosting (GB)
Accuracy	High accuracy, especially in structured datasets with strong feature importance	Moderate accuracy, dependent on kernel selection and parameter tuning	High accuracy for large datasets with deep structures but requires extensive training	Very high accuracy due to iterative refinement of weak learners
Interpretability	Moderate interpretability, as feature importance can be extracted	Low interpretability; works as a "black box" model	Very low interpretability due to complex architectures	Low interpretability; relies on ensemble models with weak learners
Computational Efficiency	Computationally expensive for large datasets due to tree-based structure	High computational cost, especially for large feature spaces	Very high computational cost; requires significant resources and training time	Moderate to high computational cost; depends on depth of iterations
Handling of Nonlinearity	Handles nonlinear relationships well by aggregating multiple decision trees	Good for nonlinear data if kernel methods are correctly applied	Excellent at capturing complex nonlinear relationships	Very effective for nonlinear relationships through iterative learning
Scalability	Scales well with medium to large datasets, but memory-intensive	Poor scalability for very large datasets due to high computation	Scales well but requires high-performance computing resources	Scales effectively but can suffer from overfitting on very large datasets
Spatial Dependency Integration	Weak spatial integration; does not inherently model spatial autocorrelation	Limited spatial modeling capabilities	Can be improved with geospatial layers and CNN architectures	Can incorporate geospatial dependencies through feature engineering

geostatistical techniques to enhance predictive accuracy in cadastral valuation. Future research should focus on optimizing these hybrid models to improve spatial consistency and support data-driven decision-making in urban planning and land management.

4 Discussion and Limitations

From the theoretical review of the methods and within the family of Machine Learning, a path of research of models with multivariate inputs for the prediction of land value is evidenced. It is also argued that the use of machine learning methods reduces work times, increases tax equity and contributes to better public land use policies.

In Colombia, not enough research has been done on the applicability of automated mass valuation, therefore, the available information does not allow a comparison between the methods. In the Latin American context, there are studies in the cadastral updating processes of Argentina [3, 8, 11, 14, 15] and Brazil [2, 9], where, they argue that Random Forest is a solid choice for estimating land values due to its ability to handle complex and nonlinear data, its resistance to overfitting, its stability and performance, its ability to interpret important features, and its scalability. However, it is important to note that choosing the best model may depend on the specifics of the dataset and the objectives of the case study.

Random Forest has a number of advantages in that it is effective in handling large data sets with many variables, but it does not take into account the spatial dependence of the data, being a key variable in the study for the prediction of land value.

The ordinary kriging method, also known as kriging interpolation, is a spatial smoothing technique used in spatial statistics and geostatistics to estimate values at unobserved locations within a spatial domain. Originally developed by Daniel Krige in the 1950s for mining applications, Kriging has evolved into a widely used method in geographic and cadastral sciences.

The kriging interpolation method is based on the assumption that the output variable is random and space-dependent, being the same stationary process with constant mean and variance dependent on distance and direction. Kriging solves a set of linear equations, known as the Kriging system, which contains semi-variances extracted from a fitted variogram function [17].

The primary Kriging variants used in property valuation include:

- Ordinary Kriging (OK): Assumes a constant but unknown mean and relies on variogram models to estimate spatial dependencies.
- Universal Kriging (UK): Accounts for spatial trends by incorporating a deterministic trend function.
- Indicator Kriging (IK): Utilized for categorical data classification, often re-levant in zoning applications.
- Co-Kriging (CK): Extends Kriging by integrating secondary variables that enhance prediction accuracy.

While machine learning algorithms like RF and ANNs are highly effective in handling complex, nonlinear valuation relationships, they often lack an inherent capacity to model spatial dependencies. The integration of Kriging with machine learning bridges this gap, leading to more robust and spatially aware valuation models.

The comparative evaluation of machine learning algorithms for automated mass valuation underscores the strengths and limitations of different methodologies. Random Forest (RF) and Artificial Neural Networks (ANNs) exhibit high accuracy and scalability, making them suitable for large-scale valuation tasks. However, their limited

Table 3. Performance Comparison of Machine Learning Models in Mass Land Valuation.

Model	Accuracy	Interpretability	Computational Efficiency	Handling of Nonlinearity	Scalability	Spatial Dependency Integration
Random Forest (RF)	High	Moderate	High	Strong	High	Weak
RF + Kriging	Very High	Moderate	Moderate	Strong	Moderate	Strong
Artificial Neural Networks (ANNs)	Very High	Low	Moderate	Very Strong	High	Weak
ANN + Kriging	Very High	Low	Moderate	Very Strong	Moderate	Strong

ability to integrate spatial dependencies necessitates enhancements. By incorporating Kriging, both models significantly improve spatial dependency integration, leading to more precise and geographically coherent valuation outputs. The hybrid approaches, RF + Kriging and ANN + Kriging, demonstrate superior predictive performance, reinforcing the importance of geostatistical techniques in automated mass valuation. Future research should explore further refinements to these hybrid models to enhance computational efficiency while maintaining high accuracy and robustness in diverse cadastral environments.

5 Conclusion and Future Work

The objective of this article was to determine a model of Machine Learning techniques based on a systemic review of the information available in the Colombian and Latin American context.

The integration of machine learning into mass valuation processes offers significant advantages, including reduced processing time, improved tax equity, and enhanced policy decision-making. Among the various machine learning algorithms explored, Random Forest (RF) and Artificial Neural Networks (ANNs) emerge as the most effective for automated mass valuation due to their ability to capture complex, nonlinear patterns in property data.

The similarity of results achieved by ANNs with Kriging in mass valuation processes is evident, for example, in [16] the improvement of RF compared to ANN is only one digit centesimal. In particular, it has been suggested that ANN should be used when we have large volumes of data, which in our context can be associated with large cities.

RF provides high accuracy and interpretability by leveraging multiple decision trees, making it a reliable tool for valuation in structured cadastral environments. However, it struggles with capturing spatial dependencies, which can be mitigated by integrating geospatial interpolation techniques like Kriging. On the other hand, ANNs exhibit exceptional capabilities in recognizing nonlinear dependencies and high-dimensional relationships, making them well-suited for property valuation in heterogeneous urban landscapes. Despite their superior performance, ANNs suffer from high computational demands and lack interpretability, necessitating hybrid modeling approaches that incorporate explainable AI techniques.

Future research should focus on refining machine learning models by integrating spatial dependency factors, optimizing computational efficiency, and enhancing interpretability. Additionally, empirical validation of these models across diverse cadastral datasets is essential to establish standardized methodologies for automated mass valuation in Colombia and beyond.

References

1. Erba, D., Piumetto, M.: Para leer el suelo urbano: catastros multifinalitarios para la planificación y el desarrollo de las ciudades de América Latina, p. 7. Lincoln Institute of Land Policy, Cambrige (2016). https://coilink.org/20.500.12592/xm9gbr. Accessed 29 Oct 2024
2. Eguino, H., et al.: Catastro, valoración inmobiliaria y tributación municipal: Experiencias para mejorar su articulación y efectividad, vol. 235, pp. 14–17. Banco Interamericano de Desarrollo (2020). https://doi.org/10.18235/0002437
3. Carranza, J., Salomón, M., Piumetto, M., Monzani, F., Montenegro, M., Córdoba, M.: Random forest como técnica de valuación masiva del valor del suelo urbano: una aplicación para la ciudad de Río Cuarto, Córdoba, Argentina, p. 10. Anales de 13 Congreso Brasilero de Catastro Multifinalitario y gestión territorial (2018)
4. Concejo Nacional de Política Económica y Social [CONPES].: 3958 de 2019, Estrategia para la implementación de la política pública de catastro multipropósito, Colombia (2019)
5. Concejo Nacional de Política Económica y Social [CONPES].: 4071 de 2022, Declaración de importancia estratégica del proyecto de inversión: Actualización y gestión catastral nacional, Colombia (2022)
6. Resolución 070 del 2011.: Por la cual se reglamenta técnicamente la formación catastral, la actualización de la formación catastral y la conservación catastral. Article no. 97. Colombia (2011)
7. da Silva, A., Fernandes, R.: Smart governance based on multipurpose territorial cadastre and geographic information system: an analysis of geoinformation, transparency and collaborative participation for Brazilian capitals. Land use policy 97-104752 (2020). https://doi.org/10.1016/j.landusepol.2020.104752
8. Piumetto, M., et al.: Técnicas algorítmicas y Machine Learning para la Valuación Masiva de la Tierra de la provincia de Córdoba. Revista de la Facultad de Ciencias Exactas, Físicas y Naturales **6**(2), 49–52 (2019)
9. de Oliveira, A., Bandeira, S., Silva, C.: Estimativa de desempenho de métodos de aprendizado de máquina baseados em árvores de decisão na valoração do solo no município de Fortaleza, Brasil. Revista Valorem **1**(1), 1–15 (2022). https://doi.org/10.29327/2290393.1.1-1
10. Breiman, L.: Random forests. Mach. Learn. **45**, 5–32 (2001). https://doi.org/10.1023/A:1010933404324
11. Carranza, J., Piumetto, M., Salomón, M., Monzani, F., Montenegro, M., Córdoba, M.: Valuación masiva de la tierra urbana mediante inteligencia artificial. El caso de la ciudad de San Francisco, Córdoba, Argentina. Vivienda y ciudad (6), 90–112 (2019)

12. Kim, J., Lee, Y., Lee, M., Hong, S.: A comparative study of machine learning and spatial interpolation methods for predicting house prices. Sustainability **14**(15), 9056 (2022). https://doi.org/10.3390/su14159056
13. Bilgilioglu, S., Yilmaz, H.: Comparison of different machine learning models for mass appraisal of real estate. Surv. Rev. **55**(388), 32–43 (2023). https://doi.org/10.1080/00396265.2021.1996799
14. Cerino, R., Carranza, J., Piumetto, M., Bullano, M., Donalisio, V., Monzani, F.: Propuesta metodológica para la valuación masiva del suelo urbano.: Aplicación espacial del algoritmo Quantile Regression Forest. Vivienda y ciudad (8), 261–274 (2021)
15. Monzani, F., Montenegro, M., Piumetto, M., Cordoba, M., Salomon, M., Carranza, J.: Técnicas geoestadísticas aplicadas a la valuación masiva de la tierra urbana: el caso de la ciudad de rio cuarto, provincia de córdoba. Anales de 13 Congreso Brasilero de Catastro Multifinalitario y gestión territorial (2018)
16. Tziachris, P., Aschonitis, V., Chatzistathis, T., Papadopoulou, M., Doukas, D.: Comparing machine learning models and hybrid geostatistical methods using environmental and soil covariates for soil pH prediction. ISPRS Int. J. Geo Inf. **9**(4), 276 (2020). https://doi.org/10.3390/ijgi9040276
17. Oliver, M., Webster, R.: A tutorial guide to geostatistics: computing and modelling variograms and kriging. CATENA **113**, 56–69 (2014). https://doi.org/10.1016/j.catena.2013.09.006
18. Hong, H., Choi, H., Kim, W.: A house price valuation based on the random forest approach: the mass appraisal of residential property in South Korea. Int. J. Strateg. Property Manag. (2019). ISSN 1648-715X/eISSN 1648-9179
19. Adetunji, A.B., Akande, O.N., Ajala, F.A., Oyewo, O., Akande, Y.F., Oluwadara, G.: House price prediction using random forest machine learning technique. Procedia Comput. Sci. **199**, 806–813 (2022). https://doi.org/10.1016/j.procs.2022.01.101
20. Xin, Y.: Application of optimized support vector machine model in tax forecasting system. J. Funct. Space **2022**, 6212579 (2022). https://doi.org/10.1155/2022/1234567
21. Almaslukh, B.: A gradient boosting method for effective prediction of housing prices in complex real estate systems. In: International Conference on Technologies and Applications of Artificial Intelligence (TAAI) (2020). https://doi.org/10.1109/TAAI51410.2020.00047
22. Forys, I.: Machine learning in house price analysis: regression models versus neural networks. In: 26th International Conference on Knowledge-Based and Intelligent Information & Engineering Systems (2022). https://doi.org/10.1016/j.procs.2022.09.078
23. Idris, I., Mustapha, A., et al.: Application of artificial neural network for building feature extraction in Abuja. Int. J. Multidisc. Curr. Educ. Res. (IJMCER) (2021). ISSN 2581-7027
24. Casas, A.: Propuesta Metodológica para Calcular el Avalúo Catastral de un Predio Utilizando Redes Neuronales Artificiales. Tesis Maestría en Geomática. Universidad Nacional de Colombia (2014)

Web Development Based on Design-Transfer Through Client Adaptations

Jonathan Delgado Guerrero[1,2](✉), Leandro Antonelli[3,4], and Diego Firmenich[5]

[1] Fac. de Informática, UNLP, La Plata, Argentina
jonathan.delgadog@info.unlp.edu.ar
[2] SENESCYT, Guayaquil, Ecuador
[3] Lifia, Fac. de Informática, UNLP, La Plata, Argentina
lanto@lifia.info.unlp.edu.ar
[4] CAETI, Facultad de Tecnología Informática, Universidad Abierta Interamericana, Buenos Aires, Argentina
[5] Departamento de Informática, Facultad de Ingeniería, UNPSJB, Comodoro Rivadavia, Chubut, Argentina
dafirmenich@ing.unp.edu.ar

Abstract. This article presents a methodological framework in order to integrate interaction patterns validated during the development of web software to contribute to reducing the differences between user interface design and software development. The proposal is based on three aspects: (1) a systematic method to link documented interaction patterns (such as online validation, multi-step flows) with functional requirements during the requirements engineering process; (2) an experimental tool that uses customer adaptation to convert high-fidelity prototypes (designed in Figma/Sketch) into semantic and modular HTML/CSS/JS code, including business logic linked to interaction patterns, and (3) a testing approach that combines the System Usability Scale (SUS) with case studies to validate the effectiveness of the method. The iterative process encourages collaboration between users, designers and developers, prioritizing consistency between user expectations and technical specifications. The tool's architecture comprises modules to import design metadata, enrich components with pattern-based rules, and generate reusable code. The contributions lay the foundation for future research in pattern-based design automation and its integration into software development environments.

Keywords: Interaction Requirements · Design-transfer · Client Adaptation · High fidelity proto-typing

1 Introduction

The software development process involves the design of the user interface, which is carried out by designers who have to consider various inputs such as business rules, design trends and user technology. This is known as prototyping.

V. Agredo-Delgado et al. (Eds.): DECISIONING 2024, CCIS 2369, pp. 212–223, 2025.
https://doi.org/10.1007/978-3-031-91690-8_17

The complexity of the prototype depends on the scope of the project and the quality of the requirements. High complexity and good quality of the requirements will cause an increase in the time and cost consumption of the software. A low-complexity prototype will have a shorter development time, but the cost will depend on the quality of the requirements.

The prototype development, with focusing on the user interface, makes use of a variety of prototyping tools and technologies that range from support for building a basic abstraction of what the user interface will be, to a tool that provides a more elaborate deliverable (such as navigation components, styles) that can be used to have a more approximate idea of the user interface in execution.

These components represent rules or validations that are part of a requirement obtained following a requirement engineering methodology. For example, if a requirement is to make a wire transfer, it will involve creating a user interface with input fields for data validation and feedback. These fields are individual components with their own behavior, layout, and relevance to the requirement.

In the last decade, more high-fidelity prototyping tools have been developed. This is mainly due to the community of researchers in human-computer interaction and the creation of sketch-based environments. There is also an aspiration to combine the speed and flexibility of computer-aided tools with graphical capabilities.

The transfer of user interface (UI) design to code is a process in web development that involves the transformation of visual representations, generated in tools such as Figma or Sketch, into operational code (HTML/CSS) that accurately represents the designer's intention. This procedure not only aims to emulate the aesthetics, but also to maintain the interactivity and accessibility established in the prototype. For example, a button that includes hover animations and real-time validations needs to be converted into code that includes both the visual styles and the relevant JavaScript events.

Having a high-fidelity prototype in the early stages of software development can provide more concrete insight to the end user. It may also allow for improvements or adjustments prior to the coding phase. User participation can help refine requirements and incorporate scenarios that were not detected in the requirements gathering process.

During the development phase, transferring design validated by the end user to code could facilitate its reusing, thus reducing time and future errors with the differences between the prototype and the built software. Design transfer involves converting the visual representation of the prototype into HTML code and writing CSS code to manage the style sheet.

Today, these high-fidelity prototyping tools offer the ability to perform prototype inspection from a web browser. This enables the use of client-side adaptation techniques that allow extracting these components with more specific details that turn a visual design artifact into a reusable artifact for the developer.

A mechanism that allowed the transfer of its validation logic specified in a requirement in addition to transferring the design into code could benefit the software development team by providing a more elaborate code aligned with what is requested or expected by the end user. This way, the aim is to design mechanisms that allow discovering, classifying and enriching the components of a user interface.

This article proposes a methodology to incorporate interaction design patterns as part of the requirements. Furthermore, it suggests creating an experimental tool to transfer this design and behavior to reusable components for future application improvements or new requirements. This methodology guarantees a reduction in software development time by having functional design and behavior components at the beginning of the development phase.

2 Related Work

Modern web software is based on methodological and technological approaches that look to optimize the relationship between design, requirements, and implementation. In this context, specialized literature has explored various strategies to close gaps between prototyping and functional code, although challenges persist in the integration of detailed interactions and the automation of workflows. This section discusses key contributions in three critical areas: 1) Model-based web engineering, which addresses prototyping through high-level transformations; 2) Client-side adaptation, focused on techniques to manipulate and enrich interfaces in real time; and 3) Machine learning, which explores code generation from visual representations. Although these approaches have advanced in aspects such as agile iteration [1, 2] or responsive multi-device [3, 4], limitations in the specification of granular behaviors and the reuse of components highlight the need for hybrid solutions.

The present work enters discussion, proposing a framework that integrates documented interaction patterns with client-code adaptation tools, in order to cover identified gaps in the relationship between design and software development [5].

2.1 Model-Driven Web Engineering

There are proposals that allow providing guidance on the selection of a certain type of prototype given the dependence on the complexity of user-developer communication [1, 6]. Thus, we have methodologies that create an agile methodology with a prototyping modeling strategy through model-driven mockups to allow reversing the development process. Therefore, an iterative process based on prototyping with the characteristics of a model-driven design (Model-Driven Web Engineering) [2, 7, 8].

A similar approach is taken in the design of accessible user interfaces using the agile WebTDD methodology, focused on continuous user participation in development cycles [3]. Due to the scope of the study, this methodology was used to represent the navigation and interaction between the application components. A domain-specific language (DSL) was used to generate tests and track changes in requirements, while mockups were used for interface analysis, design, and prototyping [9].

There are also studies focused on combining iterative design with user-centered design strategies that pursue using this methodology in the planning, analysis, and design phases; mainly to build models of interaction, behavior, and the voting scheme with the objective of determining user feedback and using it as input for new iterations as a contribution to the user-centered design [10].

Another application of methodologies is presented in a case study in which incremental design is used together with web modeling (Web Model Refactoring - WMR and Web Quality Evaluation Method - WebQEM) to improve the usability of an application, focusing mainly on the use of WMR during the analysis, design and evaluation phases of the incremental design [11].

These works do not center on providing interaction details regarding data-related visual components. They focus primarily on schematic representation and navigation. These aspects are important for usability and should be addressed in later phases of the software life cycle, which are more related to coding [5].

2.2 Client-Side Adaptation in User Interface Development

Client-side adaptation is used to extract and augment design metadata, allowing for fluid code generation. This technique allows interfaces to be manipulated in real time, directly in the browser, by injecting scripts that modify the DOM (Document Object Model) or intercept user events. Its main advantage lies in the ability to enrich prototypes without altering the original source code, facilitating rapid iterations based on direct feedback from users or stakeholders [12, 13].

There are works that involve using client-side adaptation to create prototyping tools that improve collaboration in web redesign activities [3, 12]. Similarly, client-side adaptation is applied in the user interface design to improve the user experience while taking into account the complex and current interaction with web applications that can occur simultaneously on different devices [4].

Tools like Crowdmock [14] take advantage of this approach to allow multiple users to collaborate on the redesign of interfaces through contextual annotations and visual adjustments in real time, without the need to access complex development environments.

In projects like Wamri [15], client adaptation is used to empower end users in the customization of user interfaces, allowing them to define interaction rules through simplified visual languages. These systems transform user modifications into reusable artifacts, such as CSS or JavaScript snippets, that can be integrated into the standard development flow. This approach not only democratizes interface design, but also reduces the workload on technical teams by outsourcing minor adjustments to the users themselves. These artifacts are used in the creation of conventional web applications and augmentation artifacts.

2.3 Machine Learning in Code Generation

Recent efforts [16–18] apply convolutional neural networks (CNN) to turn sketches into code. To do this, they use a technique for detecting basic components that can be transferred to code. There are methodologies to identify the basic components that are commonly used throughout the software development process [19, 20].

A key limitation of current CNN-based approaches is their focus on structural fidelity over semantic richness. While these models excel at mapping sketches to functional HTML/CSS elements, they often overlook contextual nuances such as ARIA roles, keyboard navigation sequences, or responsive design considerations. For example, a sketched navigation bar might be translated into a <div> with inline styles rather than a semantic <nav> component with proper landmark roles, undermining accessibility compliance. To address this, emerging frameworks are exploring hybrid models that combine computer vision with natural language processing (NLP) to infer intent from annotations or adjacent text in sketches. By training datasets on accessible design systems—such as Google's Material Design or IBM's Carbon—these models could generate code that adheres to WCAG guidelines by default, bridging the gap between visual prototyping and inclusive development.

This form of representation of elements from a smaller and indivisible level that aims to structure prototyping through modular components (atoms, molecules, organisms) promoting its reusing and, has recently been used as a first approach to the detection of components from which to create new components using composition and grouping. As an example, recent works use it to detect a representation of an HTML element sketched on a sheet of paper to convert it to code and also to evaluate the classification algorithms used, and they do it through machine learning.

In summary, while modern tools optimize visual design, gaps persist in: 1) generation of semantic and accessible code, 2) native integration with requirements management systems and 3) automatic translation of interaction patterns into coded behaviors. These limitations highlight the need for hybrid approaches that combine the flexibility of visual design with the precision of software engineering, as proposed in this work.

2.4 Conclusion of Related Work

Nowadays, there are methodologies for requirements gathering that are performed along with a methodology for user interface prototyping. However, there is no methodology that allows incorporating more interaction details of the visual components used in the prototype that are related to a specific requirement. Current methodologies, such as Agile or design thinking, often treat requirements gathering and prototyping as parallel yet disconnected processes.

Tools like Figma or Adobe XD facilitate visual prototyping but lack mechanisms to explicitly link interaction logic—such as button behaviors, form validations, or dynamic data updates—to specific user stories or functional requirements. This lack of agreement can lead to ambiguity where developers interpret designs without fully understanding the intended user experience. For instance, a requirement for "real-time form feedback" might result in inconsistencies.

Having more accurate prototypes could help users see how a product will perform beyond its mere visual presentation. Their input could lead to timely improvements or corrections.

Additionally, it is possible to translate validated design and behavior into reusable code, which can reduce development time by using small components to build current and future requirements. When interaction details are codified alongside requirements, they pave the way for reusable component libraries. Frameworks like React or Angular thrive on modularity, where a validated "dropdown with search" component, for instance, can be repurposed across projects. This approach not only accelerates development but also enforces consistency, as updates to a single component propagate universally. For startups or enterprises scaling digital products, such efficiency reduces technical debt.

3 Our Approach

This research proposes contributions aimed at optimizing the participation between user-centered design and technical implementation in web software development. These contributions seek to address gaps identified in current literature and practice, focusing on three aspects: 1) Designing a method that allows enriching the components of a user interface through the relationship of the interaction patterns existing in the literature as part of the requirements gathering phase, 2) Designing and creating a tool that allows extending the web visualization of the prototype created on an interface design platform through the use of client adaptation to capture the functionality of the component and facilitating the transfer of its design and behavior to HTML/CSS/JS code and 3) Evaluating the method and the tool through an SUS survey to measure its usability. Additionally, preparing a case study to evaluate them in more detail.

In summary, firstly, a systematic procedure is implemented to enhance interface elements through the structured incorporation of documented interaction patterns, such as "Wizard" or "Internal Validation", during the requirements gathering phase. This method aims to reduce uncertainties by associating each functional need with interaction pattern behaviors and the most common interface. For example, a "bank transfer" requirement would automatically link to interaction patterns such as real-time validation of fields and contextual feedback, preventing subjective interpretations between teams from various disciplines.

Secondly, an experimental tool that uses client customization methods to transform high-precision prototypes (designed in Figma or Adobe XD) into working code (HTML/CSS/JS) is created. The tool uses a Node.js parser to obtain design metadata (location, styles, hierarchies) and a rules engine to inject business logic linked to the detected interaction patterns.

Finally, a rigorous evaluation of the experimental method and tool is performed through the methodological application of evaluation techniques. On the one hand, the System Usability Scale (SUS) is applied with the objective of measuring the ease of integration in agile work processes. On the other hand, a detailed investigation examines an e-commerce project, evaluating factors such as development time, consistency between the prototype and the final product, and the decrease in code smells (e.g., duplicate CSS). These initiatives not only confirm the effectiveness of the contributions, but also establish a precedent for future studies in design automation focused on patterns, prioritizing scalability and user experience without giving up technical accuracy.

Analysis of the Proposed Contribution. Figure 1 describes the proposed approach for web software development, integrating key roles, processes and artifacts. This model reflects an iterative and user-centered methodology, aligned with requirements engineering principles. To offer a better understanding of the proposal, the roles, main activities and interaction will be detailed.

Among the roles that participate in the contribution we can find users, requirements engineer, designers and developers.

User. They are the central axis of the process. Their needs, expectations and contexts of use define the direction of the project. They provide the requirements as inputs, their

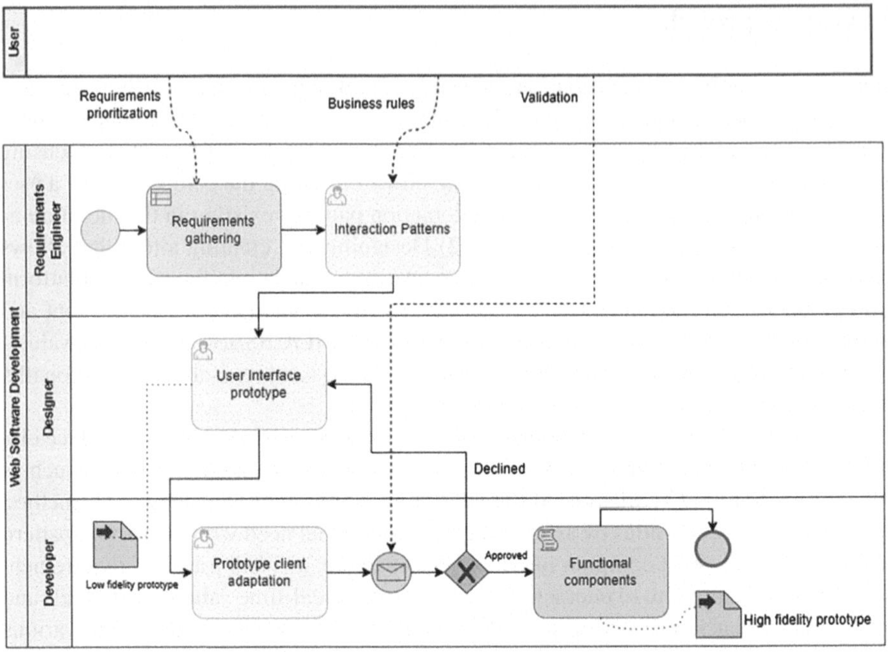

Fig. 1. Interaction of roles and activities of the proposed contribution.

prioritization, in addition to providing the business rules and being an important part of the initial validation of the user interface with the interaction patterns incorporated. Their continuous feedback is important to avoid design deviations.

Requirements Engineer. Their main function is to be the communication bridge between the user and the technical part, translating the user's needs into functional/non-functional requirements through techniques such as interviews and observations. The requirements engineer not only collects data relevant to the user's needs, but also prioritizes and validates the requirements to ensure their technical feasibility and alignment with business objectives, always with the help of the user.

Designer. They use requirements to design the user interface using prototyping tools like Sketch or Figma to deliver a low-fidelity prototype available to developers.

Developer. They are in charge of carrying out the coding of the software for which they use the low-fidelity prototype. Through the experimental tool they can extend the design by integrating the interaction patterns defined in the requirements phase in order to create a high-fidelity prototype that will finally be validated for the user, creating an iterative process of continuous improvement to refine it. When the validation is complete, there will be functional components that will be used for the following phases of software development.

Regarding the definition of the activities in which the roles participate, they are described below:

Requirements Gathering. This systematic process involves detailed documentation of functionalities, constraints, and acceptance criteria. Tools such as user stories, use case diagrams or traceability matrices are used to organize the information. The output of this stage serves as the basis for creating a correspondence matrix between the functional requirements, where the user interface intervenes with the interaction patterns.

Interaction Patterns. With this activity, the correlation matrix that allows the functional or non-functional requirements, which are related to the user interface, to be associated with the interaction patterns is established. This registered will serve as input for the design of the user interface and the specification of the interaction patterns for web development. For example, if the functional requirement involves the entry of a cell phone, interaction patterns such as notifying the format to be entered, or the result of an internal validation of the entered data notified on the screen, could be used.

User Interface Prototype. These can be low fidelity (wireframes), in this activity the designer based on the functional/non-functional requirements uses a design tool such as Sketch or Figma to capture the user interface [21].

Prototype Client Adaptation. In this phase, the prototype undergoes iterative reviews with the client/user. The developer uses the experimental tool that allows extending the low-fidelity prototype through the definition of the interaction patterns and the experimental tool to create a high-fidelity prototype that, in addition to meeting the functional/non-functional requirements, already contains implementations defined by the interaction patterns.

Functional Components. Once the prototype is validated, the functional components of the system are developed. These modules (e.g., buttons, inputs, that already apply interaction patterns) are implemented following modular and scalable development practices. The integration of these components with the adapted interface ensures consistency between the frontend and the user interface design, meeting technical requirements [22].

The proposed model is not linear, but iterative. For example, if during the adaptation of the prototype unforeseen requirements are identified, the process can return to the requirements gathering phase. Furthermore, interaction patterns evolve as new needs are discovered, reflecting an adaptive approach [23]. The collaboration between the requirements engineer, designers and developers is constant, guaranteeing that developments based on user interface designs faithfully reflect user expectations [24, 25]. The current contribution describes a structured approach to web software development, integrating key roles, processes and artifacts. This model reflects an iterative and user-centered methodology, aligned with principles of requirements engineering and agile design.

Method for Enriching Requirements with Interaction Patterns. The suggested technique incorporates verified interaction patterns in the creation of interfaces through three sequential phases. 1) Trend detection: A catalog of models is chosen (e.g., Wizard, real-time validation) that is based on the software domain, the context of use and the profile of the users. 2) Needs assessment: Functional and non-functional requirements related to the interface are analyzed and prioritized, breaking them down into goals, actors, and related patterns. 3) Ordered mapping: A correspondence matrix connects requirements (rows) with patterns (columns), granting aptitude levels (e.g., Likert scale 1–5). As an example, a "product search" requirement relates to data management models, defining text fields and filters.

This approach guarantees coherence between design and technical needs, optimizing decisions in later phases of the software development cycle (SDLC). The matrix acts as a guide for designers, reducing deviations and code smells (e.g., duplicate CSS). The method prioritizes multidisciplinary collaboration, scalability and user experience, closing gaps between conceptual design and technical implementation.

Architecture of the Experimental Tool. The proposed experimental tool is based on a modular structure that mainly incorporates three levels: 1) The import and analysis level, which uses Fig-ma/Sketch's own application programming interfaces (APIs) to obtain design metadata (location, styles, component hierarchies) and convert them into a standardized JSON structure. 2) Behavioral enhancement level, in which a Node.js-based rules engine links previously established interaction patterns (e.g., inline validation, tabbed navigation) to visual elements. For example, a form extracted from Figma has JavaScript logic added to verify fields in real time, according to requirement specifications. 3) Code creation layer, which uses client-side augmentation to create custom templates to generate semantic HTML (with ARIA tags), modular CSS (with BEM methodology) and reusable React components, ensuring consistency between design and Development.

Validation and Transfer from Design to Code. After the high-fidelity prototype has been created, it is implemented in an interactive web platform that incorporates a contextual voting module. End users and stakeholders have the opportunity to experiment with key functionalities (e.g., shopping flows, dynamic filters) and provide feedback through a feedback system linked to specific elements (e.g., "The confirmation button is not properly visible"). Voting is measured using indicators such as satisfaction (Likert scale) and task completion time, giving priority to modifications in elements with low acceptance. After validation, the tool automatically exports the accepted components to a Git repository, accompanied by technical documentation that specifies dependencies and use cases. This procedure makes it easier for programmers to directly incorporate artifacts into the environment.

4 Research Methodology

The research will begin with a qualitative approach focused on the review of literature on user interface design transfers through interaction patterns. The goal is to derive a solution using client-side adaptation techniques and evaluate its effectiveness in web development.

The next step is to design a method to discover, classify, and enrich UI components.

Next, an experimental software tool will be created and implemented to adapt the discovered components, which will be tested through a case study. The final stage consists of conducting an experiment to evaluate, adjust and improve the developed method and tool.

5 Conclusions and Future Work

This study seeks to define a method that integrates interaction design patterns, existing in the literature, with the requirement, and converts them into inputs for the development of prototypes. This will allow users to have a better understanding of the final product and make improvements or corrections early in the SDLC with user participation. It would be beneficial to create an experimental tool to transfer this design to reusable components. With this method, a reduction in development time is sought by having functional components from the beginning, and by integrating validated interaction patterns in the requirements engineering process, a more precise specification of interface behaviors is achieved, reducing ambiguities that traditionally lead to costly reinterpretations during coding. The proposed methodology not only systematizes the relationship between functional requirements and design solutions, but also promotes a common language between designers, developers and stakeholders, facilitating more effective multidisciplinary collaboration.

The experimental tool proposes to automatize the transition from high-fidelity prototypes to functional code by linking design metadata with pattern-based rules, ensuring that complex components, such as dynamic forms or navigation flows, are translated into functional and reusable code. This approach is particularly relevant in agile contexts, where rapid iteration and component reuse are important to meet tight deadlines and quality standards. The following lines of research focus on expanding the scope and applicability of the proposed framework: 1) integration with agile methodologies to explore the compatibility of the method with agile frameworks; 2) automatic selection of interaction patterns using artificial intelligence, by analyzing functional/non-functional requirements and using machine learning techniques to automatically associate the selection of interaction patterns.

References

1. Schmidt, T.S., Wallisch, A., Böhmer, A.I., Paetzold, K., Lindemann, U.: Media richness theory in agile development choosing appropriate kinds of prototypes to obtain reliable feedback. In: 2017 International Conference on Engineering, Technology and Innovation (ICE/ITMC), pp. 521–530. IEEE (2017). https://doi.org/10.1109/ICE.2017.8279930
2. Rivero, J.M., et al.: Improving legacy applications with client-side augmentations. In: Web Engineering: 18th International Conference, ICWE 2018, Cáceres, Spain, 5–8 June 2018, Proceedings 2018, pp. 162–176. Springer, Cham (2018)
3. Hertel, H., Dittmar, A., Linke, D.: Meta-level support for facilitating participation in website (re-) design activities. In: Companion Proceedings of the 12th ACM SIGCHI Symposium on Engineering Interactive Computing Systems, pp. 1–6 (2020). https://doi.org/10.1145/3393672.3398641
4. Firmenich, S., Bosetti, G., Rossi, G., Winckler, M., Corletto, J.M.: Distributed Web browsing: supporting frequent uses and opportunistic requirements. Univ. Access Inf. Soc. **18**, 771–784 (2019). https://doi.org/10.1007/s10209-017-0608-y
5. Tidwell, J.: Designing Interfaces: Patterns for Effective Interaction Design. O'Reilly Media, Inc. (2010)
6. Raptis, G.E., Katsini, C.: Transforming ideas into code: a novel approach to design-to-development workflow. In: 2023 International Conference on Computer and Applications (ICCA), pp. 1–6 (2023). https://doi.org/10.1109/ICCA59364.2023.10401412

7. Urbieta, M., Firmenich, S., Bosetti, G., Maglione, P., Rossi, G., Olivero, M.A.: MDWA: a model-driven Web augmentation approach—coping with client- and server-side support. Softw. Syst. Model. **19**, 1541–1566 (2020). https://doi.org/10.1007/s10270-020-00779-5
8. Kaluarachchi, T., Wickramasinghe, M.: WebDraw: a machine learning-driven tool for automatic website prototyping. Sci. Comput. Program. **233** (2024). https://doi.org/10.1016/j.scico.2023.103056
9. Medina, N.M., Burella, J., Rossi, G., Grigera, J., Luna, E.R.: An incremental approach for building accessible and usable web applications. In: Web Information Systems Engineering–WISE 2010: 11th International Conference, Hong Kong, China, 12–14 December 2010. Proceedings 2011, pp. 564–577. Springer, Cham (2010). https://doi.org/10.1007/978-3-642-17616-6_49
10. Hussain, Z., et al.: User interface design for a mobile multimedia application: an iterative approach. In: First International Conference on Advances in Computer-Human Interaction, pp. 189–194. IEEE (2008). https://doi.org/10.1109/ACHI.2008.24
11. Olsina, L., Rossi, G., Garrido, A., Distante, D., Canfora, G.: Incremental quality improvement in web applications using web model refactoring. In: Web Information Systems Engineering–WISE 2007 Workshops: WISE 2007 International Workshops Nancy, France, 3 December 2007 Proceedings 8, pp. 411–422. Springer, Cham (2007). https://doi.org/10.1007/978-3-540-77010-7_39
12. Aldalur, I.: Web augmentation: a systematic mapping study. Sci. Comput. Program. **232**, 103045 (2024). https://doi.org/10.1016/j.scico.2023.103045
13. Rodríguez-Calero, I., Daly, S.R., Burleson, G., Sienko, K.H.: Prototyping strategies to engage stakeholders during early stages of design: a study across three design domains. J. Mech. Des. **145**, 041413 (2023). https://doi.org/10.1115/1.4056815
14. Firmenich, D., Firmenich, S., Rivero, J., Antonelli, L., Rossi, G.: CrowdMock: an approach for defining and evolving web augmentation requirements. Requirements Eng. **23**, 33–61 (2018). https://doi.org/10.1007/s00766-016-0257-3
15. Marticorena, L.G., Morales, L.A., Antonelli, L., Rossi, G., Firmenich, D.: Development iterations based on web augmentation and context tasks. Multimed. Tools Appl. **82**, 11793–11817 (2023). https://doi.org/10.1007/s11042-022-13694-2
16. Aşıroğlu, B., et al.: Automatic HTML code generation from mock-up images using machine learning techniques. In: 2019 Scientific Meeting on Electrical-Electronics & Biomedical Engineering and Computer Science (EBBT), pp. 1–4 (2019). https://doi.org/10.1109/EBBT.2019.8741736
17. Dave, H., Sonje, S., Pardeshi, J., Chaudhari, S., Raundale, P.: A survey on Artificial Intelligence based techniques to convert User Interface design mock-ups to code. In: 2021 International Conference on Artificial Intelligence and Smart Systems (ICAIS), pp. 28–33 (2021). https://doi.org/10.1109/ICAIS50930.2021.9395994
18. Arefin, M., Hossen, K.M., Khan, R.: pic2code: generating HTML Code from Handwritten Picture. In: 2023 26th International Conference on Computer and Information Technology (ICCIT), pp. 1–6 (2023). https://doi.org/10.1109/ICCIT60459.2023.10441098
19. Frost, B.: Atomic Design. Brad Frost Web (2016)
20. Wang, Y., Luo, L., Liu, H.: Bridging the semantic gap between customer needs and design specifications using user-generated content. IEEE Trans. Eng. Manag. **69**, 1622–1634 (2022). https://doi.org/10.1109/TEM.2020.3021698
21. Chen, J., et al.: Wireframe-based UI design search through image autoencoder. ACM Trans. Softw. Eng. Methodol. (TOSEM). **29**, 1–31 (2020). https://doi.org/10.1145/3391613
22. Shamat, N.A., Sulaiman, S., Sinpang, J.S.: A systematic literature review on user interface design for web applications. J. Telecommun. Electron. Comput. Eng. (JTEC) **9**, 57–61 (2017)
23. Kaluarachchi, T., Wickramasinghe, M.: A systematic literature review on automatic website generation. J. Comput. Lang. **75**, 101202 (2023). https://doi.org/10.1016/j.cola.2023.101202

24. Bexiga, M., Garbatov, S., Seco, J.C.: Closing the gap between designers and developers in a low code ecosystem. In: Proceedings of the 23rd ACM/IEEE International Conference on Model Driven Engineering Languages and Systems: Companion Proceedings, pp. 1–10 (2020). https://doi.org/10.1145/3417990.3420195
25. Feng, K.K., Li, T.W., Zhang, A.X.: Understanding collaborative practices and tools of professional UX practitioners in software organizations. In: Proceedings of the 2023 CHI Conference on Human Factors in Computing Systems, pp. 1–20 (2023). https://doi.org/10.1145/3544548.3581273

What the Semantic Web Can Do for Cognitive Digital Twins: Challenges and Opportunities

Mario Lezoche[1] and Diego Torres[2,3](✉)

[1] University of Lorraine, CNRS, CRAN, 54000 Nancy, France
mario.lezoche@univ-lorraine.fr
[2] LIFIA, CICPBA-Facultad de Informática, UNLP, 1900 La Plata, Argentina
diego.torres@lifia.info.unlp.edu.ar
[3] Departamento de CyT, UNQ, Bernal, Argentina

Abstract. The Cognitive Digital Twin is an advanced version of the Digital Twin model. It integrates cognitive computing technologies to create systems that not only connect but also reason, learn from past experiences, and make informed decisions. The integration of machine learning algorithms and artificial intelligence allows cognitive digital twins to process and interpret data. This cognitive capability enables the digital twin to function with a layer of intelligence that mimics human cognitive abilities, making the system adaptable to its environment and capable of handling complex decision-making processes autonomously. The cognitive features of cognitive digital twins are crucial as they enable the system to predict future states, identify potential problems before they occur, and suggest mitigating actions. Furthermore, the use of semantic web technologies can facilitate advanced analytics and machine learning within cognitive digital twins. This article offers a rapid literature analysis of how Semantic Web approaches can support several aspects of cognitive digital twins models.

Keywords: Cognitive Digital Twins · Semantic Web · Industry 4.0

1 Introduction

The concept of a Digital Twin represents an important advancement in how we perceive and interact with the physical world through digital models. From a scientific perspective, the Digital Twin is fundamentally an elaborate and dynamic software model that accurately mimics a physical object or system [1]. This model continuously updates and evolves in response to data from sensors and other inputs, essentially living parallel to its physical counterpart [2]. Digital Twins' science hinges on synthesizing real-time data streams, advanced simulations, and analytics to enable understanding, learning, and reasoning. This dynamic simulation environment allows for real-time diagnostics, predictive analytics, and operational optimization, providing a robust framework for research and experimentation.

Technologically, the Digital Twin leverages state-of-the-art IoT frameworks, cloud computing, and machine learning algorithms to create a live, functional replica of the

V. Agredo-Delgado et al. (Eds.): DECISIONING 2024, CCIS 2369, pp. 224–237, 2025.
https://doi.org/10.1007/978-3-031-91690-8_18

studied object or system [1]. At its core, it integrates various data sources continually collected from the physical twin through sensors and other monitoring technologies. These data sources are then processed and analyzed within a cloud-based platform that supports high volumes of data inflow and complex computational algorithms. The technology stack is fundamental as it must handle not only massive and continuous data streams but also provide the computational power required to model and simulate complex physical systems accurately.

From an industrial point of view, the significance of Digital Twins cannot be overstated. They are increasingly becoming a cornerstone of Industry 4.0, offering profound benefits across various sectors, including manufacturing, automotive, aerospace, and healthcare [3]. In manufacturing, for instance, Digital Twins improve product quality and yield by enabling the real-time monitoring and control of factory operations [4, 5]. They also predict future states and process outcomes, reducing downtime and enhancing operational efficiency. In the automotive and aerospace sectors, they facilitate the detailed simulation of products under various stressors and conditions to predict performance and prevent failures. The healthcare industry benefits by using (Human) Digital Twins [6] to create personalized treatment plans for patients by simulating medical interventions and predicting their outcomes without any risk to the patient.

Overall, the intersection of scientific research, technological advancements, and industrial application in the realm of Digital Twins enhances operational efficiencies and opens new avenues for innovation and development. This integration is significant, forming the backbone of next-generation engineering and operational strategies. This first part of the introduction sets the stage for discussing the profound impact of Digital Twins across various domains, highlighting their role as not just tools of replication but also as instruments of innovation and efficiency in the digital age.

The Cognitive Digital Twin (CDT) [7] represents an evolution of the Digital Twin paradigm, integrating cognitive computing technologies to enable systems that are not only connected but are also capable of reasoning, learning from past experiences, and making informed decisions [7]. This cognitive capability infuses the digital twin with a layer of intelligence that mirrors human cognitive abilities, making the system adaptive to its environment and able to handle complex decision-making processes autonomously.

A CDT combines the real-time data streams from its physical counterpart with a powerful, dynamic simulation model. It employs machine learning algorithms and artificial intelligence to process and interpret this data. The cognitive aspects are particularly significant as they allow the CDT to perform tasks such as predicting future states, identifying potential problems before they occur, and suggesting mitigating actions [7, 8]. By incorporating natural language processing, it can intuitively interact with human operators, providing explanations and supporting collaborative decision-making processes.

Additionally, the need for a state-of-the-art review in this field is underscored by the potential of semantic web technologies to facilitate advanced analytics and machine learning within CDTs. By structuring data semantically, CDTs can improve the efficacy of algorithms used for pattern recognition, anomaly detection, and predictive analytics. This structured data approach enables more precise models to predict equipment failure, optimize resource allocation, and even simulate complex scenarios to test potential outcomes. For example, in the energy sector, a semantic-enabled CDT can analyze relationships between weather conditions, energy demand, and production capacity to optimize grid operations without human intervention.

Furthermore, as digital twin technologies permeate more critical areas such as healthcare and public safety, the accuracy and reliability of these systems become paramount. Here, semantic functionalities not only enhance the precision of digital twins but also their explainability. Healthcare providers utilizing CDTs can benefit from systems that predict patient outcomes based on vast datasets and explain their recommendations in understandable terms, thereby improving trust and facilitating better patient care.

In conclusion, the state-of-the-art in CDTs equipped with Semantic Web functionalities is not just a technological advancement but a necessary evolution to meet the demands of modern, data-intensive industries. This part of the introduction highlights the critical need for developing sophisticated, semantically enriched cognitive digital twins that can transform complex data landscapes into intelligible, actionable frameworks that drive decision-making and strategic innovation across various sectors. This advancement is essential for harnessing the full potential of digital twin technologies in an increasingly interconnected and data-driven world.

This article introduces a rapid literature review to describe the state-of-the-art in CDTs equipped with Semantic Web functions. It is organized as follows. Section 2 describes the background of the use of CDTs in the industry and some trends in semantic web technologies. A brief description of the methodology is introduced in Sect. 3. Section 4 describes the cognitive characteristics that should be managed in a Cognitive Digital Twin. Then, Sect. 5 describes the Semantic Web technologies that will be compromised in the development and design of CDTs. Section 6 analyzes the critical components involved in CDTs. Finally, the conclusions and further work are presented in Sect. 7.

2 Background

As it was mentioned before, the rapid growth of Digital Twins and the incorporation of Cognitive Digital Twins in several fields like Industry 4.0, healthcare, and manufacturing among others offer new trends.

In the industrial context, the applications of CDTs are vast and transforming. For example, in the manufacturing sector, a CDT of a production line could continuously learn and adapt from operational data [9–11]. It could predict equipment failures or process deviations and suggest adjustments to maintenance schedules or operations to optimize performance and reduce downtime. This capability to predict and adapt in real-time is fundamental for industries where equipment failure can result in significant economic losses and safety hazards.

Similarly, in the energy sector, CDTs can be used to manage complex power generation systems [12]. By understanding the operational dynamics and environmental influences on these systems, a CDT can optimize fuel usage and energy output, reduce emissions, and predict system failures before they occur. For instance, a CDT for a wind farm could analyze data from each turbine and environmental conditions to optimize the angle of the blades and the operation of each turbine to maximize energy production based on predicted weather conditions.

In the automotive industry, CDTs are being explored for both manufacturing processes and in the vehicles themselves. In manufacturing, a CDT can streamline the assembly line, optimize logistics, and enhance quality control by learning from every component installed and every finished vehicle tested. For cars, a CDT can enhance the driving experience by learning the driver's habits and preferences, adapting the vehicle's operational characteristics accordingly, and providing personalized maintenance reminders.

These examples illustrate how the cognitive capabilities of Digital Twins are revolutionizing industries by adding layers of intelligence to traditional monitoring and simulation models [12]. The cognitive aspect not only increases the efficiency and effectiveness of these systems but also paves the way for innovative approaches to operations management, predictive maintenance, and dynamic optimization. In essence, CDTs represent a leap towards more autonomous, intelligent systems that are proactive rather than reactive, significantly enhancing their utility in industrial applications. This part of the introduction delves into how these cognitive functionalities manifest in practical, industrial scenarios, highlighting their potential to drive substantial advancements in various sectors.

Integrating Semantic Web technologies with Cognitive Digital Twins (CDTs) represents a significant leap in the evolution of digital twin technologies, enhancing their ability to process, interpret, and utilize data more meaningfully and contextually. Semantic Web technologies [13, 14], rooted in the principles of linking data and metadata in a structured, interoperable format, enable CDTs to understand and reason about the data they process beyond mere numerical or categorical data points. This integration allows for a more nuanced and comprehensive understanding of the digital and physical worlds, facilitating advanced functionalities like automated reasoning, complex decision-making processes, and sophisticated interaction capabilities.

By incorporating Semantic Web standards, such as RDF (Resource Description Framework), OWL (Web Ontology Language), and SPARQL (SPARQL Protocol and RDF Query Language), into CDTs, these intelligent systems can achieve a higher level of data interoperability and integration. This semantic layer enables CDTs to gather data from diverse sources and understand the relationships and hierarchies within the data. As a result, CDTs can perform more complex analyses, deduce new insights, and automate decision-making processes in a context-aware manner. For instance, a CDT equipped with semantic web capabilities can understand that a temperature reading is not just a number but is related to a specific part of a machine under certain operational conditions, thereby enhancing the accuracy of its predictions and recommendations.

In the industrial domain, applying Semantic Web technologies in CDTs unlocks new possibilities for optimization and innovation. Previous works state the generation of DT from the use of Knowledge Graphs definition [15] introducing a connection from Semantic Web to DTs. Nowadays, consider the example of a smart factory, where a CDT with semantic web capabilities is implemented. This CDT can seamlessly integrate and interpret data from various production line parts, including machinery, logistics, and supply chain systems. By understanding the semantic relationships between different data points and systems, the CDT can optimize production schedules, reduce waste, and anticipate supply chain disruptions before they occur. Moreover, it can provide insights into process improvements and innovation opportunities by analyzing data holistically.

Another industrial example is in the field of energy management. A CDT with semantic web capabilities can manage an intelligent grid, integrating data from various sources, such as energy consumption patterns, weather forecasts, and renewable energy production. By understanding the semantic context of this data, the CDT can optimize energy distribution, predict demand spikes, and automatically adjust energy production from renewable sources. This not only improves energy efficiency but also contributes to sustainability goals.

Additionally, in the realm of healthcare, a CDT with semantic web functionalities can revolutionize patient care by integrating and analyzing data from electronic health records, wearable devices, and clinical studies. By understanding the semantic relationships between different health indicators, treatment outcomes, and patient histories, the CDT can provide personalized care recommendations, predict health risks, and support clinical decision-making.

Incorporating Semantic Web technologies into CDTs significantly enhances their analytical and decision-making capabilities by providing a deep, contextual understanding of data. This semantic understanding enables CDTs to function more autonomously, making informed decisions based on a comprehensive view of the data landscape. The industrial examples highlighted herein demonstrate the transforming potential of semantic-enhanced CDTs across various sectors, paving the way for more intelligent, efficient, and innovative solutions. This part of the introduction explores the synergistic combination of CDTs and Semantic Web technologies, emphasizing their impact on advancing digital twin functionalities and their application in industry-specific scenarios.

Cognitive Digital Twin technology has rapidly advanced over the past few years and has gained significant attention for its potential to transform various industries. This response will present the state-of-the-art in Cognitive Digital Twin technology, focusing on its key components, applications, challenges, and future directions.

The imperative to establish a state-of-the-art in the domain of Cognitive Digital Twins (CDTs) with Semantic Web functionalities stems from the escalating complexity and scale of data-driven operations across various industries. As organizations increasingly rely on digital twins for real-time decision-making and strategic planning, the need for enhanced data understanding and processing capabilities becomes critical. This advancement is particularly essential, where integrating cognitive and semantic functionalities can transform raw data into actionable insights, optimizing performance, enhancing predictive maintenance, and driving innovation.

The foundation of CDTs lies in their ability to dynamically simulate real-world processes, assets, and systems. However, by integrating Semantic Web technologies, these digital twins can leverage structured data and relationships enriched with domain-specific ontologies. This semantic enhancement allows CDTs to represent, understand, and reason about the operational context. Such capabilities are crucial in scenarios where decisions depend heavily on the intricate interplay of various data points and their semantic relationships. For instance, in complex manufacturing settings, a semantic-enabled

CDT can interpret the data concerning machine performance in the context of its maintenance history, operator shifts, and production cycles, offering contextually relevant and highly actionable insights.

Moreover, the rapid evolution of both the Internet of Things (IoT) and big data technologies has led to an unprecedented influx of data from multiple sources and formats. Here, the state-of-the-art CDTs with semantic functionalities can provide a cohesive framework to manage this diversity and volume effectively. By using semantic technologies, such as RDF and OWL, CDTs can create a unified view of heterogeneous data sources, ensuring that the digital twin's database is robust and comprehensible to both machines and humans. This capability is critical for providing interoperability among different systems and enhancing the scalability of digital twin technologies across various sectors.

The previous description of the rapid growth of CDTs and the semantic web and knowledge graph solutions motivated an analysis of the literature to better understand the characteristics and challenges relating to the semantic web and the world of CDTs.

3 Methodology of this Study

This study is a rapid literature review [16]. A systematic literature review was not possible at the time of this article's publication. Because the time available for this study is not compatible with a Full Systematic Reviews, to achieve our goal, we conducted a Rapid Review, and we complimented the Rapid Review process with the strategies presented in the work of Grant and Booth [17].

A rapid review (RR) is a type of knowledge synthesis that simplifies or omits components of the systematic review process to produce information quickly.

There is strong evidence that when the RR is applied correctly and complemented by a rigorous snowball process, it can produce results equivalent to those obtained through a Full Systematic Review. Rapid Reviews are complementary methods for Full Systematic Literature Review which includes a selection of recent published bibliography works from the last years and which includes the following keywords: Cognitive Digital Twins, OR [Ontology, Semantic Web, LOD].

Research questions: The purpose of this work involves two main important aspects in order to our interest. The first is the idea of "cognition" which is involved in the general idea of Cognitive Digital Twins. And the second question relates the known technologies and standards in the Semantic Web in order to be used in the architectures of the Cognitive Digital Twins that supports the cognition part.

- RQ1: Which characteristics make cognitively able a Digital Twin?
- RQ2: Which Semantic Web technologies support the Cognitive aspect in a Cognitive Digital Twin?

The search strategy generated a list of 14 articles, which are detailed in Table 1. There are 14 representative published papers that include the analysis and/or description of Cognitive Digital Twins. Some of the themes are previous to the Cognitive Digital Twins denomination; however, the need for cognition as an extension of Digital Twins is presented. In this screen, the period is from 2008 to 2022.

The analysis to answer the two research questions is detailed in the following sections.

Table 1. List of analyzed articles. Source: Authors.

Ref.	Title	Year
[18]	Next Generation Digital Twin	2018
[19]	Symbiotic Autonomous Systems with Consciousness Using Digital Twins	2019
[11]	COGNITWIN-Hybrid and Cognitive Digital Twins for the Process Industry	2020
[8]	Enhancing Cognition for Digital Twins	2020
[9]	Cognitive Twins for Supporting Decision-Makings of Internet of Things systems	2020
[20]	Actionable cognitive twins for decision making in manufacturing	2020
[7]	Cognitive digital twin for manufacturing systems	2021
[21]	Cognitive Digital Twins for Smart Manufacturing	2021
[22]	Smart Steel Pipe Production Plant via Cognitive Digital Twins: A Case Study on Digitalization of Spiral Welded Pipe Machinery	2021
[10]	A Cognitive Approach to Manage the Complexity of Digital Twin Systems	2021
[12]	The emergence of cognitive digital twin: vision, challenges and opportunities	2022

4 Cognition in Cognitive Digital Twins

The concept of cognition in Cognitive Digital Twins (CDTs) encapsulates the integration of advanced computational processes that mimic human reasoning in digital twin frameworks. This cognitive layer enables CDTs not only to replicate real-time operational data but also to interpret, learn from, and make decisions based on that data. This capability transforms digital twins from mere data mirrors into proactive, intelligent systems that can significantly enhance operational efficiency and innovation [12].

Machine learning algorithms and artificial intelligence technologies primarily drive cognition in CDTs. These technologies allow CDTs to analyze historical and real-time data to detect patterns, predict outcomes, and initiate actions without human intervention. For instance, in predictive maintenance, a CDT can analyze data from machine sensors to predict equipment failure before it occurs. By doing so, maintenance can be scheduled in a timely manner, thus avoiding unplanned downtime and extending the equipment's operational life.

Another core aspect of cognition involves natural language processing (NLP) and semantic technologies, which enable CDTs to understand and generate human-like responses [18]. This feature is particularly useful in scenarios where CDTs interact directly with operational staff or end-users. For example, in the automotive industry, a CDT could interpret diagnostic data from a vehicle and communicate potential issues and solutions in clear, understandable language to the vehicle's owner or technicians.

Cognition also encompasses the ability of CDTs to improve over time through continuous learning processes [7, 11, 19]. As these systems are exposed to more data and different scenarios, they refine their algorithms and enhance their predictive accuracy. This aspect of cognition is critical in environments where operational conditions frequently change, such as in dynamic manufacturing settings or fluid markets like energy trading [9, 18, 19]. Here, a CDT can continuously adjust its models based on new data, remaining relevant and accurate in its predictions and recommendations [20].

Moreover, integrating decision-making capabilities within CDTs represents a significant leap in their cognitive functionalities [19]. By leveraging rule-based logic along with machine learning, CDTs can execute complex decision-making processes that traditionally require human expertise [8]. In the healthcare sector, for instance, a CDT could analyze a patient's ongoing health data in conjunction with their medical history and current medical research to provide personalized treatment recommendations. Such a system not only assists healthcare providers in decision-making but also helps in monitoring patient health more effectively.

Finally, the cognitive aspect of CDTs allows for the incorporation of ethical and regulatory considerations into the decision-making process. As CDTs are increasingly used in critical and sensitive domains, embedding ethical and conscious [21] guidelines and compliance protocols within the cognitive processes ensures that the actions and recommendations of CDTs align with legal standards and societal norms.

In summary, cognition in Cognitive Digital Twins imbues these systems with their intelligent, dynamic capabilities, transforming them from static models of real-world entities into active, learning, and decision-making agents. This integration of cognitive abilities enables CDTs to perform complex analyses, learn from interactions, adapt to new information, make informed decisions, and communicate effectively, making them invaluable across a broad spectrum of industries [12].

5 Semantic Web Applied to Cognitive Digital Twins

Integrating Semantic Web technologies with Cognitive Digital Twins (CDTs) heralds a transformative approach to how data is utilized and interpreted in complex systems. By embedding Semantic Web principles, CDTs can leverage enriched, context-aware data models to enhance their analytical and decision-making capabilities. This section elaborates on the synergy between Semantic Web technologies and CDTs, outlining the mechanisms, benefits, and potential industrial applications of this integration.

At the intersection of the Semantic Web and Digital Twins, we find a powerful paradigm that enhances the functionality of CDTs through sophisticated data management and processing techniques. The Semantic Web provides a framework that makes data machine-readable across different systems via common formats and shared data standards. Using RDF (Resource Description Framework), OWL (Web Ontology Language) [22], and SPARQL (SPARQL Protocol and RDF Query Language), CDTs can define and retrieve data through rich, interoperable ontologies that describe data relationships in a meaningful way.

5.1 Data Interoperability and Integration

A core benefit of applying Semantic Web standards to CDTs is the significant improvement in data interoperability. This feature is particularly crucial in environments where multiple CDTs operate within the same ecosystem, such as in large-scale manufacturing, smart cities, or integrated healthcare systems. For instance, in a smart city, CDTs of traffic systems, public utilities, and emergency services can interlink through shared ontologies, allowing seamless data exchange and synchronization across these services. This level of integration supports more coordinated responses to city-wide events or emergencies, optimizing resource allocation and response times.

5.2 Enhanced Analytical Depth

Semantic Web technologies enable CDTs to perform beyond traditional data analysis by incorporating reasoning tools that interpret the 'meaning' of data within a specific context. This capability allows CDTs to execute complex queries that consider the relationships and attributes defined in their ontologies. In the industrial sector, a CDT equipped with semantic capabilities can analyze the operational data from a factory floor not just in isolation but in relation to historical performance data, maintenance records, and even external factors such as supply chain disruptions. Such depth of analysis facilitates predictive maintenance, optimized production schedules, and improved quality control [8].

5.3 Adaptive Learning and Personalization

The adaptive learning feature of CDTs powered by Semantic Web technologies stems from their ability to continually refine and update their ontologies based on new information and interactions. In personalized healthcare, a CDT can use semantic rules to tailor medical treatments based on a patient's genetic information, past responses to treatments, and ongoing health data. This approach not only personalizes patient care but also dynamically adjusts to new medical insights or changes in the patient's condition, thereby enhancing treatment efficacy and patient outcomes.

5.4 Question Answering in Knowledge Graphs

Knowledge Graph Question Answering (KGQA) is a popular research branch of KBQA that uses a knowledge graph (KG) as a knowledge source and uses triples to answer a question asked in natural language [23]. In KGQA, in the first stage, a question asked in natural language is translated into some semantic query representation, e.g., SPARQL. Then, that query is applied to the knowledge network, and the answers are adapted to offer them to the person who asked the question. The approaches could also be improved in combination with LLM and graph embeddings [24]. CDTs have their knowledge base described in a knowledge graph. Questions and answers are part of their life cycle.

5.5 Challenges in Implementation

Despite the advantages, the application of Semantic Web technologies in CDTs faces several challenges. The complexity of developing and maintaining detailed ontologies that accurately reflect the real world can be substantial. Additionally, the computational demand of processing and querying rich semantic data in real time can impose significant burdens on existing infrastructures. Moreover, ensuring data privacy and security is challenging, especially when handling sensitive information across interconnected systems.

5.6 Future Directions

Looking forward, the convergence of Semantic Web technologies and CDTs is set to redefine the landscape of digital twins. As these technologies mature, we anticipate more robust models of semantic interoperability that can scale across different industries and domains. Future advancements may include more automated tools for ontology generation and management, improved semantic data processing algorithms, and enhanced data security standards in semantic environments.

In conclusion, the application of Semantic Web technologies to Cognitive Digital Twins opens up a new frontier in digital modeling and simulation. This integration not only empowers CDTs with enhanced data comprehension and operational intelligence but also sets the stage for revolutionary applications across various sectors. As we continue to develop these technologies, the potential for creating more connected, intelligent, and responsive systems is immense, promising significant advances in how we interact with and manage complex systems.

6 Key Components of Cognitive Digital Twin Technology

The key components of Cognitive Digital Twin technology include real-time data collection, machine learning algorithms, artificial intelligence, cognitive computing capabilities, visualization and simulation, and optimization and control. These components work together to create an intelligent model that can accurately represent the physical asset or system, learn from its environment, and optimize its behavior.

Real-time data collection involves collecting data from sensors and other sources in real time, which is then used to continuously update the model. Machine learning algorithms are used to process and analyze the data to identify patterns, anomalies, and other relevant information. Artificial intelligence enables the model to reason and make decisions based on the data it ingests. Cognitive computing capabilities enable the model to understand natural language and interact with humans in a more human-like manner. Visualization and simulation enable the model to create a virtual representation of the physical asset or system and simulate different scenarios. Finally, optimization and control mechanisms enable the model to optimize its behavior based on the data it ingests, improving efficiency, reducing costs, and preventing downtime.

6.1 Applications of Cognitive Digital Twin Technology

Cognitive Digital Twin technology has numerous applications in various industries. In the manufacturing industry, the technology can be used to create a virtual model of a manufacturing system to simulate different scenarios, optimize production, reduce downtime, and lower costs. Similarly, in the transportation industry, the technology can be used to create a virtual model of a vehicle or transportation system to monitor performance, optimize routing, and reduce fuel consumption.

In the healthcare industry, Cognitive Digital Twin technology can be used to create a virtual model of a patient's health status, which can be continuously updated based on data from sensors and other sources. This can enable more accurate and timely diagnosis and treatment, as well as more personalized care. In the energy sector, the technology can be used to create a virtual model of a power plant or other energy system to optimize energy generation, reduce emissions, and improve efficiency.

6.2 Challenges of Cognitive Digital Twin Technology

While Cognitive Digital Twin technology has shown great promise, there are still challenges that need to be addressed. One major challenge is the integration of various systems and data sources, which can be complex and time-consuming. Another challenge is the need for high-quality data to ensure accurate predictions and optimizations. In addition, the technology is still in its early stages of development, and there is a lack of standardization and best practices, which can make implementation difficult.

6.3 Future Directions of Cognitive Digital Twin Technology

Despite the challenges, the potential applications and benefits of Cognitive Digital Twin technology are vast, and there are many ongoing research efforts to address these challenges and further advance the technology. Some potential future directions for Cognitive Digital Twin technology include the integration with blockchain, the expansion to new industries, the adoption of explainable AI, the integration with edge computing, and the development of hybrid models.

The integration with blockchain can improve data security and enable more efficient data sharing between different systems. Expanding to new industries can open up new technological opportunities, such as in the construction and agriculture industries. The adoption of explainable AI can improve transparency and accountability, enabling users to understand how the model makes decisions. The integration with edge computing can enable real-time decision-making and reduce latency. Finally, the development of hybrid models that combine the strengths of different technologies, such as Cognitive Digital Twin technology and predictive analytics, can enable more accurate predictions and optimizations.

7 Conclusions

In conclusion, the Cognitive Digital Twin is a promising technology that combines the power of digital twins and cognitive computing to enable more intelligent, adaptable, and autonomous systems. The Cognitive Digital Twin has the potential to revolutionize a variety of industries, from manufacturing and healthcare to transportation and energy.

Currently, research on the Cognitive Digital Twin is still in its early stages, and many challenges and opportunities lie ahead. Some of the key challenges include developing more advanced algorithms and models for cognitive computing, ensuring the security and privacy of data, and integrating the Cognitive Digital Twin with existing systems and processes.

Despite these challenges, the potential benefits of the Cognitive Digital Twin are significant, and researchers are working diligently to overcome these obstacles and unlock the technology's full potential. As the field continues to evolve, it is likely that the Cognitive Digital Twin will become an increasingly important tool for optimizing complex systems and processes in a variety of domains.

Cognitive Digital Twin technology is a rapidly evolving field that has gained significant attention in recent years due to its potential to transform various industries. The technology involves creating a virtual model of a physical asset or system, which is then equipped with cognitive computing capabilities, machine learning algorithms, and optimization and control mechanisms. This enables the model to learn, reason, and optimize based on the data it ingests, allowing for more efficient and effective decision-making, monitoring, and control.

The key components of Cognitive Digital Twin technology include real-time data collection, machine learning algorithms, artificial intelligence, cognitive computing capabilities, visualization and simulation, and optimization and control. These components work together to create an intelligent model that can accurately represent the physical asset or system, learn from its environment, and optimize its behavior.

One of the major applications of Cognitive Digital Twin technology is in the manufacturing industry. By creating a virtual model of a manufacturing system, the technology can simulate different scenarios and optimize the system's behavior to improve efficiency, reduce downtime, and lower costs. Similarly, in the transportation industry, the technology can be used to create a virtual model of a vehicle or transportation system to monitor performance, optimize routing, and reduce fuel consumption.

In the healthcare industry, Cognitive Digital Twin technology can be used to create a virtual model of a patient's health status, which can be continuously updated based on data from sensors and other sources. This can enable more accurate and timely diagnosis and treatment, as well as more personalized care.

Despite its potential, there are still challenges that need to be addressed in the field of Cognitive Digital Twin technology. One major challenge is the integration of various systems and data sources, which can be complex and time-consuming. Another challenge is the need for high-quality data to ensure accurate predictions and optimizations.

However, the potential applications and benefits of Cognitive Digital Twin technology are vast, and there are many ongoing research efforts to address these challenges and further advance the technology. Some potential future directions for Cognitive Digital Twin technology include the integration with blockchain, the expansion to new industries, the adoption of explainable AI, the integration with edge computing, and the development of hybrid models.

In conclusion, Cognitive Digital Twin technology is a rapidly evolving field with the potential to transform various industries through the creation of an intelligent model that can learn, reason, and optimize based on the data it ingests. While there are still challenges that need to be addressed, ongoing research efforts are focused on addressing these challenges and further advancing the technology. With continued advancements and integration with other advanced technologies, Cognitive Digital Twin technology has the potential to greatly improve the efficiency and effectiveness of physical assets or systems in the future.

References

1. VanDerHorn, E., Mahadevan, S.: Digital twin: generalization, characterization and implementation. Decis. Support. Syst. **145**, 113524 (2021). https://doi.org/10.1016/j.dss.2021.113524
2. Tao, F., Xiao, B., Qi, Q., Cheng, J., Ji, P.: Digital twin modeling. J. Manuf. Syst. **64**, 372–389 (2022). https://doi.org/10.1016/j.jmsy.2022.06.015
3. Pires, F., Cachada, A., Barbosa, J., Moreira, A.P., Leitão, P.: Digital twin in industry 4.0: technologies, applications and challenges. In: 2019 IEEE 17th International Conference on Industrial Informatics (INDIN), pp. 721–726 (2019). https://doi.org/10.1109/INDIN41052.2019.8972134
4. Onaji, I., Tiwari, D., Soulatiantork, P., Song, B., Tiwari, A.: Digital twin in manufacturing: conceptual framework and case studies. Int. J. Comput. Integr. Manuf. **35**, 831–858 (2022). https://doi.org/10.1080/0951192X.2022.2027014
5. Soori, M., Arezoo, B., Dastres, R.: Digital twin for smart manufacturing, a review. Sustain. Manuf. Serv. Econ. **2**, 100017 (2023). https://doi.org/10.1016/j.smse.2023.100017
6. Okegbile, S.D., Cai, J., Niyato, D., Yi, C.: Human digital twin for personalized healthcare: vision, architecture and future directions. IEEE Netw. **37**, 262–269 (2023). https://doi.org/10.1109/MNET.118.2200071
7. Al Faruque, M.A., Muthirayan, D., Yu, S.-Y., Khargonekar, P.P.: Cognitive digital twin for manufacturing systems. In: 2021 Design, Automation & Test in Europe Conference & Exhibition (DATE), pp. 440–445. IEEE, Grenoble, France (2021). https://doi.org/10.23919/DATE51398.2021.9474166
8. Eirinakis, P., et al.: Enhancing cognition for digital twins. In: 2020 IEEE International Conference on Engineering, Technology and Innovation (ICE/ITMC), pp. 1–7. IEEE (2020). https://doi.org/10.1109/ICE/ITMC49519.2020.9198492
9. Lu, J., Zheng, X., Gharaei, A., Kalaboukas, K., Kiritsis, D.: Cognitive twins for supporting decision-makings of Internet of Things systems. In: Wang, L., Majstorovic, V.D., Mourtzis, D., Carpanzano, E., Moroni, G., Galantucci, L.M. (eds.) Proceedings of 5th International Conference on the Industry 4.0 Model for Advanced Manufacturing, pp. 105–115. Springer, Cham (2020). https://doi.org/10.1007/978-3-030-46212-3_7
10. Lu, J., Zheng, X., Schweiger, L., Kiritsis, D.: A cognitive approach to manage the complexity of digital twin systems. In: West, S., Meierhofer, J., Ganz, C. (eds.) Smart Services Summit, pp. 105–115. Springer, Cham (2021). https://doi.org/10.1007/978-3-030-72090-2_10
11. Abburu, S., Berre, A.J., Jacoby, M., Roman, D., Stojanovic, L., Stojanovic, N.: COGNITWIN – hybrid and cognitive digital twins for the process industry. In: 2020 IEEE International Conference on Engineering, Technology and Innovation (ICE/ITMC), pp. 1–8. IEEE, Cardiff, UK (2020). https://doi.org/10.1109/ICE/ITMC49519.2020.9198403
12. Zheng, X., Lu, J., Kiritsis, D.: The emergence of cognitive digital twin: vision, challenges and opportunities. Int. J. Prod. Res. **60**, 7610–7632 (2022). https://doi.org/10.1080/00207543.2021.2014591
13. Berners-Lee, T., Hendler, J., Lassila, O.: The semantic web. Sci. Am. **284**, 34–43 (2001)
14. Shadbolt, N., Berners-Lee, T., Hall, W.: The semantic web revisited. IEEE Intell. Syst. **21**, 96–101 (2006). https://doi.org/10.1109/MIS.2006.62
15. Banerjee, A., Dalal, R., Mittal, S., Joshi, K.P.: Generating digital twin models using knowledge graphs for industrial production lines. In: Workshop on Industrial Knowledge Graphs, co-located with the 9th International ACM Web Science Conference 2017 (2017)
16. Cartaxo, B., Pinto, G., Soares, S.: The role of rapid reviews in supporting decision-making in software engineering practice. In: Proceedings of the 22nd International Conference on Evaluation and Assessment in Software Engineering 2018, pp. 24–34 (2018). https://doi.org/10.1145/3210459.3210462

17. Grant, M.J., Booth, A.: A typology of reviews: an analysis of 14 review types and associated methodologies. Health Info. Libr. J. **26**, 91–108 (2009). https://doi.org/10.1111/j.1471-1842.2009.00848.x
18. Albayrak, Ö., Ünal, P.: Smart steel pipe production plant via cognitive digital twins: a case study on digitalization of spiral welded pipe machinery. In: Colla, V., Pietrosanti, C. (eds.) Impact and Opportunities of Artificial Intelligence Techniques in the Steel Industry, pp. 132–143. Springer, Cham (2021)
19. Ali, M.I., Patel, P., Breslin, J.G., Harik, R., Sheth, A.: Cognitive digital twins for smart manufacturing. IEEE Intell. Syst. **36**, 96–100 (2021). https://doi.org/10.1109/MIS.2021.3062437
20. Boschert, S., Heinrich, C., Rosen, R.: Next generation digital twin. In: Proceedings of the TMCE, pp. 7–11. Las Palmas de Gran Canaria, Spain (2018)
21. Fernández, F., Sánchez, Á., Vélez, J.F., Moreno, A.B.: Symbiotic autonomous systems with consciousness using digital twins. In: Ferrández Vicente, J.M., Álvarez-Sánchez, J.R., de la Paz López, F., Toledo Moreo, J., Adeli, H. (eds.) From Bioinspired Systems and Biomedical Applications to Machine Learning, pp. 23–32. Springer, Cham (2019). https://doi.org/10.1007/978-3-030-19651-6_3
22. Alaoui, K., Bahaj, M.: Semantic oriented data modeling based on RDF, RDFS and OWL. In: Ezziyyani, M. (ed.) Advanced Intelligent Systems for Sustainable Development (AI2SD 2019), pp. 411–421. Springer, Cham (2020). https://doi.org/10.1007/978-3-030-36674-2_42
23. Hao, Y., et al.: An end-to-end model for question answering over knowledge base with cross-attention combining global knowledge. In: Barzilay, R., Kan, M.-Y. (eds.) Proceedings of the 55th Annual Meeting of the Association for Computational Linguistics (Volume 1: Long Papers), pp. 221–231. Association for Computational Linguistics, Vancouver, Canada (2017). https://doi.org/10.18653/v1/P17-1021
24. Huang, W.: Knowledge-based geospatial data integration and visualization with Semantic Web technologies. In: CEUR Workshop Proceedings (2019)

Author Index

V. Agredo-Delgado et al. (Eds.): DECISIONING 2024, CCIS 2369, pp. 239–240, 2025.
https://doi.org/10.1007/978-3-031-91690-8

The manufacturer's authorised representative in the EU is Springer Nature Customer Service Centre GmbH, Europaplatz 3, 69115 Heidelberg, Germany. If you have any concerns regarding our products, please contact ProductSafety@springernature.com

Printed and bound by CPI Group (UK) Ltd, Croydon, CR0 4YY
01/10/2026
02225908-0004